LOCATING CULTURAL CREATIVITY

Anthropology, Culture and Society

Series Editors:
Dr Richard A. Wilson, University of Sussex
Professor Thomas Hylland Eriksen, University of Oslo

LOCATING CULTURAL CREATIVITY

Edited by
JOHN LIEP

PLUTO PRESS

First published 2001
by PLUTO PRESS
345 Archway Road, London N6 5AA
and 22883 Quicksilver Drive,
Sterling, VA 20166–2012, USA

www.plutobooks.com

British Library Cataloguing in Publication Data
A catalogue record for this book is available from
the British Library

Library of Congress Cataloging in Publication Data
Locating cultural creativity / edited by John Liep.
    p. cm.— (Anthropology, culture, and society)
  ISBN 0–7453–1703–0 (hardback)
  1. Creative ability—Cross-cultural studies. 2. Culture. 3. Social
change.   I. Liep, John. II. Series.
GN453.L63 2000
306—dc21
                                                          00–009108

ISBN 978 0 7453 1703 8 hardback
ISBN 978 0 7453 1702 1 paperback

10 09 08 07 06 05 04 03 02 01
10   9   8   7   6   5   4   3   2   1

Designed and produced for Pluto Press by
Chase Production Services, Fortescue, Sidmouth EX10 9QG
Typeset from disk by Stanford DTP Services, Northampton

CONTENTS

Acknowledgements

The chapters in this book were first presented at a workshop organized by the Institute of Anthropology, University of Copenhagen in late 1994. The workshop was part of the research programme 'Complex Cultural Processes' at the institute financed by a major grant from the Foundation of Pure Research of the Danish Ministry of Education. The editor expresses his thanks to the participants in the workshop for constructive discussions, to the contributors, who tolerantly considered his editorial suggestions, and to the staff of the Institute of Anthropology for inspiration at a subsequent seminar where I presented the introduction. The institute has further supported the editing of this volume and contributed generously to its publication.

INTRODUCTION
John Liep

May 1995 was the fiftieth anniversary of the liberation of Denmark from German occupation during the Second World War. The Ministry of Culture had set aside generous funds for celebratory manifestations. By far the most costly and provocative project to be approved was a gigantic installation by a young artist who proposed illuminating the entire western coastline of Denmark with a single laser beam relayed from hill to hill. This performance on the midnight of peace was to continue along the German coast and thus demonstrate friendly cooperation across the border. The artist herself explained the installation as a re-creation in a new medium of the customary Danish commemoration of the liberation. This celebration originated spontaneously on the very night of German capitulation when people in many towns tore down blackout curtains and put candles in their windows.

The project immediately gave rise to heated public debate and became the dominating topic of the media during the spring. Some praised the idea of employing a new technology in this novel and striking experiment. Populist critics opposed wasting taxpayers' money on yet another outrageous scheme supposed to be 'art'. By far the most bitter opposition came from old veterans from the wartime resistance movement. To them the installation brought back memories of another spectacle. This was when Hitler's chief architect Albert Speer for the first time used searchlight beams to create a towering celestial space above a Nazi rally in Berlin.[1]

The debate throws into relief several facets of the topic of this book. We show how creativity bursts forth when elements, which were already known but apart, are brought together by inventive people in a novel way. Concrete elements of experience, such as darkness and light, are used as metaphors, for example to stand for oppression and freedom. Sometimes metaphors are conveyed by new means and moved into new spaces. But the effect of creativity depends on the social environment it occurs in and on the inner motivations of its audiences. Creative action is promoted or hindered by institutions in society and to 'move the world' it must resonate with deep emotions of people. We celebrate creativity, as I argue in this introduction, as the spark of the incessant innovation of modernity. But sometimes we shiver at the uses it may be put to. This book explores creativity from the perspective of anthropology and its sister discipline ethnology. We provide

1

new insights into the recent explosion of creativity in our world, the way creativity works and how it changes our lives.

Much literature on creativity already exists. The vast majority of it is the work of psychologists and is concerned with exploring 'the creative mind' of the individual. Psychologists aim to discover the thought processes and backgrounds of exceptionally creative people and their relations to their surroundings. Related publications discuss how conditions encouraging creativity may best be promoted in education. A special domain of research involves creativity in innovative management. Finally, creativity has been a topic of interest in the history of science. All this literature centres on the individual creator and is therefore somewhat marginal to anthropological interest. Recently, some sociologists and historians of science have viewed creativity in terms of social and cultural process and have studied the institutional framework for scientific research and its authorization (see for example Brannigan 1981 and papers in Boden 1994). This approach is much more relevant to anthropological concerns.

For the purposes of this introduction I define creativity as activity that produces something new through the recombination and transformation of existing cultural practices or forms. As I suggest below, one may envisage a continuum from small-scale everyday creativity to intensive creativity concentrated in a single place or period. Creativity involves the acceptance of the novel in a social environment (cf. the definition in Rosaldo et al. 1993:5). The term *innovation* I regard as more or less synonymous with creativity, whereas *improvisation* indicates a more conventional exploration of possibilities within a certain framework of rules.

When anthropologists propose taking up a comparative study of cultural creativity, a certain objection is likely to be brought forward. This is that creativity as a specific preoccupation of our culture and times cannot be assumed to be found as an explicit notion and a relevant issue in all cultures. To this I would say, firstly, that the problems and issues which fire the curiosity and involvement of anthropologists are always grounded in the current developments and debates of Western culture, whereafter they are brought to bear on more distant life-worlds. In a progressively international world the scientific and intellectual hegemony of the West may be increasingly challenged but it is for the present a major factor. If, for reasons appertaining to our own part of the world, we find that creativity is an interesting problem, we will set out and try to locate it elsewhere and study the conditions that promote or limit it.

Secondly, there is a global cultural field. This involves not only the *ecumene* of cosmopolitans but also the global diffusion of ideas, messages, models, art forms, etc., and their manifold local appropriations (cf. Hannerz 1992:217ff.). If creativity is proliferating in the global field it is also becoming involved in numerous local agendas.

MODERNITY, THE WORLD SYSTEM AND CREATIVITY

A discussion of cultural creativity ought to broadly situate the notion itself in culture and history. Here, I shall emphasize that the connection between the growth of creativity and the processes associated with modernity seem clear. Daniel Miller has stressed the continuous change under modernity and the creativity this demands of a humanity which now incessantly must '... forge for itself the criteria by which it will live' (1994:62). Instead of being placed in a timeless order, which came about through the original creation of the world by God, humanity finds itself in a condition where creation has moved into the present. The life trajectory of the individual and the course and shape of society are becoming a consciously human project. In the area of the West where modernity emerged, these are conditions inescapably intertwined with capitalism. The expansion of commodity exchange was accompanied by a separation of human actions from their embedding in traditional social relations. The development of a class of free entrepreneurs promoted the placing of value on risk-taking and innovation. Within this emerging class ideas crystallized about rights to self-organization and civil freedom. The quest of the Enlightenment was for liberation from the hierarchic and immobile order of *l'ancien régime*, which was followed by the emphasis of Romanticism upon individual self-fulfilment. The competition of the market place forced capitalist entrepreneurs to revolutionize the means and modes of production and to create commodities to satisfy new desires. Thus, creativity became the mark of engineers and scientists. At the same time artists became separated from the dependency on and support of feudal and ecclesiastic patrons, and had to develop individual and novel styles to compete in the market. Creativity thus took two forms, represented as the contrast between the material and the spiritual: secular, rational scientific discovery and the emotional, spiritual creativity of the artist.[2]

The historical process associated with the rise of modernity, which has engulfed and transformed the world, produced a differentiated world system. Thus the specific constellation of features (distanciation, reflexivity, trust in expert systems or whatever) that we associate with Western modernism does not penetrate with the same force, or establish itself in an identical configuration, globally. Although politico-economic and media forces impinge everywhere, they do so in different ways and with different intensities and the political and cultural institutions they confront locally are highly diverse. Thus there is not one ubiquitous modernity but several historical and contemporary versions. Miller (1994) proposed a study of comparative modernities as a timely anthropological project. His study of modernity in Trinidad sees it as no less modern or genuine than Western modernity, just different. However, it is productive to consider the conditions and limitations of modern developments in terms of a more explicit world system model. In many parts of the world, local societies have been involved for hundreds of years in long-distance trade and the penetration of the market. Strategies and ways of thinking suggestive of modernity have been widespread but the institutional apparatus of Western European modernity is lacking. In world-system terms the situation could be characterized as a 'peripheral modernity' in contrast to the 'central' form. Granted that the social processes and changes in mentality associated with modernity are in general important background factors for creativity, I will therefore argue that these factors vary with position in the world-system. In any area of the world, the conditions affecting creative developments are influenced by the specific configuration of modernity in that part of the system.

To return to the centre: with the late-modern penetration of the market into further domains of human life, the decentralization of capital, the extension and intensification of the international economy and the globalization of the media, a great many transformations of social and intellectual relations are taking place. The 'postmodern' decentering of cultural production and authorization has resulted in a dehierarchization of the cultural field. Where securely entrenched cultural elites once adjudicated what was authentic and possessed quality and originality, we now experience an acceptance of popular and exotic cultural forms in the lifestyles of the consumer society. An earlier stable hierarchy of spheres of cultural production and exchange is collapsing and formerly segregated 'high' and 'low' cultural forms are juxtaposed at a common level. This fragmentation and disintegration of the cultural field results in a proliferation of cleavages and discords of signification. But it also evinces a multitude of encounters and cross-fertilization between hitherto separate cultural forms and environments.

The expanding commoditization of culture and of display and desire have also influenced views on creativity. This has to do with the increasing reification of culture as spectacle and performance and with what is called the aestheticization of everyday life. The emerging class of 'new professionals', much involved in the mediation of culture, excels in the consumption of novelty, the event and aesthetic experience (Featherstone 1991:43ff.; Bourdieu 1984:354ff.) Breaking away from the emotional self-control and sense of 'knowing one's station' of the former *petite bourgeoisie* this broad stratum of new intellectuals and cultural intermediaries pursues ever more varied sensibilities, lifestyles and forms of distinction. In this process of manifold fleeting images, socialities and values, the boundaries and hierarchies of former cultural structures weaken. To this class the world appears as a landscape of differences, or of hybridization, and creativity becomes a regular strategy in the externalization and appropriation of objects of fascination and desire. It would indeed be strange if these broad cultural concerns did not affect the life and thinking of anthropologists too. The discipline cannot escape the cultural processes in which it is enmeshed. One should therefore be aware that the fascination with creativity (as reflected in the present volume) involves to some degree what could be called a 'gentrification' of anthropology. That is, the practitioners are themselves participants in a broad trend of Western contemporary urban experience infused by elements of fashion, aesthetics, nostalgia etc.

Where creativity was formerly located in the elevated circles of science and the secluded atelier of the artist, it now seems to be everywhere. If the term is bandied about in new forms of distinction and elitism it may as well be evoked in seemingly more democratic endeavours. If the media proclaim that creativity is to be found in the studios of designers and popular musicians, it may be claimed by the defenders of the dominated and outcast to be evident in the resistance of marginalized peoples and in the lifestyles of subcultures. Thus it has come about that creativity has been on the lips of all for some years. Löfgren's contribution in this volume provides a critical overview of the recent history of the term and its employment by social and cultural scientists in anti-hegemonic discourses.

CREATIVE DESTRUCTION

There is a strong tendency, as Löfgren notes, to regard creativity as positive. It is 'good for you', 'we can't have enough of it'. Löfgren also shows how creativity has been viewed in recent cultural studies as a 'weapon of the weak', as part of the strategy of underdogs. This attitude to creativity is attractive to most anthropologists, who feel a natural solidarity with people at the grassroots. Amidst this celebration of creativity we should, however, consider in a larger perspective the rise and proliferation of creativity in modern world history. As I have argued above, creativity in its modern sense must be seen as part of the expansion of capitalism. Marx explored on a grand scale the great contradictory processes of the unfolding of capitalism. He emphasized the great revolutionary power of the *bourgeoisie*, how it had developed hitherto unseen forces of production and created new forms of communication and knowledge. This revolution of all human conditions and relations, covering the entire globe, had created new needs and new ways of satisfying them, an immense accumulation of wealth, monuments of pro-ductivity and a world transformation of the entire life process. But this immense expansion of productive and commercial development was accompanied by what Schumpeter (quoted in Zukin 1991:4) called a 'creative destruction' on an awe-inspiring scale. Old forms of production and cooperation, old ways of life and relationships, whole classes and populations were swept away. And hand-in-hand with the growth of forces of production have gone the expansion of the destructive forces of war and the degradation and pollution of the natural resources of soil, water and air. Thus, creative construction in all its material and cultural aspects was predicated upon a creative destruction of awesome proportions and consequences.

We should therefore not look only at the bright side of creativity. It would be naive to be blind to the fact that creativity may also be employed in projects of seduction, control and domination. I have already mentioned how creativity was used effectively in the sinister imagery of Nazi public symbols and the orchestration of mass spectacles.

MODES OF CREATIVITY

Students of creativity tend to agree that there are two main forms of it. Boden (1994) distinguishes the *exploration* of a conceptual space from the *transformation* of it. She views a conceptual space as an underlying generative system that defines a certain range of possibilities – limits, contours, pathways and structure. Exploration of a system is the production of possible forms within the constraints of the system. Modifying a limitation causes a 'tweak', while the dropping or negation of a constraint effects a transformation of the system. (Boden's approach to creativity is still within a 'mental map' conception of culture and does not take account of more open, complex fields. One should also note that transformation in her sense of the term involves a major systemic change, whereas some contributors to the present volume (Friedman, Parkin) regard transformative creativity as the production of variations within a stable structural framework.) Nevertheless, one may discern a more conventional elaboration of meaning along received lines from 'true' creativity where meaningful forms are renewed or emerge through unconventional extension or application. Both Fernandez and Friedman (this volume) indicate such a division in the universe of creative activity. One may in fact see creativity as a continuum at one of whose poles it appears as an aspect of all behaviour. This is the 'invention of culture' view of Wagner (1981) where practice must always involve improvisation to adapt and develop cultural schemes to everyday conditions, which are never completely specified. Thus culture is always 'emerging'. At the other pole is 'true' creativity where highly unconventional forms emerge. This view would also distinguish a diffuse, widely distributed creativity of everyday life from concentrated bursts of creativity which, in specific environments, under certain conditions and within particular periods, give rise to centres of novel cultural productivity.

METHODS OF CREATIVITY

The production of cultural forms is not the creation of something out of nothing. Every creative effort must emanate from familiar forms and methods of production. As Barnett said: 'Every innovation is a combination of ideas' (1953:16). The immediate background is always the experience of those concerned. This is of course already a meaningful experience, constituted and felt through existing cultural forms (see also below). Life always involves gaps in and doubts about the criteria by which experience is conceived. But in periods of major change, when conventional understandings are discredited or no longer able to explain altered conditions, the need for creating new cultural schemes to account for life in the world becomes acutely urgent (cf. Fernandez, this volume).

Undoubtedly, there are structural constraints to the production of meaning, as explored brilliantly by Lévi-Strauss and others, which provide an underlying order to mythical or performative sequences of meaningful elements. Structural limitations seem, however, to concern the positional value of signs, in opposition, inversion, mediation etc., while they leave the meaningful content much more open to choice.

Fernandez explores how concrete everyday experiences provide image schema that become prototypes in categorization. Through the manipulation of metaphor and metonym, the relative resemblance to prototypes is explored in order to establish central or peripheral category membership. Thereby, more concrete experiences are employed to understand more complex situations.[3] The method of creativity is here a structured categorization. It involves some underlying principles, but the use to which it may be put, and the efficiency of the product in reconstituting the lived experience of people, is open to variability. Fernandez notes how 'true' creativity involves the use of metaphors in new ways or the invention of novel metaphors.

CONDITIONS OF CREATIVITY

As already mentioned, creativity concerns the novel combination of old ideas. Boden paraphrases Koestler (1964) to say: 'the most creative moments ... involve the recognition of a novel analogy between previously unrelated fields' (Boden 1994:97). This leads to a view of creativity as emerging in open spaces, gaps, interstitial zones (cf. Rosaldo et al. 1993:2). Focusing on creativity makes us think of a cultural field characterized by discontinuities or discrepancies which may be bridged in a search for new meaningful connections. It would also seem that the potential for the most striking and novel forms would involve the crossing of the largest cultural distance, if this could be measured.

In the classical concept of culture as a bounded and integrated system of shared meanings and values, the zone of creative potential would be located at the boundary between contiguous cultures. This leaves creativity as a phenomenon of 'culture contact' or acculturation. The current conception of culture, however, which regards a cultural field as an open and complex system, involves much more inconsistency in the field, and thus allows for creative activity to emerge at many points. When this is coupled with a practice-oriented approach to culture, much of life seems to involve a creative aspect. Here culture is seen as being continually constructed by agents testing concepts in concrete everyday projects and placing constructions upon life experiences. There is no doubt that the attention to creativity and the practice- and process-oriented approach to culture are part of the same paradigm.

However, one must question the utility of finding the potential for creativity in widespread and normal conditions, more or less in the everyday stream of cultural process. This tendency leads to the belief that creativity is everywhere. It would seem more productive to adopt a view leading to the identification of certain points or zones and certain times as presenting more favourable conditions for creativity than others. We are thus brought back to a notion of cultural inconsistency and the creative process of mediation. Fredrik Barth dealt with this problem on several occasions. A long time ago (1966) he argued that integration cannot be taken for granted in culture. Integration comes about when people transact values across boundaries, and thus gradually establish compatibility. Barth also pointed to the innovator or entrepreneur as especially concerned to identify and establish channels of conversion leading to cultural integration. This view of a cultural field comprising inconsistencies that are being explored and negotiated has much in common with current thinking.

In his work on ethnic groups, on the other hand, Barth emphasized that, despite exchange and mobility across ethnic boundaries, cultural differences between the groups persist (1969:16). One should thus look for the social boundaries between groups with differing interests to find causes for the maintenance of old barriers and the development of new.

If innovations are to become culturally relevant, they must imply reorganization of collective expression. Barth's approach implies that, at least in certain fields, ambiguities and discrepancies will provoke attempts at integration. We are then faced with the question of why culture does not become more and more integrated over time. This could indeed be the case in some instances. Where, for example, a dominant elite of literati for generations develops and refines a specific tradition of knowledge and suppresses or ignores alternative visions of the world, there may exist a well integrated body of propositions and codifications of meanings. In such regimes of entrenched authority we expect little room for transformatory creativity. Nevertheless such unchallenged hegemony, however strongly consolidated, only lasts for limited spans of time in history. Sooner or later the legitimacy of received world views will be questioned by competing formulations put forward by other social groups. Thus conditions for the development of new cultural gaps and discrepancies arise with the appearance of social groups struggling for recognition and empowerment. Here it is that new solutions and new forms of expressing them will be sought. Cultural elements from hitherto unconnected contexts will be combined here, often drawing on imports from foreign sources. But the new cultural forms are also shaped by their very divergence from or opposition to received beliefs and expressions. Creativity may thus itself give rise to cultural contrast and heterogenization.

The above argument concerned cultural discrepancies caused by social processes and class formations internal to a society. Let us return to cross-cultural confrontations where there is interference between the cultural influence of two or more sources. Here Hannerz's concept of creolization (1987, 1992:261ff.) has received attention. In creolization there is a confluence of historically separate cultural currents that interact in a centre–periphery relationship (1992:264). In this 'spectrum of interacting forms' there is a creative interplay between the 'cultural technology' in the centre and transforming meanings and expressions on the periphery. As a universal concept, I find that creolization is not very productive. Hannerz's general formulation, in which cultures are supposed to flow like initially pure substances that mingle and mix, is unfortunate. This is especially so in view of the fact that he has much to say about institutional settings and power relations in the social management of meaning. However, in the present volume Archetti derives much insight from employing a notion of creolization in a regional setting where creole processes (in terms of race and ideology) have been intense. It seems that the concept is more useful in such a specific context where it is historically relevant.

Power relations and the control of resources are of the utmost significance among the conditions for creativity. Recent sociological approaches to the study of scientific creativity have emphasized the importance of structures of authorization and justification (Brannigan 1981, Schaffer 1994). What is acceptable, fruitful and valuable is evaluated within a structure of the management of knowledge and aesthetic expression. In an authoritarian society where conventions are continually policed, we do not expect to find genuine creativity in the official culture although dissident forms may spread in 'underground' circles.[4] In other cases the evaluation of innovations may be more open and uncentralized, or the field may be characterized by the struggles of clashing interests and power bases.

The ability to search for, develop and disseminate the products of creativity also depends on access to material and intellectual resources. Hannerz (1992:206–8) stressed the importance of public institutions such as debating societies, cafés, cabarets, etc., which facilitate the critical comparison and cross-fertilization of ideas. Sustained creativity in itself demands a certain minimum level of welfare and the circulation of its products requires further resources. If a population is in a state of stark poverty, one can expect no flourishing creativity above the limited ingenuity involved in making ends meet. Although Whyte (in the present volume) describes the mushrooming of creative strategies of survival among Ugandan health workers on a 'killing wage', she also notes that this period of florescence did not occur when the need was greatest but when peace and international relief had improved conditions somewhat.

MOTIVATION AND EXPERIENCE

Some of the contributors to this volume take up the subjective and experiential aspects of creativity. Friedman argues that the receptivity of creations depends on the felt needs of the social subjects. The attribution of meaning to the world must make sense to people in terms of the local strategies of signification, but it must also take account of the motivations of the subjects. Both creators and their social groups are motivated by powerful desires grounded in the socially structured experience space they inhabit. Borofsky similarly refers to implicit habituated forms of understanding, a notion that comes close to Bourdieu's concept of habitus (1977, 1984). As Barth (1987:29) argues, creativity involves a dialectic process in which public representations become deeply personal symbols which 'give identity and direction' to subjects. Refashioned as subjective imagery, symbols may again, if accepted by the group, become objectified public culture (cf. Obeyesekere 1981 quoted in Barth 1987).

These arguments emphasize that resonance in terms of the experience of social subjects is a decisive factor for the acceptability of creations. This corresponds to the structures of justification involved in the evaluation of scientific discoveries. But whereas scientific acceptability is evaluated according to explicit paradigms and procedures, the reaction to other creations depends much more on dispositions embedded in the habitus of the subjects. This also means, as Friedman emphasizes, that creativity is not intellectual or aesthetic play, but concerns deeply felt desires and emotions at the core of experience. For him this constraint on creativity ensures a large measure of cultural continuity. However, I suggest that such very deep levels of resonance could be articulated with quite variable forms of concrete expression. Again, 'experience' is not a homogeneous straitjacket constraining subjects uniformly. Firstly, experience is not identical for differently situated subjects in a social field. Secondly, the world does not invariably conform to the habitual accommodations of the subject. Especially during periods of major social change, individuals may often find themselves uneasily habituated in the world. This is what alienation involves. The subject then experiences dissonance, doubt or incomprehension. This becomes the basis for an urge for a reconstruction of existential conceptions and revitalized forms of experiencing the world, as Fernandez argues.[5] In a similar way Hastrup discusses how creative individuals may 'bend the world' and reframe experience through what Babcock calls a 'dislocation in the economy of cultural representations' (1993:75).

CONTENT OF THE BOOK

The book contains two parts. Part I consists of six contributions that explore in a general way the dimensions of creativity and the uses of the concept in social science. James Fernandez focuses on the central concepts of prototype and metaphor and shows how they may be employed creatively in an 'argument of images' to revitalize dead or disorganized conventions. He locates cultural creativity in situations of cultural incompability between dominant and subordinate cultures, where conventions are questioned and a search is made for a new world view. Through the example of a Brazilian *candomblé* dancer's performance of *Othello*, Kirsten Hastrup explores theatre as a 'technology of enchantment'. She views theatrical performance as a specific example of how gifted individuals may alter history by reshaping experience of the world. Jonathan Friedman is more concerned with constraints on creativity. He surveys various modalities of creativity concentrating on bricolage as a recombination of elements within the framework of a more stable structure. This he sees as located in 'conjunctive' (that is embedded) world experience. Robert Borofsky investigates similar terrain by way of the neuroscientific concept of implicit memory, which he uses to show how habitual routines may involve considerable fluidity and innovation. Orvar Löfgren offers a critical overview of the use of the concept of creativity in studies of consumption. There has been, he argues, a routinization of creativity, a narrowing-down to a focus on its symbolic, innovative and aesthetic dimensions, whereas those that are more mundane or trivial have been bypassed. Finally, Rolf Lindner provides a critical view of the practices of youth subcultures and studies about them. Both subculture members and their researchers have subscribed to a notion of uncontaminated, authentic culture. Lindner also shows how a knowledge of social science enters directly into the process of subculture construction.

Part II contains six case studies from Latin America, Africa, Indonesia and the Pacific. Eduardo Archetti analyses the transformation of football and polo from imports from Britain to 'creole' Argentinian forms. The two sports developed on different class bases but were both appropriated within a conservative, nationalist ideology. Marc Schade-Poulsen takes up various social games involved in the consumption of Algerian *raï* music and the pleasures it evokes. He analyses the creative moment of its emergence and its context in changing Algerian gender relations. Susan Reynolds Whyte views the creativity involved in the commoditization of pharmaceuticals in Uganda. This is an example of how necessity becomes the 'mother of invention' in strategies of survival for health workers on a 'killing wage'. David Parkin discusses the paradox of artistic movements on Zanzibar that profess authenticity while escaping conventional rules of expression. His case study shows how rules may be replaced while the actors still experience a strong sense of cultural continuity. Another angle on cultural change and continuity is provided by Signe Howell. Based on material from the Lio people on the Island of Flores in Indonesia, she argues that modernization does not have to result in a hybrid mix but may involve a complementary coexistence of traditional and modern practices. Finally, John Liep analyses the interplay of local and external constraints and incentives in the development of the *kula* exchange system and of a social movement in the Trobriand Islands, relating these processes to the debate on the global versus the local in the Pacific.

CONCLUSION

In this survey I first considered creativity as a concomitant of modernity in terms of a historical process of incessant social and mental change. The contemporary interest in creativity is, I argue, connected to intellectual currents and developing lifestyles in late modernity or, if you will, postmodernity. Part of the search to locate creativity has thus been to consider reflexively the background to our own interest in the issue. The next step was to consider first what forms creativity may take and second where most fruitfully to locate it 'out there'.

These two questions seem linked. We may approach creativity on two levels. One mode of creativity deals with the generation of variations in a framework of commonly accepted rules. This is the small-scale or everyday production of solutions to current problems following habituated generative structures. Seen from this angle creativity is an aspect of human existence everywhere. Then there is the 'true' creativity that involves a major restructuring of the rules and a reorganization of experience. This is not ubiquitous but concentrated at a particular time and place. If 'conventional creativity' spreads like an ocean on the surface of the world, 'true creativity' rises like islands here and there.

I noted that creativity involves the bridging of gaps through the fusion of disparate cultural configurations. To locate conditions for major cultural creativity, one should therefore search for situations where there is interaction involving different values, world views and forms of expression. At the same time there must be an openness or relaxation of social control that allows for a productive cross-fertilization of perspectives. There must be, in Barnett's phrasing (1953:46), a 'conjuncture of difference' or a process of change in existential conditions that calls for reorientation. In the present time of transcultural processes, global media diffusion, migration and increasing cultural plurality in urban centres – covered by the term cultural complexity – islands of cultural creativity appear as multitudinous archipelagos in the world.

NOTES

1. In fact, the Danish project flopped as the laser technique failed to function satisfactorily.
2. In Danish school curricula this dichotomy is still reflected in the contrast between instrumental subjects such as reading, writing and mathematics and creative subjects such as music, art or woodwork. The former train children for professional skill in disciplined work, the latter develop the free spirit of the individual.
3. Already Barnett (1953:207ff.) – without the benefit of cognitive linguistics – used the term prototype in his discussion of innovative processes. He argued that precedents or prototypes as mediating mechanisms serve as a charter for integration of new experience.
4. Thus our conception of creativity is much tied up with the notion of civil liberty and the freedom of the individual.

5. Barnett (1953:72) noted that when there is an abandonment of authoritative control during periods of social and political upheaval the individual loses his orientation and finds his microcosm destructuralized. He needs to 'reorganize his experiential field'.

REFERENCES

Babcock, B.A. (1993) 'At home, no womens are storytellers: ceramic creativity and the politics of discourse in Cochiti Pueblo', in S. Lavie, K. Narayan and R. Rosaldo (eds) *Creativity/Anthropology*. Ithaca: Cornell University Press.
Barnett, H.G. (1953) *Innovation: The Basis of Cultural Change*. New York: McGraw-Hill.
Barth, F. (1966) *Models of Social Organization*. London: Royal Anthropological Institute of Great Britain and Ireland, Occasional Paper 23.
—— (1969) 'Introduction', in *Ethnic Groups and Boundaries*. Boston: Little, Brown.
—— (1987) *Cosmologies in the Making*. Cambridge: Cambridge University Press.
Boden, M.A. (1994) 'What is creativity?', in M.A. Boden (ed.) *Dimensions of Creativity*. Cambridge, Massachusetts: MIT Press.
Bourdieu, P. (1977) *Outline of a Theory of Practice*. Cambridge: Cambridge University Press.
—— (1984) *Distinction: A Social Critique of the Judgment of Taste*. London: Routledge & Kegan Paul.
Brannigan, A. (1981) *The Social Basis of Scientific Discoveries*. Cambridge: Cambridge University Press.
Featherstone, M. (1991) *Consumer Culture and Postmodernism*. London: Sage.
Hannerz, U. (1987) 'The world in creolisation', *Africa* 57: 546–59.
—— (1992) *Cultural Complexity: Studies in the Social Organization of Meaning*. New York: Columbia University Press.
Koestler, A. (1964) *The Act of Creation*. London: Hutchinson.
Miller, D. (1994) *Modernity: an Ethnographic Approach. Dualism and Mass Consumption in Trinidad*. Oxford: Berg.
Obeyesekere, G. (1981) *Medusa's Hair: An Essay on Personal Symbols and Religious Experience*. Chicago: University of Chicago Press.
Rosaldo, R., Lavie, S. and Narayan, K. (1993) 'Introduction: creativity in anthropology', in S. Lavie, K. Narayan and R. Rosaldo (eds) *Creativity/Anthropology*. Ithaca: Cornell University Press.
Schaffer, S. (1994) 'Making up discovery', in M.A. Boden (ed.) *Dimensions of Creativity*. Cambridge, Massachusetts: MIT Press.
Wagner, R. (1981) *The Invention of Culture*. Chicago: The University of Chicago Press.
Zukin, S. (1991) *Landscapes of Power: From Detroit to Disney World*. Berkeley: University of California Press.

PART I

CREATIVITY IN ACTION AND ANALYSIS

1 CREATIVE ARGUMENTS OF IMAGES IN CULTURE, AND THE CHARNEL HOUSE OF CONVENTIONALITY[1]

James W. Fernandez

CIVILIZED TIMES, THEIR CONVENTIONS, THEIR 'JEU D'ESPRIT' AND THEIR LANGUAGE GAMES

I begin with two important modern philosophers, Wittgenstein and Rorty, as a context for more grounded anthropological discussion. These philosophers are both intensely interested in language (and particularly figurative language) and sympathetic to the anthropological project.[2] I refer to the project dating at least back to Vico which understands culture as something reconstructed, largely out of the building materials of language, from that which is long given.

Wittgenstein, conversing on aesthetics, shows understanding of the compensatory – perhaps revitalizing – interest moderns take in 'creativity' (Wittgenstein 1966:8 quoted in Lurie 1991). For him as for Spengler and for Vico before him these are not creative times. He found the times overwhelmed by *convention* (a key term in this essay). Talent and cleverness abound but genius from which true creativity springs is lacking. We are too civilized and too conventional in our civilization and have lost contact with the springs of culture. Irony and a sense of the incongruous abound but the adventuresome human spirit at work in culture is lacking. We manipulate but we do not create. We play language games or entertain by tasteful 'jeu d'esprit'. But we do not understand the creative nature of games themselves and our 'jeu d'esprit' does not advance the spirit of reason in culture. We are conventional and have lost contact with the original springs of true cultural creativity. The times would seem to be ripe, for him as for Vico referring to the *ricorso*, for a return to the courage of the fundamental, that is to organic reformulations – in anthropological parlance, to 'revitalization'.

Lurie, reviewing Wittgenstein's views on creativity in culture, contrasts his 'romantic' philosophy with Rorty's pragmatism where metaphor occupies a central role in cultural creativity (Lurie 1991). It is not that Wittgenstein lacks metaphor. There is fertility in figures of speech in his argument in favor of the creative spirit.[3] But he does not as does Rorty make metaphor the basis of cultural creativity. Rorty grants to creative metaphor the power to 'break with observance, transcend the predictable and revolutionize culture'. That is its emancipatory genius.

But we cannot predict its consequences. For Rorty, 'culture is indeterminate.' We can only know creative 'genius' *ex post facto* which is to say by its consequences. We do not know beforehand what metaphors will attract attention and revolutionize culture. Many creative metaphors are put forth in cultures. Few are chosen. We cannot predict that choice and its consequences. We can talk endlessly about creativity but we can never recognize it with absolute certainty.

Because of that indeterminacy Rorty takes a negative view of tropological investigation of the kind that will be treated here – the kind that in the last several decades has made of metaphor a focus of social science investigation. For Rorty, 'To ask "how metaphors work" is like asking how genius works. If we knew that, genius would be superfluous. If we knew how metaphors work they would be like ... matters of amusement, rather than ... instruments of moral and intellectual progress' (Rorty 1987:296 quoted in Lurie 1991).

In the long run of human cultural evolution, there may be truth in this scepticism. But since new metaphors arise constantly in situations of immediate interactive need as strategic and often creative responses to these situations, they are open to relevant evaluation. The view taken here is that it is the understanding of this dynamic, the interactive dynamic of figurative discourse, that is important to anthropological understanding of creativity.

IF 'CHEMISTS HAVE THE SOLUTIONS' WHO IS BEING CREATIVE HERE? THE PLAY OF TROPES IN UNCONVENTIONAL CIRCUMSTANCES

What makes these philosophers interesting to anthropologists is their attention to the vicissitudes and vagaries, the solidarities and misunderstandings, of everyday life. Relevant to that interest is a recent argument in anthropology that has to do with social understanding and misunderstanding and implicates anthropologists in that dynamic. More particularly it has to do with metaphor, convention and creativity. I refer to an argument put forth by the late Roger Keesing in a sequence of papers from the mid 1980s until his death in 1993 (Keesing 1985, 1987, 1989).

Keesing was concerned with tendencies in interpretive and symbolic anthropology (and other anthropologies oriented to the study of meaning in culture), firstly with the tendency to over-interpret as meaningful what was simply conventional in the life experiences of members of other cultures, and secondly with the collateral tendency to over-interpret and essentialize (by exoticization processes) cultural differences. There have been other similar arguments on both these points. In recent years Dan Sperber, for example, is well known for a trenchant series of essays addressed to the first point and to the problems of anthropological exegesis and anthropological knowledge of cultural symbols (for example Sperber 1985). With respect to the second point the last dozen years have seen many arguments against the tendency, particularly with a holistic conception of culture to over-interpret cultural differences and thus exoticize the Other (Abu-Lughod 1993). But Keesing made one of the most detailed arguments against these fruits of the relativizing impulse, on the one hand, and the exigencies of professional positioning on the other. His arguments are of relevance to the present theme because of their bearing on the problem of convention and creativity in culture, particularly as that problem may be approached from the perspective of metaphor theory.

Let me first recall Keesing's argument in 'Exotic readings of cultural texts' (1989). In this article Keesing asserts that some if not many of our ethnographic accounts are misinterpretations and misunderstandings which wrongly essentialize Otherness. This is not only because both the main theories and the reward structures of anthropology encourage the discovery of the interestingly exotic and alien but because anthropologists fail to understand grammaticalization or conventionalization processes by which metaphors and other figures of speech become built into language structure in such a matter-of-fact way as to lose semanticity. Lexical forms which once may have been fleshed out with undeniable semantic colour and body become 'bleached' of their semantic content and come to serve only abstract, bare bones, relational functions (1989:465).

The motivated ethnographer, Keesing argues, in search of deep symbolic meaning, fastens however upon the possible lexical force of these merely conventional forms, interpreting out of them, falsely, complex meaning structures which they do not possess locally. Empirical ethnography becomes thereby *creative and over-determined* ethnography in the sense of interposing and substituting the ethnographer's over-elaborated structure of meaning for very limited local ones. The question arises in the ethnographic process: 'Who is being creative here?'

Keesing gives examples of this creative over-interpretation from his own Kwaio ethnography and from possible ethnographic over-interpretation of such English conventional phrases concerning 'luck' as though it were a substance or a mystic person determining outcomes. A favorite example taken from the work on metaphor of George Lakoff and Mark Johnson, whose theories Keesing espouses, concerns an Iranian student who

shortly after his arrival in Berkeley ... found ... an expression that he heard over and over and understood as a beautifully sane metaphor ... 'the solution of my problems' – which he took to be a large volume of liquid, bubbling and smoking, containing all of your problems ... He was terribly disillusioned to find that the residents of Berkeley had no such chemical metaphor in mind. (1980a:143)

Let me, however, cite my response (Fernandez 1989) to Keesing's argument, published in the same issue of *Current Anthropology*. It bears on the issue of creativity in culture. While granting Keesing's salutary

strictures on ethnographic monism and excessive relativism and essential-
izing of the Other, I sought to balance his argument somewhat differently.
I did not wish for Keesing's focus on the deadness of metaphors trapped in
convention and idiomaticity to overlook the constant 'invention' or
'creation' of culture, that is the 'social use' to which metaphors are
constantly put in difficult, that is unconventional, human circumstances in
problem solving and in building world views, even cosmologies.

My 15 years of research among African societies with religious
movements undergoing revitalization (Fernandez 1978, 1982) had
convinced me of the pervasive human capacity to escape and revitalize
convention, to creatively enliven dead metaphors or discover new ones, and
to build social and cultural structures on that basis. I argued that the study
of the conventional structures and asemanticity of dead metaphors should
be complimented by field study of the lively 'play of tropes' in culture
(Fernandez 1986). In the 'division of labor' in the human sciences of which
Keesing spoke – he was arguing for anthropological commitment to inquiry
informed by cognitive linguistic science – the study of such creative play falls
to anthropology as a primary task. 'Playfulness' in culture is as much if not
more our subject matter as 'planfulness'.

For example, about the same time as I was formulating my CA response,
in early 1989, I noticed a bumper sticker appearing around university
campuses: 'Chemists have the Solutions', a creative enlivening play upon
just that 'dead' metaphor which Lakoff and Johnson and Keesing had
employed to clinch their conventional argument. While we should not read
lively meaning into dead metaphors, at the same time we should not ignore
the lively, once and future figurality of these forms. A conventional
metaphor, one whose 'shock of recognition' has been forgotten or is ignored,
is always subject to the play of revitalization – a play that should be of
particular interest to anthropology:

[While a foreigner's] reading of a chemical metaphor into the idiomatic English, 'I
have a solution to my problems' [may be mistaken] any reader can recognize the
poetry and potential illumination in such 'mistakenness' ... the [dead] metaphors in
our [language] can be ceaselessly brought back to life in many 'foreign' ways. And in
that sense language is a reservoir of potential for revitalized understanding. Revitalization movements themselves are full of such new readings of the conventional and
the idiomatic ... In these movements people who have been made 'foreign' to
themselves and their circumstances often find a 'path' out of their alienation by
creative metaphor ...

Nor should one suppose that revitalization processes are strange and unusual. Of
great variety, small and large, they happen all the time, in language as in religion, as
an enlivening reaction to the overbearing 'conventionalization' or routinization of
life. (Fernandez 1989:471)

The point is that anthropologists, especially, should complement the
cognitive enterprise and its search for bare semantic structures, its
attunement to the ordering of convention, to 'planfulness' that is, with the

anthropological enterprise and its attention to those recurrent moments and movements in which something old is persuasively revived or something new and lively and colourful is created out of or in the presence of – to use the metaphor Keesing evokes – the 'bleached bones' of the past. Our attunement should be to 'playfulness'.

WHERE CREATIVITY LIES: THE STRUCTURE OF CREATIVE METAPHOR AND THE DYNAMIC OF THE CATEGORICAL

While I may argue here for attention to 'playfulness' – or the play of tropes – in culture, I am not arguing that such 'play' (or any 'play' for that matter) escapes all structural constraints and thus is no challenge to systematic understanding. Creative and revitalizing play occurs within conventional structures – or better, structures arrived at by convention – even if expressively struggling with them or against them in order to overcome them. It should be understood in relation to them. Let me turn to the structural problem.

When one says the 'structural problem' one evokes first the structuralist argument, that is, the notion that life is a situation of 'unwelcome contradictions', sets of oppositional dilemmas, which we seek to escape but which we are able only to transform into other oppositions. We can creatively manipulate the elemental oppositions of the human situation and we can transform them. But we do not escape them.

In the structural view these creative transformations take place within various kinds of narrative structures. In the Lévi-Straussian approach these are complex myths in which the difficult and challenging oppositions between nature and culture, man and woman, life and death, etc. are worked out in transformative cosmological scenarios. After three or four decades of structuralist argument we have a good idea of what the narrator of a creative narration looks like from the structuralist view. He or she would look like the Cuna shaman in Lévi-Strauss's classic article (1963), who takes and narrativizes a difficult situation of suffering (impeded birth in this case) and, projecting it out as a cosmic struggle, temporarily resolves it. The creative person from this perspective would be a transformer by narrative of anomalous situations hung up on unresolved contradictions. He or she would be a master narrator.

But recalling Roger Keesing's argument, let us consider what creativity looks like from the perspective of the kinds of language structure – that is the structure of metaphor – focused on by himself and the cognitive linguists he attended to. Keesing holds – as do metaphorists in general – that all languages are pervaded by metaphor and that the literal–metaphorical dichotomy misleads by ignoring the degree to which literal expressions are metaphors whose figurative force has been forgotten and which have become conventional expressions in the structure – often in the grammatical

structure – of language. (We have already discussed the place of conventionalization, the death of metaphor as it were, in this theory and argued for
attention to playful revitalization.)

Structural theory focuses on the structure of cognitive categories and
upon how the tropes – metaphor and metonymy primarily – make use of
these structures: predicating, in the instance of metaphor for example,
elements from those source categories that are richly provided with meaning
upon elements in target categories that are lacking in meaning; or, in the
instance of metonymy, using elements from within a category to stand for
other elements in the category, or for the whole category, in order to grasp
it. It is these category manipulations that are referred to by the phrase 'the
play of tropes', or 'the dynamic of the categorical'. Anthropologists and social
scientists generally must be interested in this dynamic since such categorization processes are fundamental to social dynamics.

Without detailing an entire theory of inter- and intra-category predicative
dynamics, it is important in relation to the problem of creativity to recognize
that modern cognitive theory replaces the Aristotelian organization of
categories by reference to distinctive – necessary and sufficient – defining
features of membership. It does so with the notion of prototypicality, that is
with the notion of central and peripheral membership of categories. That is,
a category may contain members with few distinct features in common yet
which are related to each other by resemblance of some sort to the prototype.
It is metaphor that plays along the lines of these resemblances, extending
metaphorically, for example, the category or prototype of the father, the
biological father, to political leaders (the Father of his country), priests
(Father Jerome), deities (Our Father who art in Heaven), geography
(Fatherland) and so on. There is something elementally creative in being able
to contemplate an extended category of such diverse membership on the
basis of resemblance to prototype and not on the basis of common defining
features. Creativity we might say by the lights of this revised notion of
categorical logic has very much to do with the location and the extension of
prototypicality rather than the violation of a principle of inclusion and
exclusion of membership on the basis of conventional defining features.

A second element in this theory has to do with underlying experiential
images (called image schema) that we possess as a consequence of our
human temporal, spatial, visual and kinesthetic experience of being the kind
of creatures we are, living in the kind of world we live in. These are prototype
experiences upon which and out of which we come to understand more
complex or more abstract experiences.[4] These underlying prototypic images
are metaphorically transformed and used to give meaning to a great variety
of more abstract experiences we have difficulty understanding but which in
some way can be seen to resemble them. We use, to take an obvious example,
the underlying image of space-time movement to speak of changes in
emotional state. We say that we are moved by an experience. There is a
fundamental creativity involved here in the transformation of our baffled

understanding of complex experience by predicating a prototypical experience upon it.

An example of this creative elaboration or transformation is found in the foundational argument of Lakoff and Johnson (1980b). Take the case of a complex everyday activity of intellectuals: 'theorizing'. Theorizing is usually understood by reference to the prototypical activity of putting things together or pulling things apart and hence building something. Theories are buildings and to theorize is to build a structure (or, postmodern wise, to deconstruct it).

As Lakoff and Johnson point out (1980b:471–2) the conventional metaphoric elaboration makes use of the foundation and the shell or supporting structure. And we speak, as above, of the foundations of a theory and of its structure. That is the used part of the conventional metaphor. But there are also unused parts of any metaphoric extension, in this case the roof, rooms, staircases, hallways, plumbing, air-conditioning, etc.

Now, as we have said, a certain creativity, we may call it creativity1, lies in understanding theorizing in terms of the prototypical activity of putting things together constructively. Creativity2, however, involves making use of the conventionally unused parts of an established and now conventional metaphor of understanding. For example,

- 'His theory has thousands of little rooms and long winding and windy corridors' (Lakoff and Johnson).
- 'His theories are baroque and lack classical rigor and control.' Or 'His theories are frightful Gothic structures covered with Gargoyles' (Lakoff and Johnson with a little help from their friend).
- 'It's a drafty theory he is developing there full of holes.'
- 'His theory of language structures is a charnel house containing only the bare bones of human communication.'

Lakoff and Johnson (1980b:472) distinguish three different kinds of imaginative or creative2 metaphor that escape convention and lie outside the used parts of our normal conceptual systems:

1. Extensions of the used part of a metaphor: 'These facts are the bricks and mortar of my theory.'
2. Instances of the unused part of the conventional metaphor: 'His theory has thousands of little rooms and long winding and windy corridors.'
3. Instances of a novel metaphor which does not have a conventional presence in our normal conceptual system but suggests a new way to think about something: 'Classical theories are patriarchs who father many children, most of whom fight incessantly.'

We will return in conclusion to this typology of creative metaphor. What we have here in each instance of creativity2, we might add, is revitalized metaphor – metaphor rescued by unusual and unconventional extension.

It happens all the time and its occurrence is, in my experience, one of the pleasures – the pleasure of human creativity – of ethnographic field work. I turn now to review some relevant materials from my own ethnographic work in Africa.

AFRICAN SERMONIZERS: THE TRANSCENDENT (WORLD-SHAKING) IMPLICATIONS OF CREATIVE ARGUMENT

In my ethnographic work, particularly in Africa, I have tried to be especially attentive to 'revitalizing' discourse. From very early on (1965) I understood that discourse, or 'subtle words', most frequently in the form of sermons, as revitalizing in the sense that it impacted positively on local senses of wellbeing and on social relationships (Fernandez 1966a, b). Such an easy assertion covers very complex issues which I cannot fully clarify here though I attempted to do so at length in my various ethnographies of these African movements.

I can say a few things of relevance to the topic of cultural creativity. I was working among societies that were living disadvantageously along the expanding fire front of the Western political–industrial–commercial imperium, first in the dependency of the colonial order and then in the dependencies of the post-colonial first-world–third-world order. The sermons I investigated were surely creative in that they employed unconventional language which took advantage of the implication system, as previously discussed, and thus played upon the normal colloquial use of terms (Fernandez 1966a; 1966b; 1982, ch. 19). They presented in their arguments enlivened images of self and situation to their auditors. And I investigated the way these enlivened images provided, at least during ritual worship, a different world in which to live and act efficaciously from the disadvantaged one in which these African spiritualists were actually living.[5] The consequences of this enlivened or revitalized discourse I argued was a new world. In this I followed an enduring argument in metaphor theory that maintains that metaphors are not simply helpful restatements of the literal reality but suggest to the imagination, if they do not actually bring into being, other worlds. Indeed the object of these African religious leaders was to one degree or another the reinvigoration of either a spiritual world lost or abandoned during colonial and post-colonial hegemonies, or the discovery and entry into the new spiritual world trumpeted but inhibited by the double bind of missionary evangelization.

Of course, it was not by word alone that these revitalized worlds were brought into being but by the intricate and absorbing image-rich ritual activity of these movements. Nevertheless the religious leader's sermonizing words were very efficacious. Allowing for the fact that these multitudinous African movements were highly various in their pretensions to world creativeness, the point is that in all cases the 'new' worlds they were bringing into being were produced out of a creative language that was playing on the implications already contained in their proverbial wisdom and in colloquial expression – the conventional organizational metaphors of their culture or the imbibed missionary ones unconventionally extended.

The problem of 'newness' in creativity is a problem that lies, to be sure, in the very definition and etymology of the term creation itself. For creation is a word which has two basic meanings: firstly to cause to exist or form out of nothing, as in the biblical sense of God's or some other demiurge's power of 'newness'; and secondly to produce a work of craft or thought along unconventional lines. It is this latter sense of creation, the manipulation of the conventional, that I address here. The creator in this sense is the unconventional one. Such a definition places our focus as social thinkers precisely where it belongs: on the cognitive and social problem of convention and unconventionality.

The challenge to creativity in the context of African religious movements, then, was the challenge of conventions associated with social disorganization and culture denial or culture loss. The truly creative religious leader, in this context, was the unconventional one whose words and organization of ritual action offered amelioration – not to say transformation – of conventional yet anomic social relationships, and a vision of a world invested with meaningful cultural content – either traditional or acculturated or, as in most cases, a syncretism of the two. His or her challenges were the discredited conventions of the traditional life-world, on the one hand, and the disadvantageous and racist–colonialist conventions of the colonial and post-colonial world on the other. His creative power lay in such ameliorative or transformative power over convention.

But to have put the challenge to creativity in that way is also, for our part, to have paid fealty to a set of theoretical conventions in anthropology. I do not doubt the insight and perhaps predictiveness they provide. Still they ride roughshod over the experience of everyday life in these religious movements where, in my experience, no equivalent concept of creativity was ever considered or discussed. Here it seems to me that the truly creative analysis of these movements lies in an analysis of the argument of images characteristic of them and how that argument escapes conventionality and brings, by a kind of transcendence, a transformed world to the imagination. It is that ethnographic 'creativity' that I have tried to understand and to reproduce in my ethnography.

CREATIVE ANTHROPOLOGICAL ARGUMENT IN IMAGES OF CULTURE

Before concluding our discussion of the relation between creativity, transformation and transcendence we may take a brief meditative moment. By simply reversing the terms in the title to this paper, I want to make reference to the creativity in images of (scientific) argument that is integral to our sense of perceptive progress in anthropology, as is the case in social science disciplines generally. Insofar as our arguments are not mainly statistical, mathematical or otherwise formal, an important part of our capacity to offer new ideas or revitalize old ones – and the same problem of 'newness' applies here as discussed above – lies in our ability to offer 'new' images of culture: to coin 'new' metaphors.

Hyman (1966) almost half a century ago pointed out how the master thinkers in the social sciences – Marx, Frazer, Freud and Weber – were animated by compelling underlying organizing metaphors of thought. Subsequently Nisbet pointed out how pervasive various versions of the organic metaphor have been, since classical times to the present, in thinking about social change in history (1969). And more recently Salmond has examined the favourite orienting metaphors that occur in anthropological thinking (1982). The most-cited anthropological thinkers of our age (as of any other) have nearly all been particularly fertile metaphorizers. And we often associate them with certain particular metaphors, whether it is Frazer's prowling priest-king, eventually to be slain in the struggle for succession, or Victor Turner's 'social drama' or 'flow of social life', or Clifford Geertz's 'cockfight' or his 'turtles all the way down', or Pierre Bourdieu's 'jazz musician', intended to replace the 'social automaton' metaphor in order to capture the 'regulated improvisation' of the interacting *habiti* realizing themselves in social life.

A reading of the anthropological literature, both ethnographic and ethnologic, is always an endlessly interesting enterprise for a metaphorist, given the many creative metaphors employed by our colleagues, by which they grasp the complexities of life in society in relation to culture. Let me give just one more, since it seeks to address the plain hard reductive work that goes into ethnographic writing itself. It is David Plath's imageing of the reduction of the accumulated field material in the field notes we customarily bring back from a successful field trip as akin to the laborious melting-down by the Curies of tons and tons of pitchblende into a few beads of radioactive radium (Plath 1990).

In short, when we treat of the 'creative argument of images in culture' as a necessary focus of our ethnographic task we are bound at the same time to reflect on our own 'creative anthropological argument in images of culture'. We are bound to recognize that progress in social thought, a sense of 'newness', is a consequence of creative revitalization in our ability to capture the imagination of our fellow social thinkers.

CONCLUSION: THE LOCATIVE AND THE INTERLOCATIVE

In the modern world creativity is an engrossing word and a constant preoccupation! In part no doubt the interest in 'creativity' is a function of the kind of economic system and market economy we all participate in with its emphasis on 'creative' consumption energized by 'planned obsolescence', with its enticement of 'shoppers' by a constant turnover in fashionable products. We are ruled by fashion, and fashion, by definiton, is 'creative'. The most pervasive kind of that sort of creativity is 'creative' marketing of the fashionable such that the consumer is made uncomfortable about last year's models although they may have many years of service left in them. The creative play of fashion is profoundly 'planful' in our market of 'unplanned' economies.

While it is important to be aware of that set of material conditions and modes of production and consumption that are the backdrop if not the groundwork for any contemporary interest in creativity, in the case of the argument made here I have wanted to locate creativity differently – not in relation to the market but in relation to the problem of conventionality, and the need for escape from convention found in revitalizing transformation and transcendence. And I have wanted, as far as creative discourse is concerned, to make clear that the use of the figurative – which is a 'playfulness' deeply imbedded in human thought – is creative only by reference to the conventional and that which is implicit in it.

But, of course, the problem of conventionality and the need to escape from it must also be located. The revitalization movements which I have studied, and their creativity, must be located on the front lines between expanding dominant cultures and subordinate cultures which they seek to control and which they usually deprecate. So the creativity I have experienced is to be located as a 'culture contact' or acculturation or syncretism phenomenon – a reaction on both sides of the cultural lines of battle mentioned to a disturbing awareness of different cultural perspectives, and the interrogation of one's own cultural conventions that such awareness brings with it. We can simply define creativity, therefore, as the product of needs arising out of and located on the frontiers of cultural incompatibility where questions arise about centeredness or peripheralization, domination or subordination.

Of course, the specific location of my fieldwork on revitalization cannot supplant our more interlocative discussion where we developed a typology of type 1 and type 2 creativities as well as typologies of the unconventional in creative expression. For more than locations and typologies we need analytic tools to use in the interlocative enterprise. We need, for example, to use the concept of domains and of *inter*domain and *intra*domain relationships. And we have to understand the dynamic of these inter–intra relationships. That is, we have to understand the energy of the kind of creativity in which we are interested in terms of the dynamic of the categorical. And we have to understand category not in terms of Aristotelian logic but rather in terms of the Wittgensteinian logic of family resemblance – prototypes or central types on the one hand and peripheral membership or peripheral types on the other. That is because, in the situations of African acculturation and revitalization where my fieldwork has been located, we find matters of resemblance brought into profound question. We find, we might say, disturbing awareness of peripheralization and loss of prototypicality. And that has energized the creation by a kind of 'deep play'[6] of revitalized worlds. We might thus also say, at least by the lights of that ethnographic experience, that creativity is animated by the search for prototypicality and more particularly a lost prototypicality.

But might not that search – to return to the philosophers with whose animadversions on creativity we began – be typical of all intellectuals whose characteristic malaise is the sense of lost prototypicality, or even the loss of the vital power of prototypicality in the presence of the anaesthetized or moribund but still overmastering hand of routine and uninspiring convention?

As for anthropology, hardly a conventional discipline, we return again to Keesing's important question. May not our abhorrence of conventionality and our mandate to explore and explicate the unconventional be driving an unacceptable ethnographic creativity? Perhaps! Precautions are in order. But while Roger Keesing labels the consequences of that creativity an exaggerated exoticism he also peripheralizes its importance. We have, on the contrary, sought to locate this world-creating playfulness at the very centre of both the human condition and the anthropological task.

NOTES

1. This chapter is written in remembrance of Roger Keesing (1935–1993). He and his anthropological work were exemplary on a number of counts: for his devoted long-term commitment to the highly detailed and knowledgeable ethnography of a single people, the Kwaio; for his commitment not only to their ethnography but to their wellbeing, which led to his creation of and contribution to a Foundation to protect their interests; for his crisp theoretical argument; and for his profound sense of anthropological problems. Though in this essay I offer different perspectives on some of his arguments I recognize their importance and the informed way in which he posed them and pursued them. They are vital questions, or at least they raise the question of vitality in human interlocution. Thus I salute him by returning to engage an argument he posed effectively.
2. As in Wittgenstein's careful reading of Frazer, and Rorty's frequent sympathetic mention of 'ethnography' as the unique means humankind possesses for creating some semblance of solidarity on a world basis (Rorty 1989; Wittgenstein 1975).
3. As in the following criticism couched in mechanistic metaphor of the faculty of taste: 'The faculty of taste cannot create a new structure, it can only make adjustments to one that already exists. Taste loosens and tightens screws, it does not build a new piece of machinery. Taste makes adjustments. Giving birth is not its affair' (Wittgenstein 1985:59–60, quoted in Lurie 1991).
4. There is, incidentally, a universalizing theory of human nature here which in part (along with the theory of conventionalization or grammaticalization) leads to Keesing's conservative view of human diversity, and of human creative potentiality. It also explains his anti-relativistic stance. He, like the cognitive linguists influential in his argument, believes in, and has sought to work out, universal patterns in the logic of categorization.

5. Here I followed a theory of the consequences of metaphoric predication put forth by Samuel Levin (1977, 1988).
6. The reference is to Clifford Geertz's notion developed in 'The Balinese Cockfight', an article which identifies, one might say, a fundamental (deep) world creating playfulness in the human equation (Geertz 1973).

REFERENCES

Abu-Lughod, L. (1993) *Writing Womens' Worlds: Bedouin Stories*. Berkeley: University of California Press.
Fernandez, J.W. (1965) 'Symbolic consensus in a Fang reformative cult', *American Anthropologist* 67:902–29.
—— (1966a) 'Unbelievably subtle words: representation and integration in the sermons of an African reformative cult', *Journal of History of Religions* 6:43–69.
—— (1966b) 'Revitalized words from the parrot's egg and the bull who crashes in the kraal', *Proceedings of the American Ethnological Society for 1966*:53–64.
—— (1978) 'African religious movements', *Annual Reviews in Anthropology* (1978):195–234.
—— (1982) *Bwiti: An Ethnography of the Religious Imagination in Africa*. Princeton: Princeton University Press.
—— (1986) *Persuasions and Performances: The Play of Tropes in Culture*. Bloomington: Indiana University Press.
—— (1989) 'Response to R. Keesing: Exotic readings of cultural texts', *Current Anthropology* 30:470–1.
Geertz, C. (1973) 'Deep play: notes on the Balinese cockfight', in *The Interpretation of Cultures*. New York: Basic Books.
Hyman, S.E. (1966) *The Tangled Bank: Social Science Theory as Imaginative Writing*. New York: Grossett and Dunlap.
Keesing, R. (1985) 'Conventional metaphors and anthropological metaphysics: the problematic of cultural translation', *Journal of Anthropological Research* 41:201–17.
—— (1987) 'Anthropology as interpretive quest', *Current Anthropology* 28: 161–76.
—— (1989) 'Exotic readings of cultural texts', *Current Anthropology* 30: 459–79.
Lakoff, G. and Johnson, M. (1980a) *Metaphors We Live By*. Chicago: University of Chicago Press.
—— (1980b) 'Conceptual metaphor in everyday language', *The Journal of Philosophy* 77:453–86.
Levin, S. (1977) *The Semantics of Metaphor*. Baltimore: Johns Hopkins Press.
—— (1988) *Metaphoric Worlds: Conceptions of a Romantic Nature*. New Haven: Yale University Press.
Lévi-Strauss, C. (1963) 'The effectiveness of symbols', in *Structural Anthropology*. New York: Basic Books.
Lurie, Y. (1991) 'Geniuses and metaphors', *The Journal of Aesthetics and Art Criticism* 49:225–33.
Nisbet, R. (1969) *Social Change and History: Aspects of the Western Theory of Development*. New York: Oxford University Press.
Plath, D. (1990) 'Fieldnotes, filed notes, and the conferring of note', in R. Sanjek (ed.) *Fieldnotes: The Makings of Anthropology*. Ithaca: Cornell University Press.
Rorty, R. (1987) 'Unfamiliar noises', *Proceedings of the Aristotelian Society*. Supplementary 61:283–96.
—— (1989) *Contingency, Irony and Solidarity*. New York: Cambridge University Press.

Salmond, A. (1982) 'Theoretical landscapes: on cross-cultural conceptions of knowledge', in D. Parkin (ed.) *Semantic Anthropology*. ASA Monographs No. 22. London: Academic Press.

Sperber, D. (1985) *On Anthropological Knowledge: Three Essays*. New York: Cambridge University Press.

Wittgenstein, L. (1966) *Lectures and Conversations on Aesthetics, Psychology and Religious Belief* (ed. C. Barrett). Oxford: Basil Blackwell.

—— (1975) *Remarks on Frazer's Golden Bough*. Atlantic Highlands: Humanities Press.

—— (1985) *Culture and Value* (ed. G. von Wright). Oxford: Basil Blackwell.

2 OTHELLO'S DANCE: CULTURAL CREATIVITY AND HUMAN AGENCY[1]

Kirsten Hastrup

In anthropology, the notion of creativity has received renewed attention in recent years. Partly in response to the general historicization of the subject matter which took place during the 1980s, anthropologists have turned towards the processes of change inherent in any society. Cultural creativity is investigated as an ever-emergent feature in the world (Wagner 1981), and it is generally acknowledged that the 'healthy perpetuation of cultural traditions requires invention as well as rote repetition' (Rosaldo et al. 1993:5).

One could not agree more, yet there is still a slight feeling of an inherently marginal positioning of the creative element in culture. Just as suffering has been placed on the painful periphery of the normal (Davis 1992; Hastrup 1993), creativity has been put aside with the playful. One reason why this lopsidedness persists is the tendency to use the arts as exemplary cases of creativity. Whether decorative, performative or literary, the hallmark of the arts is precisely their creativity, at least within Western notions of art. And this, of course, is why they present themselves so forcefully as exemplars of cultural creativity. Like other exemplars, the creative element in art also points to wider spheres of relevance, however, as I hope to demonstrate in this chapter, in which my point of departure will be a theatrical event.

My ambition is to identify a point of historical dynamism, which is at the same time structure and event. Instead of studying social processes, hailed as the legitimate heirs to our interest after the death of structures and cultures, as just so many other (constructed) empirical objects, I suggest that we see 'processes' as the active principles in any event, action, or social world. This is a way to truly counterbalance the previous emphasis on entities, or 'results' of processes. In other words, I want to explore cultural creativity as a way in which 'newness' enters the world. My aim is to explore this as a particular feature of human agency, in keeping with recent epistemological considerations (Hastrup 1995a). In a recent article Robert Paine has discussed two kinds of newness: 'the new' of discovery and 'the new' of invention (Paine 1995:52–4). Discoveries are predicated by previous conceptualizations; the discovery of a new tribe is predicated by the concept of a tribe, and that is the big invention. 'Whereas discovery implies that the nature of the thing found was previously known, with invention we find the ontologically new' (ibid.:53). In my exposition I take 'creativity' to be an instance of invention in this sense.

As simultaneously structure and event, creativity connects to both space and time. Mixtures, encounters and contacts between people and cultures are made in space, but their effect, in terms of the newness they entail locally (and, indeed, by the same stroke, globally), belongs to time. Creativity is not only to discover or innovate, although this may be part of it, it is to reach a new potentiality by finding the ontologically new.

My argument centres around the world of dramatic performance; I discuss the potential of theatre and drama for creative intervention in the world. Moving into the sphere of artistry does not take us out of the mundane, however, since I agree with Gell when he suggests that the various arts are 'components of a vast and often unrecognized technical system, essential to the reproduction of human societies', identified as a 'technology of enchantment' (Gell 1992:43). Reproduction, as we know, is never mere replication; cosmologies are always in the making (Barth 1987). Thus, the arts, and theatre among them, may be seen as just exemplary cases of cultural creativity in a more general sense. Far from being an argument for a separation of the 'creative' from the dullness of ordinary social life, my aim is to reintegrate the two, and to suggest one possible answer to the question of how newness is produced in the world, and history made from what T.S. Eliot has called the 'still point of the turning world'.

In this article I am balanced on the edge of words, which are generally too literal for my purpose, which is to locate a centre of creative force in society. 'If words have any meaning, then there cannot be a discourse of action: there is only a discourse which states action and which, unless it is to fall into incoherence or imposture, must never stop stating that it is only stating action' (Bourdieu 1990:33). Yet the subject is sufficiently important to seek a balance on this edge, however unstable it might be. By way of introduction I shall present an instance of dramatic creativity: the case of Othello.

OTHELLO

In the early seventeenth century William Shakespeare wrote the drama *Othello, the Moor of Venice* (1604–5). His inspiration was a short story by the Italian author Giovanni Battista Giraldi. Shakespeare dramatized the story by condensing it in time, from months to days, and by complicating the psychology of Othello, from a cynical to a loving, even 'honourable' murderer. Many people will know the dramatic scene between Desdemona and Othello in the fifth act, which ends with Desdemona's death, and from our learned emotional dispositions most Europeans understand both the jealousy and the terror involved.

In the late nineteenth century, Shakespeare's play was used as the backbone of the libretto (by Arrigo Boito) for Giuseppe Verdi's opera, first performed in 1887 in Milan. Verdi's *Otello* keeps close to Shakespeare's drama, while of course adding the dimension of music. The libretto of the opera is probably as well known as the original drama, not least the tense dialogue between Otello and Desdemona, he accusing her of adultery, she pleading innocence. In paintings, too, the death of Desdemona has often been portrayed; in a well-known print (by G. Noble) we see the black Moor somehow crumbling away under the weight of his deed, while a heavenly light reaches the pale Desdemona.

Already at this stage we have a feeling of a never-ending creative process, each artful transformation addressing the same theme, if through distinct repertoires and art forms. The feeling reflects a primary sensation of looking into a hall of mirrors, which is patiently waiting for us to enter. Recently yet another transformation of Othello saw light. Eugenio Barba, director of Odin Teatret, a Danish/international group theatre, created a new play, *Othello*. It was first shown publicly in Brazil in August 1994; I myself was among the audience.

The play opens with a fragment of Verdi's opera, and an elegantly dressed black man enters, reading Shakespeare's *Othello*. He gets carried away by the story and shifts from silent reader into the main characters in an increasing tempo. He enacts Othello, Desdemona and Iago according to Boito's words, changing from one character to another, building dialogues between them and reacting to the characters he interprets. Meanwhile, Verdi's opera is commented upon, counterpointed or replaced by the traditional rhythm of the *candomblé* drums: drums that in other contexts represent the Orixas (Afro-Brazilian gods).

The performer himself is a child of candomblé. Augusto Omolù, whose second name is the name of an Orixa, as he rather shyly explained, grew up in a *terreiro* (the ceremonial space of the candomblé) in Bahia, and moved on from the street culture and the artistry of *capoeira* (a mixture of dance and martial art) to classical (European) ballet and modern dance. In his work he now combines these traditions into impressive performances, dancing to Orixa rhythms with the precision of classical ballet and the inventiveness of modern dance. The result is an impressive performance, with the three drums constantly reminding one about the cultural space beyond the actual stage; there is a distinct feeling of condensed power in those drums, power that transmitted itself to the dancer.

It seems that Augusto Omolù personifies the 'creole', referring to a quality of multidimensional spaces, inhabited by people equipped with two or more repertoires for communication (Carrington 1992). But what about the Moor of Venice then? He certainly had more than one cultural repertoire; he was even black. And Shakespeare and Verdi, did they not live in multidimensional spaces? Certainly, Shakespeare drew on several cultural registers, related both to social classes and to different historical situations, quite apart from his obvious dramatic licence; and this produced in *Otello* a double time scheme, not to say temporal and logical inconsistency, which has been much debated by his critics (G. Taylor 1990). Is Shakespeare's art, therefore, 'creole', or is it just art?

Ulf Hannerz (1987) defines creolization as a conversation between cultures, a conversation that has often gone on for quite some time, allowing people to form their lives according to several systems of meaning. More often than not, if we are to believe Hannerz, the conversation has taken place between unequal partners. This is how creolization amounts to a creative reinterpretation of the dominant or 'central' culture in the subdominant or 'peripheral' one (Hannerz 1989). With Shakespeare and Verdi we are well placed within the central culture, it seems, while with Eugenio Barba's recent production of *Othello*, we seem to have a clearer case of asymmetrical cultural conversation, the white director somehow transporting his native tradition of Italian opera to the black culture of Brazil. Here, the native dancer creatively reinterprets the opera, if we take the notion of creolization at face value.

Yet, at closer inspection the term makes little sense. This is not only because I am focusing upon a particular instance, an event, while Hannerz deals with long-term processes; I would argue that either way, 'creolization' must be both structure and event. The principal weakness of the term is its derivation from an obsolete notion of cultures as localized yet portable wholes, which may mix in unequal ways. I think that the model of creolization as a creative reinterpretation of the dominant culture in the periphery is a fantasy that belongs to that very same dominant culture.

The creative powers of the main characters in the trajectory of Othello as told here – the author, the playwright, the dramatist, the composer, the director and the dancer – do not stem from their mixing of repertoires or drawing upon diverse cultures but from their ability to create something truly new, which stands on its own feet. They do not merely discover another world and incorporate it into well-known categories; they invent a new beginning. So also for Omolù's performance, which is described thus in the printed programme:

> The performance is based exclusively on the codification of the Orixa dances: all gestures, steps and movements originate from the dances of the saints and gods of the Candomblé religion.
>
> In the performance the Orixas are different manifestations of the human passions which animate the main episodes of the play ...

The dancer has his own perspective, of course. Let us hear Augusto Omolù's own voice, to make this a true conversation. When asked about his way of seeing his dance, Augusto answered (quoted from my notes of 15 August 1994):

> I transform the Orixas – or my image of it because I never received a Saint – into art. I am not letting the Orixas come through in the performance. It is this transforma-

tion which is the challenge for the actor: to go out of the ritual and to become a character in another story. In the beginning it was difficult because the images stuck with me. Even when I dance to Verdi I still hear the drums.

This is not a creative creole speaking; this is a professional performer, not compromising his tradition but living it in different, and separate, ways. The paradox of acting, which is also the paradox of living, is that 'performance consciousness' does not destroy the reality of the action (Dening 1993:85). The authenticity of Omolù's dance does not depend on his being within the ritual, but on his being in command of its force and able to direct it towards his own goal. It is this directive force which is at the centre of whatever creativity is inherent in Othello's dance.

This was to be confirmed when, nine months later, I again saw the performance. This time the stage was set in northern Sweden, and while the programme read the same, the actual performance seemed to have changed. It was smoother, more finished; less candomblé and more Omolù in some way. The paradox of Omolù's name being an Orixa name actually reflects the paradox of his performative genre. The 'dance' is not necessarily generic; just as the game of *capoeira* defies the category (Lewis 1995), so in fact may Othello's dance, as related to and in some sense deriving from the candomblé. The distance to candomblé seemed to have increased from Brazil to Sweden; even Omolù's words were subtly different. As if rehearsed many times, he now very willingly told his own story, and the origin of his (god's) name. He also told how, when a person begins to dance, he has not been taught. One knows the elements but not how to dance. 'One has the energy, but not the perfection of movement' (quoted from my notes of 19 May 1995).[2]

What these words describe is far removed from the ritual, from which only the separate elements of the Orixa dance (mainly particular movements or codified images, like the movement of a snake or the holding up of a hand in front of the face as if it were a mirror) survive the transformation into a professional and coherent performance. The ritual itself is not performance, but the elements of the ritual are transposed into Othello's dance. They are in some way 'discovered' by the director and the audience, and thus made to fit the known category of a stage performance. The 'new' was discovered and invented at the same time. Omolù's dancing of Othello made something happen, which had far less to do with a mixture of cultures in conversation than with his strong scenic presence – amounting almost to a double agency.[3] It is this presence which authenticates his play, and increasingly so as his technical mastery grows.

A comparison may help to clarify the point I am getting at. One evening, during the same session of theatre anthropology at which *Othello* was first performed, a Candomblé group of about 30 dancers were brought in to perform their ritual, under the leadership of a *Mâe de Santo* (Mother of the Saint). Everything was apparently authentic – except that it was not. The ritual outside the *terreiro* turned into a performance of Afro-Brazilianness. It was transformed into folklore in the process, and the experience was one of a simulacrum, reflecting the process of alleged 'whitening' and 'folklorizing' of the ritual happening – even in Bahia, the regional centre of the Afro-Brazilian religion. No longer forbidden, the *terreiro* groups have quickly learnt to open up for spectators, even to apply for money from the tourist board. I am not blaming them, of course; I am concentrating on the contrastive experience of the theatre performance, that felt authentic and deeply moving, and the ceremonial candomblé dance, as performed outside the *terreiro* for a 'tourist' audience, which felt fake and somehow almost degrading. My point is that creolization in itself is not creative; by its rein-terpretation of local culture in terms of another, maybe dominant, culture it may create something 'new' – but only by discovery, by incorporating the strange into the already known. Creativity, as I see it, is different from this kind of mixing in space. It goes beyond the encounter of repertoires; it moves, and makes the direction of history shift at one level or another, by making people experience the ontologically new.

DRAMATIC EMBODIMENT

One reason why Othello's dance moves its audience is to be found in the technical mastery of the dancer. It is, indeed, a technology of enchantment. The enchantment is of a peculiar nature; it is not a simple emotional trans-ference. As Paul Spencer has put it:

> the dance creates an illusion of emotions that are not really felt, but only imagined as in a novel or a play or a painting, and revealed through symbols. Rather than symptoms of real emotion expressed though spontaneous gesture, one has symbols of perceived emotion, of will, conveyed by the artist through contrived gestures as he created a virtual world. (Spencer 1985:7)

Enchantment is the result of the virtual world. The technology of enchantment is the technique by which the dancer convinces the audience about the reality of the virtual world; in other words the technique by which he produces the illusion of 'presence' in this other world. The illusion is achieved by a mastery of the body-in-life (cf. Hastrup 1995c).

At one level, the technology covers no more and no less than an essential objectification of the body; while for most people the body is 'absent' in the sense that it recedes from direct experience (as the eye avoids the gaze), for the dancer the presence of the body is essential (cf. Leder 1990). Ordinarily, we are only aware of our bodies when they do not function or are in pain; at such moments the bodies become objectified by the thinking subject's wanting to redress the painless state. The dancer experiences this objectification as part of his technical mastery, and it is this objectification which makes possible something absolutely new (Lewis 1995:234). While people in general more often experience an absence of the body (Leder 1990; cf. Hastrup 1995b), actors, athletes and dancers must bring their body into focus and work 'with' it. This implies that the unconsciousness connected to the (recessive) body, which has displaced it from our notions of the 'self', is transformed into an acute awareness of the bodily limits and potentialities. In the training of performers, the technology of enchantment becomes embodied.

Through this dramatic embodiment, the actor enters another state of possible actions, a new point of stillness. Far from being empty, it is a stillness full of promise. As Antonin Artaud put it, in his critique of traditional theatre: 'Our petrified idea of the theatre is connected with our petrified idea of culture without shadows, where, no matter which way it turns, our mind (*esprit*) encounters only emptiness, though space is full' (Artaud 1958:12). The theatre is particularly forceful in stirring up shadows, left out by referential language, yet to move the spectators the shadows must connect to their own experience of the unspeakable.

I have no intention of simply likening the world to a theatre or to fall into facile and reductionist metaphors of stages and role-playing, implying that everyone is free to choose his or her favourite role. They are not, of course. Nor are we simply playing out our lives according to Goffman's metaphors of onstage and offstage as two separate domains of acting, one of deliberate deception, the other of true character. What matters in the present connection, is to see theatre as an experimental situation, a telescoped social drama. As Victor Turner once remarked, theatre produces an experience of heightened vitality (Turner 1986:43). This is owing to the 'presence' of the actor, not only in body but in life. The actor embodies creativity, because of his 'dilated' presence (Barba 1985; Barba and Savarese 1991). The dilated body of the actor is what takes the spectator into the unknown lands of his own experience. The actor can reveal only what is already true, even if it belongs to the unknown side of things (Grotowski 1969:194–5).

True theatre thus takes us close to the Romantic idea of imagination as 'a creation which reveals, or as a revelation which at the same time defines and completes what it makes manifest' (C. Taylor 1989:419). The brilliance of theatre is that it represents experience and offers conventions of interpretation at the same time; it works, not by replication of experience, but by condensing it, and adding the larger-than-life quality which redresses reality (Dening 1993:89). Through vicarious experience, theatre takes us close to the 'new' – in a close parallel, as it happens, to anthropological fieldwork.

As Phyllis Gorfain wrote in her analysis of Hamlet's significance for the audience (and for anthropology): '*Hamlet* ... brings us closer to the chaos from which it protects us, even while it displays the epistemological paradox it presses: knowing through not knowing' (Gorfain 1986:217). It is part of our common humanity that we are imaginable to one another (Shweder 1990:18), yet to make this unity experientially accessible takes a creative effort. As revelation, *Othello* completes and defines a multiple identity, but only in so far as it resonates with prefigured, if not yet known, suppositions.

38   *Locating Cultural Creativity*

Performative or poetic imagination may move the world by its driving at the unknown side of things, the so far unspoken reality. As Eduardo Archetti has written about the Argentinian tango: 'the authors of the tango texts were important forces in the creation of a cultural universe mainly centred on gendered social relations and representation' (Archetti 1994:107). By explicating the implicit, the tango became formative in the construction of Argentineness; the masculine narrative came to occupy a primordial place in the constitution of national culture (ibid.:116). In a similar vein from Indonesia, Anna Lowenhaupt Tsing has shown how an individual Meratus woman through her own spiritual world challenges the dominant male model of shamanism, thereby contributing to 'an emerging Meratus conversation on gender, creativity and power' (Tsing 1993:124). Both of these examples, and scores of others, point to the fact that cultures are discursively constructed, and that poetic creativity provides a channel for improvisation and imagination. This capacity for the opening of new ground is due to the parallactic power of poetic language: its ability to transcend fixed meanings by taking us into the dynamic zone of indeterminacy, that is the zone where the emotions and motives of the agents are significantly beyond the scope of exhaustive and accurate verbal description (Friedrich 1986:2).

Similarly, theatre exploits what I like to call the performative parallax inherent in the displaced experience of the stage. *Othello* exploits the theatricality of global history-making and puts it to dramatic effect. The theatrical frame gives 'force' to our experience, too often represented in bland narrative (cf. Rosaldo 1986; Dening 1993:81). The force is due to the fact that by way of dramatic embodiment and scenic presence, theatre makes us experience an experience, which we cannot, therefore, narrate away.

THE PROPHET

Whether we speak of a linguistic or a performative parallax, it is due to social agents. There are no speech or other acts without speakers or actors. Yet at the same time, the meaning of these acts is of necessity a public feature. Meaning cannot be private. Had the Argentinian tango-makers or the Indonesian poet not spoken within a conversational community, their inventive verses could have been discarded as irrelevant, maybe mad. We are, therefore, bound to consider the place of the individual agent within the creative cultural process.

From my perspective, acting on stage is but a special instance of social action in general. Action in this double sense does not necessarily imply actual movement in space or talking aloud. Action is everywhere in life. As Stanislavski wrote: 'On the stage you must always be enacting something; action, motion is the basis of the art ... of the actor; ... even external immobility ... does not imply passiveness. You may sit without motion and at the same time be in full action' (Stanislavski 1963:7–8). The human as bodily presence is the locus of – and the pretext for – action. Action is not conceivable as a mental category; it is materialized, expressed by a 'body-in-life', evidently much more than a body merely alive (Barba 1985:13).

Like language, the body serves as a depository of deferred thoughts

> that can be triggered off at a distance in space and time by the simple effect of replacing the body in an overall posture which *recalls* the associated thoughts and feelings, in one of the inductive states of the body which, as actors know, give rise to states of mind. (Bourdieu 1990:69)

In theatre, the audience 'recalls' unknown thoughts and feelings by way of vicarious bodily experience.

Theatrical performances are telescoped social performances, and as such our general notions of agency as linking the individual to a community apply equally to both. Theatre provides a social drama of heightened vitality because it condenses the agents' energy, not because it transforms it into something different. Agents, whether actors on stage or in life, are self-interpreting and reflexive humans, for whom motivation is governed as much by implicit moral evaluations as by disengaged minds (C. Taylor 1985). Double agents are even more so.

In a view of culture which allows for shadows and corporeal depth, instead of reducing it to a unilineal narrative, agency is responding to motivation, not simply acting intentionally. Motivation is a symbolic capital which moves. Symbolic capital is a means for transubstantiating real relations of power, and for producing real effects, without any apparent expenditure of energy (Bourdieu 1991:170). The parallaxes referred to above are symbolic capital in this sense.

These parallaxes share a number of features with metaphor. Metaphor hinges on the *use* of language, rather than its *meaning*, according to Donald Davidson. By way of a literal use of words, metaphor makes us see *as* rather than see *that*. 'Metaphor makes us see one thing as another by making some literal statement that inspires or prompts the insight' (Davidson 1984:263). Metaphor is not a wastebin for the not properly understood. Rather, it is a prime element in our structuring of experience; it is a pervasive mode of understanding by way of projecting particular patterns or connections onto the unprecedented (Johnson 1987:xiv et passim). The frightening indeterminacy of experience is transformed to a temporary making of sense.

This is what true theatre achieves, by making us experience the experience. The implications are profound, because 'the metaphoric sentence expresses a proposition; but the *seeing as* response that it inspires is not a propositional attitude' (Cavell 1986:495). Briefly, in Davidson's terms, 'words are the wrong currency to exchange for a picture' (1984:263). The picture created by theatre, and, indeed, the theatricality of living in general, makes us aware of the possibility of distance between outward signs and internal realities, and liberates us from the trap of literalness and mimicry.

The 'dreamwork' of metaphor, evoked by Davidson, implicitly points to a feature of condensation and displacement inherent also in Freud's analysis of dreams (Cavell 1986). Condensation and displacement are prominent features of a theatre that moves its audience. In their turn, the audience makes use of imagination as a capacity for understanding the unprecedented experience. Imagination in this sense is part and parcel of any rationality that we might claim. Even innovation is a rule-governed behaviour: 'the work of imagination does not come out of nowhere' (Ricoeur 1991:25); it resonates with previous experience.

Just as poetry may have its master tropes, so theatre may have its key expressions. In both cases, the limits – of natural language or of ordinary bodily action – are explored and altered. This is true creativity, a creativity that reveals. Thus, amongst poets and dancers of creative power we find those 'gifted individuals who have bent the culture in the direction of their own capacities', of whom Ruth Benedict once spoke (1932:26). It seems to me that Augusto Omolù personifies precisely this: creativity is a process that takes place between 'gifted' individuals and their culture. The individual gift is wasted if it does not resonate with the community. To be creative is not merely to invent or to innovate but to make a new kind of understanding possible by revealing what is already partly sensed.

We are once again balanced on the edge of words, between the analytical void of the anonymous, collective and tradition-bound creativity of the *Volksgeist*, and the equally empty myth of the alienated genius. Avoiding these extremes we may insist that culture itself is a creative process to which individual human agents contribute. Their contribution may be smaller or greater, but creativity always implies a 'dislocation in the economy of cultural representations' (Babcock 1993:75). Cultural creativity is a feature of a dynamic world in which social position is derived from the position of signs rather than the reverse (to paraphrase Zygmunt Bauman 1971:287, quoted in Babcock 1993:90). In the creative process, the poetic is not separate from the politic: by challenging cultural stereotypes, the gifted individual bends culture his or her way. In the words of Sapir, 'creation is a bending of form to one's will, not the manufacture of form *ex nihilo*' (Sapir 1924:418). In this respect, creativity differs from magic, which Mauss identifies as precisely creation *ex nihilo* (Mauss 1972:141). In the case of Othello's dance, the dancer bends the form of candomblé to his profesional will.

Creative agency in my view is a capacity to bring the yet unknown to effect by way of imaginative power. Not totally unlike Kroeber's 'genius', who is a 'channel' for cultural expression (Kroeber 1969:16), and much like Ardener's 'prophet', who expands language to accomodate the new world (Ardener 1989; Hastrup 1989), the creative individual expands the community's awareness of itself. One way of exploring the implications of this is to unfold the notion of imagination in Romantic terms while not necessarily discarding the Enlightenment ethos. The act of reasoning itself implies imagining within a social and cultural context. Understanding is an *event.* We 'intimate' unprecedented incidents or other worlds by means of imaginative projections from previous experience. As previously related, a theory of imagination is an important ingredient of any theory of rationality. Once we have abandoned the demand for a disembodied rationality, imagination need no longer be excluded from our vision of the processes of understanding. Creativity is emergent in any reflection upon society.

While so far a logic of creativity seems to have been a contradiction in terms, we can now see that even novel connections come out of past experience. Imagination provides the metonymical and metaphorical links between previous experience and new events and expressions. The logic of imaginative creativity is not distinct from the logic of reasoning; they are aspects of the same capacity for intimation, which is part of our being 'cultural'. Imagination is both constitutive and creative. It is a process, central to any event of understanding.

And because it is 'principally metaphoric reasoning that makes it possible for us to learn from our experience' (Johnson 1993:3), theatre may have an important role to play in the raising of the implicit consciousness of the world to a fuller awareness of our own position within it (cf. Hastrup 1995d). Awareness creates new possibilities for social agency. From the centre of the hurricane, the genius of theatre projects potentiality all around. The still point of the turning world is laden with dramatic density for the community to explore.

CREATIVITY AND AGENCY

In the argument so far, I have moved freely between the world of theatre and the world of culture. I have argued that theatre may be seen as telescoped social drama, expressing moments of heightened vitality in culture, and that theatre, therefore, provides us with an experimental situation. Truly, cultural creativity is condensed in drama, yet the drama also provides a kind of comment upon the culture: the act of dramatization is always selective. Theatre, therefore, 'reflects back' upon culture in a particular, poetic, way (cf. Hastrup 1992).

In contrast to mimesis, the poetic modality of theatre is truly creative; it is making not faking (cf. Turner 1982b:88). Theatre exposes what the contrastive ('surrounding') culture is not. It mocks, reverts, makes counter-claims and creates. Art is not just a sign or a means of communication – communicating, or replicating culture – but a particular mode of thought, expressing what is not otherwise said (cf. Geertz 1983:120). In the words used earlier, the theatrical idiom brings the otherwise 'unknown' to the fore. Art, such as poetry and theatre, is particularly powerful in achieving this contrastive effect, yet culture itself also functions as art, thereby testifying to the parallel between theatre and culture.

Culture as well as language is a structure in process involving meanings and contexts, and many of the relations among its symbols are analogous in part to poetic figures. It follows that culture itself, of which language is only a fairly obvious part, is, to a significant degree, a work of art. Obviously, then, it is the more artistic universes of this collective work (that is, poetry strictly speaking and the other arts) that most profoundly differentiate languages and cultures – to the extent that they capitalize on these linguistic and cultural uniquenesses. By a seeming paradox, it is also precisely in art that languages are made most accessible to each other, partly because it inspires the virtuoso and the individual response to the virtuoso. (Friedrich 1986:53)

The poetic power of language, and of art, marks difference while also overcoming it. In a mimetic modality, an optical illusion of sameness makes no room for synthesis. In contrast, a poetic modality creates a panoptical space, a space within which one may overlook the whole world from a particular position. In our case it is the position of theatre. While mimesis presents self *as* other (Taussig 1993), and portrays the subject as the sole object of desire, poesis shows self *and* other in their intersubjective relationship.

Poetic theatre is non-linear; while actions or acts are of course played out in a linear fashion, the power of synthesis inherent in the performance as well as in poetry makes the spectator hold them in the imagination as a totality (cf. Friedrich 1986:128). It is the conjunction which makes us 'know' – without necessarily knowing the implications. Such is also the power of Othello's dance, which in many ways operates like the Balinese cockfight, as analysed by Geertz: 'Enacted and re-enacted ... the cockfight enables the Balinese, as read and reread, *Macbeth* enables us, to see a dimension of his own subjectivity' (Geertz 1973:45). The dance, like any play 'becomes a mirror of problems of inquiry, but it does not make an inquiry itself' (Gorfain 1986:216).

As in periods of crisis or rapid change, so also in moments of dramatic density there is a breakdown in the way in which language itself is understood (cf. Crapanzano 1992:289). The bond of signification is broken; the world becomes momentarily unspeakable. This effective reframing (and the frame is of course part of the event) is what makes the world new. The creative human agent works by reframing, not illustrating, the mundane world, whether on stage or in life.

By way of concluding this chapter, I shall return to the notion of cultural creativity in relation to human agency. Theatre is a space which consciously reframes human experience. Yet focusing on the agent allows us to emphasize the profound continuity between acting on stage and living in the world, if only because of the dialectic between performing and learning identified by Victor Turner: 'One learns through performing, then performs the understandings so gained' (Turner 1982a:94). From the ringside of the theatre, Constantin Stanislavski also warned the actor: 'Always act in your own person ... You can never get away from yourself. The moment you lose yourself on the stage marks the departure from truly living your part and the beginning of exaggerated, false acting' (Stanislavski 1963:91). Even if theatre produces an experience of heightened vitality, this vitality is apprehensible only through a continuity with lived experience in general.

The creativity of theatre is not inherent in the drama itself, but in the effect it has upon the spectators. In its points of dramatic density – achieved through performative parallax – the spectators experience the potentiality of the moment. In a parallel fashion, cultural creativity is located neither in culture as such nor in its creolization, but in the moment when someone's imaginative power makes possible the intimation by the community of a new reality. *Othello* moves the specator, not because a black Brazilian dances to a white Italian's music, but because the dancer touches ground in a shared human capacity for imagination, which transcends preconceived notions of both Brazilianness and Italianness, of candomblé and opera.

Meaning is always emergent, and each moment contains a 'surplus' of possible successors. Only one next step can be made, however. In theatre, the vicarious experience of the surplus historicity of any moment leaves a lasting trace upon the spectator – which words in themselves could not achieve. The experience of experience displaces the individual from his or her life history. Outside theatre, the dislocation in the economy of relevant expressions may redirect history by challenging what so far seemed self-evident.

The key position attributed to (vicarious) experience in the example of theatre points to the fundamental epistemological point that most of what we study in anthropology is located not in the things but in our experience of them (C. Taylor 1985:47). Experience is what motivates the agent. Cultural creativity is intimately linked to human agency, as the capacity to respond imaginatively to new experiences – and thereby to find the ontologically new.

NOTES

1. An earlier version of this article was presented at the international conference on 'Locating Cultural Creativity', held by the Institute of Anthropology, University of Copenhagen, October 1994, under the title 'Theatrum Mundi'. I owe thanks to the participants for constructive comments, notably to James Fernandez of the University of Chicago. Later, Eugenio Barba and Patrice Pavis read and contributed to the argument. For the final revision, and the tightening of the argument I am particularly grateful to Felicia Hughes-Freeland, and to the editor John Liep.
2. The terms used by Omolù here are influenced by the work of the International School of Theatre Anthropology, founded by Eugenio Barba (see Barba and Savarese 1991, and Hastrup 1996).
3. The notion of 'double agency' is developed further in Hastrup (1997).

REFERENCES

Archetti, E. (1994) 'Models of masculinity in the poetics of the Argentinian tango', in E. Archetti (ed.) *Exploring the Written: Anthropology and the Multiplicity of Writing*. Oslo: Scandinavian University Press.

Ardener, E. (ed.) (1989) *The Voice of Prophecy and Other Essays*. Malcolm Chapman. Oxford: Blackwell.

Artaud, A. (1958) *The Theater and its Double*. New York: Grove Press.

Babcock, B.A. (1993) 'At home, no womens are storytellers: ceramic creativity and the politics of discourse in Cochiti Pueblo', in S. Lavie, K. Narayan and R. Rosaldo (eds) *Creativity/Anthropology*. Ithaca: Cornell University Press.

Barba, E. (1985) *The Dilated Body*. Rome: Zeami Libri.

Barba, E. and Savarese, N. (1991) *The Secret Art of the Performer: A Dictionary of Theatre Anthropology*. London: Routledge.

Barth, F. (1987) *Cosmologies in the Making*. Cambridge: Cambridge University Press.

Baumann, Z. (1971) 'Semiotics and the function of culture', in J. Kristeva, J. Rey-Debove and D.J. Umiker (eds) *Essays in Semiotics*. The Hague: Mouton.

Benedict, R. (1932) 'Configurations of culture in North America', *American Anthropologist* 34:1–27.

Bourdieu, P. (1990) *The Logic of Practice*. Cambridge: Polity Press.

—— (1991) *Language and Symbolic Power*. Cambridge: Polity Press.

Carrington, L.D. (1992) 'Images of Creole space', *Journal of Pidgin and Creole Languages* 7 (1):93–9.

Cavell, M. (1986) 'Metaphor, dreamwork and irrationality', in E. lePore (ed.) *Truth and Interpretation: Perspectives on the Philosophy of Donald Davidson*. Oxford: Blackwell.

Crapanzano, V. (1992) 'Maimed rites and wild and whirling words', in *Hermes' Dilemma and Hamlet's Desire: On the Epistemology of Interpretation*, Cambridge, Massachusetts: Harvard University Press.

Davidson, D. (1984) 'What metaphors mean', in *Inquiries into Truth and Interpretation*. Oxford: Clarendon Press.

Davis, J. (1992) 'The anthropology of suffering', *Journal of Refugee Studies* 5:149–61.

Dening, G. (1993) 'The theatricality of history making', *Cultural Anthropology* 8:73–95.

Friedrich, P. (1986) *The Language Parallax. Linguistic Relativism and Poetic Indeterminacy*. Austin: University of Texas Press.

Geertz, C. (1973) *The Interpretation of Cultures*. New York: Basic Books.

—— (1983) *Local Knowledge*. New York: Basic Books.

Gell, A. (1992) 'The technology of enchantment and the enchantment of technology', in J. Coote and A. Shelton (eds) *Anthropology, Art, and Aesthetics*. Oxford: Clarendon Press.

Gorfain, P. (1986) 'Play and the problem of knowing in *Hamlet*: an excursion into interpretive anthropology', in V. Turner and E.M. Bruner (eds) *The Anthropology of Experience*. Urbana: University of Illinois Press.

Grotowski, J. (1969) *Towards a Poor Theatre*. London: Methuen.

Hannerz, U. (1987) 'The world in creolization' *Africa* 57 (4):546–59.

—— (1989) 'Culture between center and periphery: toward a macroanthropology', *Ethnos* 54 (3/4):200–16.

Hastrup, K. (1989) 'The prophetic condition', in M. Chapman (ed.) *Edwin Ardener: The Voice of Prophecy and Other Essays*. Oxford: Blackwell.

—— (1992) 'Out of anthropology: the anthropologist as an object of dramatic representation', *Cultural Anthropology* 7 (3):327–45.

—— (1993) 'Hunger and the hardness of facts', *Man* 28:727–39.

—— (1995a) *A Passage to Anthropology: Between Experience and Theory*. London: Routledge.

—— (1995b) 'Il corpo motivato', *Teatro e Storia* 10:11–36.

—— (1995c) 'Incorporated knowledge', in T. Leabhart (ed.) *Incorporated Knowledge: The Mime Journal* 1995:2–9.

—— (1995d) 'The inarticulate mind: the place of awareness in social action', in A. Cohen and N. Rapport (eds) *Questions of Consciousness*. London: Routledge.

—— (ed.) (1996) *The Performers' Village: Times, Techniques and Theories at ISTA*. Copenhagen: Drama.

—— (1997) 'Theatre as a site of passage: some reflections on the magic of acting', in F. Hughes-Freeland (ed.) *Ritual, Performance, Media*. ASA Monographs 33. London: Routledge.

Johnson, M. (1987) *The Body in the Mind*. Chicago: University of Chicago Press.

—— (1993) *Moral Imagination*. Chicago: University of Chicago Press.

Kroeber, A. (1969) *Configurations of Culture Growth*, Berkeley: University of California Press.

Leder, D. (1990) *The Absent Body*. Chicago: University of Chicago Press.

Lewis, J.L. (1995) 'Genre and embodiment: from Brazilian *Capoeira* to the ethnology of human movement', *Cultural Anthropology* 10:221–43.

Mauss, M. (1972) *Towards a General Theory of Magic*. London: Routledge and Kegan Paul.

Paine, R. (1995) 'Columbus and anthropology and the unknown', *The Journal of the Royal Anthropological Institute* 1:47–65.

Ricoeur, P. (1991) 'Life in quest of narrative', in D. Wood (ed.) *On Paul Ricoeur: Narrative and Interpretation*. London: Routledge.

Rosaldo, R. (1986) 'Ilongot hunting as story and experience', in E. Bruner and V. Turner (eds) *The Anthropology of Experience*. Washington: American Ethnological Society.

Rosaldo, R., Lavie, S. and Narayan, K. (1993) 'Introduction', in S. Lavie, K. Narayan and R. Rosaldo (eds) *Creativity/Anthropology*. Ithaca: Cornell University Press.

Sapir, E. (1924) 'Culture, genuine and spurious', *American Journal of Sociology* 29:401–29.

Shweder, R. (1990) *Thinking through Cultures*. Cambridge, Massachusetts: Harvard University Press.

Spencer, P. (1985) 'Introduction: interpretations of the dance in anthropology', in P. Spencer (ed.) *Society and the Dance: The Social Anthropology of Process and Performance*. Cambridge: Cambridge University Press.

Stanislavski, C. (1963) *An Actor's Handbook*. New York: Theater Art Books.

Taussig, M. (1993) *Mimesis and Alterity: A Particular History of the Senses*. London: Routledge.

Taylor, C. (1985) *Human Agency and Language*. Cambridge: Cambridge University Press.

—— (1989) *Sources of the Self: The Making of the Modern Identity*. Cambridge: Cambridge University Press.

Taylor, G. (1990) *Reinventing Shakespeare: A Cultural History from the Restoration to the Present*. London: Hogarth.

Tsing, A.L. (1993) 'Riding the horse of gaps: a Meratus woman's spiritual expression', in S. Lavie, K. Narayan, and R. Rosaldo (eds) *Creativity/Anthropology*. Ithaca: Cornell University Press.

Turner, V. (1982a) *From Ritual to Theatre*. New York: PAJ Publications.

—— (1982b) 'Dramatic ritual/ritual drama', in J. Rub (ed.) *A Crack in the Mirror: Reflexive Perspectives in Anthropology*. Philadelphia: University of Pennsylvania Press.

—— (1986) *The Anthropology of Performance*. New York: PAJ Publications.

Wagner, R. (1981) *The Invention of Culture*. Chicago: University of Chicago Press.

3   THE IRON CAGE OF CREATIVITY: AN EXPLORATION

Jonathan Friedman

WHY CREATIVITY?

Creativity has become something of a slogan among latter-day Birmingham cultural sociologists and their more seasoned allies, the cultural studies crowd. There has been a clear move from the study of working-class culture to the aesthetics of everyday life. While Birmingham certainly flirted with abstract structural Marxism, their interests lay more in the direction of the concrete, since they, unlike many Marxist sociologists, were trying to gain a purchase on reality in the street, so to speak – although one may have reservations about the nature of their ethnography, which, except for some of the research reports, was explicitly focused on issues of popular culture rather than on the more complete social analysis that one expects from anthropology. First, culture was ideology; then it became the primary source of resistance; and now it has become a fabulous circus of confused identity, hybridity and pastiche. Today there is a kind of imaginary merger of members of this group, some members of the Subaltern group of historians, literary historians and philosophers and large segments of the postmodern caucus, under what has become the aegis of *cultural studies*.[1]

WHAT ARE WE TALKING ABOUT?

I have to start off this way because I have no idea what the concept of creativity ought to be referring to. Often the fact of novelty is central; the notion of the *ex nihilo* is a clear fascination in our world. It harbours the heroic so dear to the intellectual heart or, perhaps, ego. Creativity in the arts has been represented in such terms, the terms of genius, of discovery of the unprecedented. On closer analysis, the question of the *ex nihilo* is not such a simple one. In anthropology much of what may appear as novelty is in fact a question of transformation, of variation, in other words, of new combinations and constructions of previously present elements and relations. To begin with we might distinguish between the truly discontinuous and the transformative kinds of creativity. This distinction is itself based on conflating

46

what are perhaps very different kinds of processes. The invention of relativity theory cannot be deduced from classical mechanics although many of its properties can be understood as a solution to the problems of the former. There is probably no way to deduce classical from baroque music. But the processes involved in these historical transitions are not contained within the narrow field of the models or musical patterns involved. That is, classical music owes much of its content to other sources than those of the Baroque, even as many of its formal qualities are indeed continuous with the latter. Similarly Einstein found his solutions to the limitations of classical theory in pre-Socratic philosophy rather than simply developing them out of the materials of classical physics itself. But in some broader sense we must still consider the extent to which novelty might be a question of finding new combinations, new gestalts where none existed previously, but where in some sense the combinations were a potential. This does not imply that such creative changes are predictable, only that they are intelligible in structural terms. The transformative notion of creativity is more common in anthropological inquiry, although here too it has rarely been examined in a systematic fashion. Lévi-Strauss in *The Savage Mind* (1966) goes quite a way toward analysing one notion of transformative creativity, demonstrating the play of variation in structure and attempting to grasp the field of potential creation via combinatorial schemes such as the totemic operator. He makes a systematic distinction between three kinds of variation: bricolage, art and science, three kinds of 'logic' that are present universally in varying quantities and locations in society. Bricolage refers to the purest notion of variation on theme by mere recombination. As a form of knowledge it consists of reducing realities to the same fundamental relations, so that the world is made over into a given structure, no matter what its inherent properties. In bricolage, the fundamental relations are embedded in the concrete realities themselves and have no independent existence. These relations are not the product of a search for connections in the reality at hand, but an assimilation of that reality to a preordained structure. Science is the converse of bricolage. It seeks discontinuous models to account for the same realities, that is, by finding previously unknown relations in those realities. Its models must be abstract so as to be able to grasp the difference between the model and that to which it refers. It is driven by the need to achieve better accounts, by a constant desire to replace current models. Art is said to lie in between bricolage and science. It is discontinuous insofar as it is the product of the individual artist's vision of the reality at hand, a vision whose goal is to say something about the world, to discover novel connections in the world as in science; but the insights are embedded in the concretely represented realities themselves, as in bricolage. From the structuralist point of view, bricolage has a higher degree of predictability than either art or science, because it is limited primarily to a single semantic field.

In the following I shall try to unpack the relevance of structuralism when understood as embedded in social experience rather than as a mere intellectual technique.

STRUCTURE AND FORM

There are innumerable phenomena that can be described as creativity. In the most basic, if not trivial, sense it refers to what congeries of structuralists and mathematicians once discussed in terms of combinatorics, that is, the production of new structures out of a finite set of common elements, constrained by a set of rules. In the trivial sense, creativity can be defined as random recombinations of formerly combined elements. Random combinatorial processes, of course, are without information, that is, without structural properties – nothing specific can be said about them. Now much of the discussion of creativity in cultural studies refers to what I would call constrained combinatorics: the elaboration of styles, of modes of speaking, music, hybridity (as we now call it) in ethnicity, food etc. In such processes there are evidently subjects at work creating new combinations, and the combinations are constrained by the universe of meaning these subjects inhabit – this is even more so where the combinations are commodities that have to appeal to consumers. Even where it is a question of social identities, of lifestyles and language, combinations need to resonate if they are to become socially viable. They have to make sense in other people's lives. But we duly take note, for the time being, that there are indeed combinations. We also note that cultural studies and anthropologists who have dealt with and praised such combinatorial activity have usually only witnessed the products rather than the processes by which they are produced. The process of combination has not been the focus of these studies. Rather the fact of creativity seems to be enough. Thus, the cultural creativity of an urban multi-ethnic slum may be celebrated as if it were a work of art, but there is little analysis of the actual processes of generation. The latter could be achieved by applying the structuralist model extended to include the relation between fields of social experience and the actual construction of cultural variation. In such an approach the 'sociological armature' in Lévi-Strauss's terms is the experiential base of cultural production. By not clearly situating the point of cultural production, some very strange misinterpretations may arise. Some of the discourse on hybridity harbours precisely this kind of misinterpretation. The intellectual's aerial view of urban life may easily mistake a highly conflictual and violent reality for a fabulous cauldron of creativity. Some anthropologists have been quite prone to this kind of language in which the urban is described as a complex of perspectives that are sometimes in conflict with one another. Hannerz, who treats the question of urban creativity precisely in terms of high and popular cultural products, while ignoring the social class structures and deeper cultural frameworks involved, is able to dismiss the social conflicts that arise even in the upper echelons, in which police harassment and murders are involved, with typical culturalist bias: 'Such signs of conflict may all be regrettable in themselves, and yet it would be difficult to deny that the clashes between perspectives have also contributed to the vitality of cultural processes in these three cities' (1992:213). This might be extended to the urban slum, which has certainly been a source of creativity, from sounding to rap – a whole series of artistic innovations. But viewing these from above, from the point of view of products or even commodities, belies the conditions under which they are brought forth. The understanding of creativity must pass through the social and existential conditions that are its foundation. The cultural celebrationists need their Oscar Lewis and Mike Davis to bring them back to earth.

THE IRON CAGE: THE CONSTRAINTS ON CREATIVITY

To the extent that creativity is not a question of random recombinations we must understand the constraints that account for such departures from randomness.

Meaning

The attribution of meaning to the world involves creation of form and its replication in various situations via mappings from one domain to another, by means of metaphor or more generally by means of homologies. This is not a matter of playfulness since it is often deadly serious, involving, as we shall see below, the generation of cultural schemes out of social experience. Meaning creation as a social phenomenon is constrained by its receptivity in a relevant population, its capacity to make sense for others. When post-cargo cults appear in Papua New Guinea they often depend upon reorganization of meaning attribution; wealth is to come from America dropped by planes; such wealth is the product of fertility – the fertility of money, the fertility of human sexuality. *Paua hauses* are constructed where the young engage in sex and cash collected from cult members is 'tipped back and forth between two large basins' (May 1982:46). Money is buried in cemeteries to make it increase. Cargo cult fraud is a genuinely legal category. The Peli movement referred to here attracted a large population. The meanings constructed by its leaders were eminently recognizable to their followers.

Desire

The creation of new connections is motivated and the motivation has also to be susceptible to reproduction in a larger group. The Peli cult was triggered by economic decline after promises of development. It might be said to be a development movement itself. It began as its leaders protested against the existence of cement survey markers on a nearby mountain top, which, they claimed, prevented the flow of life force into the valley below. They also protested against missionaries who only gave them the religious Bible while keeping the *bisnis* Bible for themselves. Motivation, grounded in powerful desires, selects from the available connections, driving the creation of homologies and metaphoric extensions.

Social Experience

The substrate of both desire and meaning is social experience, that is the shared experience of the world that is the content of lived realities. This is not just any experience, but a largely unconscious, or conjunctive experience, as Mannheim called it (see below). He distinguishes between the communicative and the conjunctive as forms of knowledge. The former refers to context-free knowledge that can be transmitted without reference to context. The latter refers to context-bound knowledge that is only partially formulated. This is a distinction we shall develop below.

Conditions of Reproduction and Transformation of Social Experience

If the substrate of desire and meaning-production is socially shared experience, the latter has as its conditions of existence, the social processes that either maintain or transform those experiences. This is most often a question of degree. Modern cargo cults harbour modern discourses on development, chain-letter games and even what might appear as fraud, while being driven by a powerfully felt need to absorb external 'life-force' which imbues the objects of the modern sector. The political structures may have been altered to a large degree, as well as the economic conditions of local reproduction, but some basic forms of sociality and strategies of meaning attribution (signification as practice) have been maintained as they are embedded in social relations that have not been dissolved.

The image I am trying to convey here is one in which creativity is set off against both its combinatorial/structural and motivational constraints in order to close in on the process itself. The argument is primarily oriented toward highlighting the experiential foundation of creative activities as we discussed them earlier on. But this raises the serious methodological issue of how one gains access to experience.

CONJUNCTIVE EXPERIENCE AND THE ANTHROPOLOGY OF EXPERIENCE

There is clearly a move in anthropology today toward a more experience-based understanding of cultural realities, that is, of social specificities. It is a move away from a strictly cognitive and Cartesian view to one that places emphasis on what is popularly known as embodiment, embodied experiences in which mental–material oppositions dissolve into more holistic under- standings of social life. This shift, as is usual in social science, passes itself off as something new and even revolutionary. In stressing that our Western categories abstract and decontextualize the Other, and that even the concept of culture, in the plural sense, is a product of the modern project (Ingold 1993:217–21) that objectifies the world by carving it up into fragments, we are confronted with what is characterized as a reformulation of the anthro- pological project, no longer to study, compare and analyse cultures as sets of distinct cognitive schemes, but to grasp the 'cultural' (Borofsky 1987) resonance, and the nature of social existence as a practical and sensual relation to the world.

Of course the critique of Cartesianism is something of a tradition in the West although it has only rarely informed anthropology. We need only recall the phenomenology of Merleau-Ponty and his students, the early existen- tialism of Sartre, the philosophies of Heidegger and Husserl and further back in our Western Cartesian past, the arguments of Spinoza, Fichte and Hegel. In only a few cases were these individuals occupied with empirical research, but they had a significant influence on the social sciences. The work of the early Chicago School and its later developments in sociological ethnography, including grounded theory and ethnomethodology, strive for an under- standing of the immediate experiential constitution of social life. In Germany there was a series of earlier, important works by Scheler (1992) and following him, Mannheim (1982) and Schutz (1972), which provided much of the foundation of the later developments in the United States. The Karl Mannheim of this period, before 1920, is especially significant – not the sociologist of *Ideology and Utopia* (1976), but the author of *Structures of Thinking* (1982) which was a more or less forgotten work, which remained unpublished until the 1980s. The latter part of this work, on what he called the foundations of a 'cultural sociology' was pivotal for a number of researchers including Elias and Lukacs, who participated in Mannheim's seminar and who actually did fieldwork 'in the street' so to speak. Mannheim develops an opposition between what he calls the conjunctive and the com- municative. The former refers to the embedded, implicit organization of experience and knowledge of the world that lies 'beyond words' but which is the shared social experiential basis of culture and which presents a central methodological problem of documentation. The conjunctive is rooted in what Mannheim calls *Erfahrungsraum*, the space of socially shared experience. The communicative refers to the more or less context-free forms of knowledge and experience. Of course no experience can be context free, but social contexts can be so controlled and ordered as to have a minimum of contextual content.

While Mannheim is not terribly clear about this, I would suggest that we should not confuse the social in the sense of objective social field, and the social in the sense of structured experience. Thus the existence of a more or less context-free, that is, explicit, form of communication is itself dependent upon a structuring of a larger social field or context. The distinction between conjunctive and communicative is a distinction between social forms of experience, both being equally *social*. The two forms of experience or knowledge are also simultaneities in that any one experience contains both communicative and conjunctive aspects. In very different language, the Freudian analysis of therapy as containing both an explicit communicative content and a submerged process of transference and counter-transference, has been defined by Lacan (1966) as the simultaneity of the symbolic and the imaginary relations maintained with others. The imaginary here, the highly cathectic complexes of image-based investments in the other/Other which are usually repressed, is a form of conjunctive experience or knowledge. They are pre-linguistic in the pre-Oedipal child and sub-linguistic throughout the rest of life, and they inform the basic life-orientations of the subject, penetrating his/her symbolic practice. This penetration is the 'golden road' of psychoanalysis. It is the way in which the conjunctive enters the communicative, the way deeper relations are established in the everyday forms of relatedness, and it is the major problem for any ethnography that seeks to grasp other people's experience worlds which can only occur via the explicit behaviour to which we have access. The conjunctive is, thus, not another autonomous or observable reality. It is a set of properties, or structures, of social reality.

Now there are methods of gaining access to the conjunctive that have been developed by sociological ethnographers. Mannheim himself referred to the 'documentary method', and this has in turn been developed by others, most explicitly by Bohnsack (1991), who combines techniques drawn from conversation analysis with a rigorous interpretative approach, in order to understand the structures of shared experience. This approach has been used in the analysis of interview material, from life histories to group interviews (the latter are favoured, as they give free play to interacting subjects). The analysis reveals that 'people don't know what they know', and it is this latter knowledge that is the basis of interpretation. The importance of the documentary method for anthropologists is that it produces a text that can be interpreted by others. This is a far cry from the anthropologists' field notes, which are largely private and are used in unspecified ways to arrive at ethnographic interpretations. On the other hand this kind of approach is at present very much bound to recorded texts. However it might well be combined with more rigorous observational procedures that also lead to the production of documents. Participant observation, in this approach, needs to be made explicit and accessible to the research community.

Recent developments in cognitive anthropology, and other approaches at the borderland between anthropology and linguistics, have expressed a similar set of concerns. Metaphor analysis, the conversation analysis of the ethnomethodologists, and context analysis have all stressed the need to move away from the purely cognitive, to take account of the linkages among experiences, motives, strategies and representations. The general orientation combines a certain methodological precision with a focus on the relation between socially organized experience and cultural creativity. The well-known example from Lakoff and Johnson (1980), 'time is money', is used to explore the social experience that is its foundation. The argument is that that which allows the metaphor to achieve a certain resonance in our lives has to do with the way our experience of time is organized by our experience of money. The metaphor is not simply a cultural model, but a motivated insight and a productive one at that, since it generates a whole family of related expressions: 'saving time', 'wasting time', 'investing time', etc., that highlights the potential mapping of similar properties. One may go further, as Strauss and Quinn (1994) seem to suggest, as sound, smell and tactile sensations are also mapped into complexes of experience that motivate cultural production (creativity) – the positing of novel connections in reality. A serious limitation of this approach, inherited from the ethnomethodologists, is that the experiential complexes investigated are often, for methodological reasons, extremely limited in scope. Bohnsack has, in principle, attempted to overcome this limitation by combining conversation analysis and related methods with a broader focus on life orientations, or life projects; that is, a heavier interpretive programme.

STRUCTURALISM AND EXPERIENCE

The reason for the preceding discussion about questions of method is to locate the problem of experience as an accessible research area and to argue for a shift of focus of research from the objects of culture, to the substrate which generates such objects, be they artefacts or texts. This is not an exercise in method, however, but a set of suggestions on the nature of creativity as a social phenomenon. The course of these suggestions leads to unusual examples which are important for their shock value. Let us return to structuralism. Lévi-Strauss has for some years been classified as an enemy of the study of experience. He has, of course, expressed his lack of interest in the understanding of the emotions, since he understands their content aspect as interesting only in their specific social forms, and the latter are accessible whereas the former are merely the content-aspect of the latter. But there is more here than meets the eye. Lévi-Strauss after all is the product of an era and an intellectual milieu in which phenomenology was central, and he has often expressed his debt to the great phenomenologist Merleau-Ponty. Let me try to reveal the experiential in Lévi-Strauss by standing his most intellectualist work, *The Savage Mind*, on its head. I propose that the central argument of this book is based on a phenomenological interpretation of the relation between personhood and cosmos/nature. This is expressed in the unlikely model of the 'totemic operator'. The latter posits the totality of nature as consisting of a set of concrete species. These species are then successively divided into subspecies, and then into body parts that are homologous in relation to one another. The body parts are then recombined into new composite species that eventually become new and very individualized wholes in particular persons. The human individual is a highly specific combination of the concrete totality of nature, via a process of detotalization and retotalization. Every person is a specific combination and no person is like another. But at the same time every individual is merely a particularization of the concrete universal. All the properties of the individual are always-already-contained in the pre-existent universe. This can be read out of practices of naming whereby a child is given a series of names that indicate the history of pregnancy, personality traits, physical characteristics, critical events in terms of totemic beings, their characteristics and activities. Individuality is the materialization of the potential. It is thus not new in any discontinuous or absolute sense, only in a combinatorial sense. These relations, however, structuralist in their expression, are descriptions of a crucial existential reality, one in which the person is truly embedded in the collectivity of which he is a variation rather than an independent atomic unit. The person is the expression of the basic characteristics of the natural world. He belongs to the public, to society. He is not an empty subject who takes on roles, but a concrete manifestation of the already known. This powerful and clearly existential scheme is the foundation of totemic combinatorics and of the bricolage of *The Savage Mind*, that which makes an apparently formalist set of permutations into a deeper human unity. Where such existential schemes are dominant operators of social life we should expect to find that their symbolic production, their social structural variations over time, and their mythical products express a symphony of variations on a basic set of themes. In this interpretation, however, this symphony, as in music in general, is a kinaesthetic rather than a mere aesthetic or structural phenomenon. That is, the meanings inherent in the variations resonate deeply with people's experience of their world. Where such unity does not exist, as in so-called modern society, regions of existential resonance are more restricted.

GENERATIVITY AND EXISTENTIAL RESONANCE

The phenomenon of combinatorial generativity is one of the foremost forms of social creativity that has been studied by anthropologists. If fields of existential resonance can sometimes be said or assumed to characterize entire communities, it is where their forms of sociality embrace the entire collectivity embedding them in the same set of social experiences. More likely than not, and certainly in conditions of modernity, such fields are very much smaller and often more difficult to maintain as they are not institutionalized. They may also overlap in various degrees. The formation of black blues ensembles may be said to depend on more general shared sets of experience, but the emergence of the ensemble itself involves the development of a set of mutually adapted responses that operate non-reflexively and enable the group to improvise in a way that might not otherwise be possible. The formation of song ensembles might be said to be of an even more spontaneous character where the shared experiences are embedded in the self-same field. The incredible improvised counterpoint of African Pygmy music is an extraordinary example of this kind of group *habitus.*

HAWAIIAN BRICOLAGE

Hawaiians like to 'talk story', it is said, but they do not engage in psychological conversation and self-analysis. Talking story is literally talking story, telling of significant events. In the following, I examine a series of well-known stories about Captain Cook, Jesus and Spanish visitors before Captain Cook, from South Kona on the Island of Hawaii. Now in some contexts the fact that the Spanish arrived in Hawaii before Cook is a separate affair. But in the following stories, the themes of Cook, Spain and Jesus are brought together in a single series of stories, the 'real story' of Captain Cook.

In Hawaiian communities Christianity has played a crucial therapeutic role, as well as providing an interesting focus of identification, not merely through Jesus as such, but through Jesus as representative of Ancient Israel *in Hawaii*. Hawaiians in Kona maintain a contradictory set of interpretations of their origins. On the one hand there is a strong local rootedness that transforms the outside into the inside by assimilation and adoption. On the other hand there is an identification with the larger world, that which extends to the horizon where the gods dwell and which is a source of power and identity, not as foreign but as higher being.

1. Hawaiians come from afar, from Kahiki, from Ancient Israel, from over the sea. There are many migration stories of the origins of Hawaiians. The standard traditional forms talk of a place called Kahiki (but is this Tahiti?) which is associated with the land beyond the horizon, but there are several alternatives that are referred to. In more recent forms, influenced by missionary presence, the migratory movement took them from Israel over India and into the Pacific.
2. Jesus came from heaven/overseas to the 'lost tribes' which were *his* tribes. The identification with Jesus is part of the larger and older migration relation. Jesus is also from Ancient Israel.

What this implies for the formally accepted 'myths' of Cook's arrival in Hawaii is explored below.

The following stories are from a tape made in the kitchen of an elderly woman, a *kupuna* of a small fishing village. She and her distantly related niece set out to tell me the real story of Captain Cook at Hawaii. The several versions were the results of a rapid succession of interpretive discussions in which the story was elaborated upon. The entire session took about half an hour and displays a combinatorial virtuosity reminiscent of Lévi-Strauss but with the speed of a short-order cook (no pun intended). At each phase of the presentation it seemed to my interlocutors that they were filling in the story so that I would better understand it.

Version 1 There was a Spanish shipwreck here in the eighteenth century (date). Only two children survived and they were taken in. They were married to aristocrats. That is why some of us are more light skinned. You know that aristocrats are often lighter than commoners. That is also why some of us have Spanish names.

Version 2 There was a Spanish shipwreck here before Captain Cook, up at Kealakekua Bay. Everyone died but two children who we saved. The boy was brought up by the *ali'i* (chiefs) and was adopted to Maui. The girl was brought up here as a high *kahuna* (priestess). They were brother and sister and each became great in their own realms. The boy became a great warrior and the woman a famed priestess. When Captain Cook came the people mistook his sails for the Makahiki cross and believed that he was a great chief descendent of Lono. But they discovered that he was no such person and so they killed him.

There is a more elaborate version of this story in which Jesus is combined with Captain Cook in an interesting way. The story envisions Cook's visit as a false repetition of the return of Jesus:

Version 3 The Makahiki cross you know came originally from Jesus who came to Hawaii with his teachings. Hawaiians awaited his return over the centuries. There was a Spanish shipwreck here in the eighteenth century, here at Kealakekua Bay. Everyone died but two children who we saved. The boy was brought up by the *ali'i* and was adopted to Maui. The girl was brought up here as a high *kahuna*. They were brother and sister and each became great in their own realms. The boy became a great warrior and the woman a famed priestess. When Captain Cook came the people mistook his sails for the cross and were ready to accept him as their god, as Jesus. But the priestess who then lived on the upper slopes as did *kahuna* of high status, sent a message down to the Bay in which she warned the Hawaiians that this was not the real Jesus but an imposter. That is why he was mistrusted and eventually killed ... because he was an imposter, not the real Jesus.

In these stories there are two core versions, one dealing with the relation to Jesus and the other with the relation to the Spanish. Cook is a reference point and a point of contrast, that is, before Captain Cook we had other overseas visitors. Not only that. We are descended in part from them, in good cognatic fashion. The story of the shipwreck is a common theme from the Big Island, especially from Ke'ei, the area just to the south of Kealakekua Bay where Cook met his death. Some versions of this story were collected early in the century and they are considered part of the traditions of the Spanish in the islands. In the third variant of the story we have a more elaborate version of the way in which the Spaniards are incorporated into Hawaii. In all versions there is a brother–sister pair, who become part of Hawaiian society, either by marriage or by upbringing, in this case, clearly by *hanai*, or adoption. They are lighter in complexion, and therefore of higher status, and their arrival explains the phenotypic difference between aristocrats and commoners. That this event also explains the occurrence of Spanish names in Hawaii is an interesting example of time compression, referred to below, in which the existence of Spanish at the end of the past century can be equated with centuries-old connections. The equation of male to female as warrior to priest is also part of the sibling dualism characteristic of Hawaiian mythology and kinship. Finally the arrival of Captain Cook is another event, a misunder-standing juxtaposed to the account of the arrival of the Spanish as the inversion of its circumstances. The Spanish children are saved by the Hawaiians, but Cook is mistaken for the god Lono, a mistake that leads to his death. The Spanish children arrive by mistake as well, but the mistake is not one of misinformation in relation to the Hawaiians, rather a physical mistake or perhaps a mishap. The Spanish children are brought *up* by the Hawaiian aristocracy, while the false God, Cook, is brought down by the same aristocrats. The fourth version links all the previous versions of the story. Returning to version 3 and Jesus, for whose return the Hawaiians have waited for centuries, the arrival of the Spanish children follows, and finally the arrival of Captain Cook. This time he is not mistaken for Lono but for Jesus, and for the same reason, i.e his sails and the form of his mast. The connection to the Spanish *kahuna* enables the Hawaiians to realize that Cook is not Jesus, but an imposter. That is why he was mistrusted and eventually killed. Now these four versions were told to me in the order presented below, an order that establishes a playful process of elaboration on the core themes discussed here. There are always innumerable openings to new interpreta-tions and stories, loose ends so to speak, but in any one series we can appreciate the processes of combinatorial variation.

There is a structural consistency about the themes that is pertinent to understanding the nature of this local knowledge. The primary discourse, that of descent, organizes the relations between Hawaiians and both Jesus and the Spanish. Jesus does not merely come for a visit, although the transfer of his teachings is central. Jesus is clearly associated with the migration of the tribes of Israel. The Spanish are also assimilated via marriage and adoption, which in Hawaii consists in the production of kin by means of 'feeding' *hanai*. The adoption aspect is reinforced by the taking up and then bringing up of the children from overseas. Here, of course, is the parallel theme of migration from overseas. This motif of assimilation via descent is present in much everyday talk about origins, as we shall see below. This is, of course, precisely the principle analysed by Sahlins (1981), whereby the god Lono or Cook is incorporated into the identity of the chief Kalani'opu'u via his sacrifice. It is expressed in the adoption by the *ali'i* of British clothing and names, and by the association of Britain with Kahiki. The appropriation of Cook, however, is negated in the village stories, which represent in a certain sense a subaltern perspective that might be more in line with a cosmological opposition between *ali'i* and *maka'ainana* (commoners), one where Cook is a false image, not a true *kino lau* (reincarnation) of either Lono or Jesus and is thus a kind of imposter. This is the same cosmology that divides the world into a pre- and post-Tahitian period, the latter being associated with the coming of warfare and human sacrifice, the former with fertility and peace, with chiefs who are of the people rather than opposed to them. Thus aristocratic identity pegs itself to Cook and Britain, while commoner identity associates itself to a true Lono, to Jesus, even to the Spanish, certainly not to violence and conquest. But this opposition is partial at best in the stories. In a system of oppositions of this sort, the oppositions are always relative. It may be that Cook is associated with the demise of Hawaiian society in this discourse so that he cannot be treated as a true icon of the system. For Hawaiians, who have lost their sovereignty, their lands and their language, Cook may well represent a discontinuity, and is thus no source of descent, except perhaps for the aristocracy. The difference between the two models of incorporation is shown in Table 3.1.

Table 3.1   Models of incorporation

Aristocratic Model: sacrificial appropriation	Commoner Model: appropriation via kinship
The foreign Chief–God, is Lono. Captain Cook is identified with Lono. Cook-as-Lono represents Kahiki which is thus equated with England, the home of the gods.	Jesus is Lono, the saviour and champion of the 'people'. Jesus represents the Hebrews who are the ancestors of the Hawaiians.
Cook is killed and *sacrificed* and by this means incorporated into the chiefly lineage.	The Hawaiians are the descendants of Jesus and his people. Israel is the ancient home of the people. Jesus is thus incorporated via descent.
Hawaii is thus incorporated into the British realm, via the politics of its chiefs.	The Spanish are children from a shipwreck who are incorporated by adoption and then by marriage to Hawaiians. Their descent relation is one of cognation.
The act of incorporation is also an act distinguishing chiefs from commoners, identifying the relatively endogamous high chiefs with the foreign gods.	Cook is no Jesus and no Lono but an imposter. His death is thus no sacrifice, no act of incorporation for the commoners.

The models are united in their opposition within a larger commoner scheme in which Cook might well be an aristocrat, more appropriately linked to the war god Ku. In any case he is on the side of the invaders in a society split between the original Hawaiians and the invaders from Tahiti, Brittanee, etc. This expresses the class division of Hawaiian society which is reinforced by status/class endogamy, so that commoners, by and large are not related to aristocrats.

The second consistency, already touched upon above, is the coming of the overseas visitors, on a cyclical basis. The annual cycle is thus extended to the repetition of the Visit and the incorporation of the Visitor into the being of the Hawaiians. Lono, Jesus, the Spanish and Cook, constitute a series of substitutions that either replicate, transform or negate the original visit. Variations might be said to exist on a continuum from descent, peaceful, via marriage and/or adoption to descent, agonistic, via sacrifice to the negation of kinship. The third consistency is the parallel dualism, brother–sister–warrior–priest(ess) which in the classical Cook story becomes the opposition Ku–Lono. The fact that the opposition is included within the sibling unity might also be interpreted as a statement of the specific form of the relation, its antagonistic intimacy, which is present in so much of the Hawaiian mythology of succession.

This play on the three themes of Jesus, the Spanish and Captain Cook, was, as I indicated, communicated with a certain virtuosity. It was not the result of elaborate discussions. On the contrary, the versions were themselves elaborated much like music is improvised, the different versions being enunciated in rapid succession and in a kind of responsive dialectic, building up the final (for the time being) version. The structuralist appearance of this variation, its form, is dependent on the relation between the enunciators and the semantic field of the stories. This relation might be likened to the relation of the jazz musician to the thematic and harmonic material out of which he creates his musical variations. This is a relation of intimacy that permits the kind of non-reflexive virtuosity that characterizes the process of mythical variation.

CONCLUSION

Creativity in the structural sense can be understood as the improvisation of structural variation. It is structural insofar as it is intelligible to those who participate in the social world in question. Creativity is only recognized in terms of its constraints. It is the latter that determine the nature of its intelligibility. The constraints are products of an organization of shared experience, of shared implicit attributions of meaning to the world. In Mannheimian terms, this kind of creativity is only possible in conjunctive terms. The degree of conjunctivity does not necessarily depend on the density of social interaction, as Mannheim might have assumed (that is,

Gemeinschaft), but on its quality. Thus it might be argued that in homogenizing nation states, the sharing occurs via an already stabilized set of practices and identifications to which the formation of the nation is linked. The national imaginary is all that is required to establish the ground for such resonance. This is not, however, the 'imagined community' of Anderson, not at least in the usual interpretation. It is not an image, a construction forced upon the 'people' from the top down. Rather it is an articulation between local sociality and the larger public sphere. It is an imaginary in the Lacanian sense insofar as it is heavily laden with libidinal investment, forming a continuum between the subject and the image itself.

Creativity, as we have used the term here, is not the mere fact of novel combinations, although this may appear to be the case in discussions that are wholly intellectualistic, that is, concerned primarily with form as product. Creativity combines insight, the combinatorial and emotional resonance. In order for it to function socially it must contain all of these phenomena. The creative act must uncover something new in reality that is expressed in a specific new combination of meanings as well as a libidinal investment in the new combination.

Creativity, then, is not really about freedom and the liberation from constraint. The latter is randomness or even chaos, that is, a state of increasing entropy. Creativity, on the contrary, is negentropic. It is about the way in which worlds are produced and expressed and the latter are tightly bound by the constraints of content and communication that make creativity a social phenomenon rather than a mere individual idiosyncracy. Rooted in subjective experience and expressive of the conjunctive properties of the social world, creativity is truly the inhabitant of an iron cage. As the famous American revolutionary Thomas Paine expressed it, 'Men have free will, but the will is not free.'

NOTES

1. Cultural studies, of course, provided an important alternative to the social sciences of the 1970s. Studies of culture were very weak in sociology and anthropology was showing no interest in modern social processes in the West.

REFERENCES

Anderson, B. (1983) *Imagined Communities: Reflections on the Origin and Spread of Nationalism.* London: Verso.
Bohnsack, R. (1991) *Rekonstruktive Sozialforshung: Einfürung in Methodologie und Praxis.* Opladen: Leske und Budrich.
Borofsky, R. (1987) *Making History: Pukapukan and Anthropological Constructions of Knowledge.* Cambridge: Cambridge University Press.
Hannerz, U. (1992) *Cultural Complexity: Studies in the Social Organization of Meaning.* New York: Columbia University Press.

Ingold, T. (1993) 'The art of translation in a continuous world', in G. Palsson (ed.) *Beyond Boundaries*. Oxford: Berg.

Lacan, J. (1966) *Écrits*. Paris: Seuil.

Lakoff, G. and Johnson, M. (1980) *Metaphors We Live By*. Chicago: University of Chicago Press.

Lévi-Strauss, C. (1966) *The Savage Mind*. Chicago: University of Chicago Press.

Mannheim, K. (1976) *Ideology and Utopia*. London: Routledge.

—— (1982) *Structures of Thinking*. London: Routledge.

May, R.J. (1982) 'The view from Hurin: the Peli association', in R.J. May (ed.) *Micronationalist Movements in Papua New Guinea*. Political and Social Change Monograph No. 1. Canberra: Australian National University Press.

Sahlins, M. (1981) *Historical Metaphors and Mythical Realities: Structure in the Early History of the Sandwich Islands Kingdom*. Ann Arbor: University of Michigan Press.

Scheler, M. (1992) *On Feeling, Knowing, and Believing: Selected Writings*. H. Beshady (ed.). Chicago: University of Chicago Press.

Schutz, A. (1972) *The Phenomenology of the Social World*. London: Heinemann.

Strauss, C. and Quinn, N. (1994) 'A cognitive/cultural anthropology', in R. Borofsky (ed.) *Assessing Cultural Anthropology*. New York: McGraw Hill.

4   WONDERING ABOUT WUTU

Robert Borofsky

How does one locate 'cultural creativity'? Where does one search? Just trying to define the phrase – so one has a clear sense of what one is after – is enough to muddle the process. Regarding culture, for example, Hatch notes: 'Even though the term has been discussed in countless books and articles, there is still a large degree of uncertainty in its use – anthropologists employ the notion in fundamentally different ways' (1973:1). Likewise, ambiguity surrounds creativity. My dictionary equates creativity with inventiveness, bringing something new into being, originating. (As Friedman suggests in this volume, novelty seems central to it.) But how does one differentiate what is new from what is different, a variant of the old? And, related to this, is creativity something special or can almost everything we do be viewed as, in some sense, creative?

In anthropological quandaries of this sort, it is often wise to build one's conceptual castle from the ground up rather than from the sky down. Let me turn to a particular incident observed during fieldwork – one perhaps many anthropologists have run into in the course of their research – in an attempt to unravel some of the ambiguities involved. The example may seem insignificant, one of those odd cases that might be passed over as a careless mistake. I would suggest, however, that less is more here, for in intensively exploring this one, small incident, we gain a better sense of what is involved in locating 'cultural creativity'. The incident concerns 'Wutu', a popular Pukapukan tale, and Tai's rendering of it. (Tai is a Pukapukan assistant.)

To facilitate the grasping of certain points made below, let me begin by breaking the Wutu story into its constituent units – following Lévi-Strauss (1963:206–31) – and presenting it in its fullest form:

(1) Wutu goes to an isolated spot, (1a) specification of location, (1b) specification of reason, (2) he goes to sleep, (3) ghosts come to where Wutu is, (4) they make a plan to eat him, (5) they carry him away in a large wooden bowl (*kumete*), (6) they sing a chant (or chants): (6a) a chant centering around the phrase 'ko wutu, ko wutu' , (6b) a different chant centering around the phrase 'tau laulau ma tau pala' , (7) Wutu makes a plan of escape, (8) he defecates inside the wooden bowl (so the bowl will be heavy when he climbs out of it), (9) Wutu climbs on to a tree reaching across the path, (10) the ghosts continue on to their selected spot (10a) specification of location, (11) the ghosts prepare to eat Wutu, (12) the ghosts throw down the wooden bowl, (13) the

ghosts are covered with faeces, (14) Wutu escapes from the ghosts, (15) Wutu runs away to another location, (15a) specification of location he runs to, (16) the ghosts chase him, (17) Wutu is safe, and (17a) specification of reason why Wutu is safe.

In *Making History* I discuss Tai's rendering of the tale. His initial interview

indicated he possessed a rather limited knowledge of the Wutu story. Later, after we had listened to over thirty informants tell the story to us, I asked Tai one evening what he thought of the versions we had heard together. He noted that people had told a variety of accounts regarding where the ghosts intended to carry Wutu. Tai, however, felt the majority of the people had agreed with what he viewed as the correct version – that the ghosts were carrying Wutu to a place called Te Aumaloa. This surprised me considerably. I recalled no one ever telling the story this way. In discussing the matter with him, he did not mention specific individuals by name. But he conveyed the clear impression that many people told the legend in such a manner. The version he suggested made considerable sense. [It solved a logistical problem regarding how Wutu could escape without bumping into the ghosts again.] But when I checked over the accounts we had heard together, none of them mentioned the ghosts carrying Wutu to Te Aumaloa. (Borofsky 1987:124)

Is this creativity? Tai offers his own version of the story – one no one else told. (It is a version, however, which I believe many Pukapukans would find reasonable.) Exploring deeper, is obscuring one's creative role a creative act too – as when Tai asserts that he heard his version from other people we interviewed? Where on the continuum of cultural creativity should we place such assertions? Are they obvious creative efforts that enlarge the Pukapukan cultural corpus or are they more akin to 'standard', everyday Pukapukan practice – nothing unusual?

CONCEPTUALIZING CREATIVITY

We might well want to label as creative Tai's assertion regarding Te Aumaloa. He makes sense of a logistical ambiguity in the Wutu tale in a novel, yet quite reasonable, way that overlaps with the 'creativity' described by other contributors to this volume. While Archetti does not trace cre-olization through specific individuals, one might still point to a parallel between Tai's tale and what Archetti refers to, in his chapter, as the 'creative synthesis of the old and the new'. Similarly, one might perceive a parallel to the 'adventurous designs' Parkin refers to in Zanzibarian furniture and to the 'innovative ways' Ugandans use therapeutic commodities in Whyte's analysis. These cases suggest we might see creativity as involving, to follow Fernandez, the 'location and extension of prototypicality'. Liep, too, perceives creativity in unconventional extensions and applications.

But I would be cautious in leaving cultural creativity at this. Certain subtleties exist which need be taken into account, which need to be explored further. Creativity, for example, is tied to knowing. (It extends what we know in new/different/original/transforming ways.) We must remember that more than one way of knowing exists. Exploring alternative forms of knowing – moving, that is to say, beyond a traditional anthropological framework to draw on the insights of neuroscience for example – extends the discussion (if I might play with the word a moment) in a creative way.

IMPLICIT KNOWING

Increasing evidence in neuroscience suggests that at least two types of memory – and I would extrapolate to two types of knowing – exist among humans: one termed implicit (or non-declarative or procedural) and the other explicit (or declarative or relational). According to Schacter:

Implicit memory is an unintentional, nonconscious form of retention that can be contrasted with explicit memory, which involves conscious recollection of previous experiences. Explicit memory is typically assessed with recall and recognition tasks that require intentional retrieval of information from a specific prior study episode, whereas implicit memory is assessed with tasks that do not require conscious recollection of specific episodes. (1992:559)

Explicit or declarative memory, Squire (1992:232) states, 'provides the basis for conscious recollections of facts and events ... [It is] termed "declarative" to signify that it can be brought to mind and that its content can be "declared".' He goes on to say:

Nondeclarative memory includes information that is acquired during skill learning (motor skills, perceptual skills, cognitive skills), habit formation, ... [and] other knowledge that is expressed through performance rather than recollection. Experience can cumulate in behavioral change but without affording conscious access to any previous learning episodes or to any memory content. (Squire 1992:233)

One can readily perceive the difference between the two types of memory in amnesia. Patients suffering from amnesia have lost their explicit, but retain their implicit, memory. Implicit memory, I would note, also appears to belong to an older and less differentiated part of the human brain (see Reber 1992, cf. Donald 1991, Reber 1993).

Much of what we discussed in the workshop from which this volume originated referred to explicit knowing – to what informants could readily discuss in explicit terms. In turning to implicit knowing, we need to take note of two critical traits.

First, implicit understandings are demonstrated through performance. The implicit's concern with habituated, unconsciously embedded experiences overlaps nicely with Bourdieu's (1977:214) concept of 'habitus' (see also ibid.:72–95, Mauss 1973:73), with Bergson's 'habit memory' (1988), and with Mannheim's conjunctive experience (1982). Hastrup quotes Turner: 'one learns through performing then performs the under-standings so gained' (this volume).

Second, it is critical to note that performance-based patterns develop from the perception of seemingly invariant or co-variant occurrences. (I say seemingly because cultural perceptions obviously affect what is and is not perceived of as similar.) People build up abstract conceptualizations of their experiences as a result of certain elements remaining the same (or varying collectively together) through a repeated set of activities.[1] This is what Squire (1992:234) refers to when he suggests it is 'the information that is invariant across many trials [that] is important'. And this is what Hasher and Zacks (1984:1381) imply when they state: 'recent work demonstrates that conceptual knowledge depends directly on frequency information'. This trait nicely fits in with the concern in this volume – especially in Fernandez's chapter – with prototypicality. Rosch, one of the prominent researchers on the subject, notes – in a suggestive statement that encourages further research – that prototypes centre around repeated experiences, around the habituated (Rosch 1978:37, 30, 35).

No one would dispute the importance of attending to the invariant, the habituated, routines of everyday life. But clearly not everything experienced in a day or in a week is invariant. The general invariant patterns just referred to will not get one through even a single day. There are always new problems, new conditions, one needs to cope with. Let me take an example, framed in terms of implicit knowing, that most of us are familiar with – driving.

People at first learn to drive through a set of explicit instructions. With practice and repetition, however, the ability to drive becomes implicit and people then have a hard time explaining exactly how they perform it. (Many rituals, I would note, become rote – in a similar way – through repetition, and are understood more on an implicit/performance level than an explicit/intellectual one; see Keesing (1982), for example.) To quote Dreyfus and Dreyfus (1986:30): 'We usually don't make conscious deliberative decisions when we walk, talk, drive, or carry on most social activities ... the expert driver becomes one with his car, and he experiences himself simply as driving.'

If you drive to work using the same route every day, you acquire an implicit memory pattern of the route. You probably could shut your eyes and experience driving the whole route visually and kinaesthetically. But in real life you could never – I would repeat *never* – drive to work with your eyes shut. There are too many unexpected occurrences that disrupt your habituated routine. Our implicit memory patterns, then, are what might be termed 'rough' understandings. They are only part of what one experiences in everyday life. More is needed to get through the day, to accomplish the task at hand, than habituated, implicit memory patterns.

That 'more' is where creativity comes in. I am going to complicate the frame I am using here in a moment, so I will try to be careful. I do not mean to confuse. Creativity, I am saying, involves going beyond the habituated. It moves beyond the standard, repeated routines of everyday life.

This brings us back to 'Wutu'. The perspective helps clarify certain ethnographic data relating to the story. And yet, as often occurs in such situations, it also complicates the problem as well.

Let me begin with how the perspective clarifies. If, in normal anthropological style, we attempt to find the tale's generalized pattern – so we have a readily recordable version to present to others – we discover that different people tell the tale in noticeably different ways. And if we try to make some statistical sense of these differences by focusing on what they all share in common, we discover that they share rather little. So little is shared, in fact, that one might suggest that perhaps no tale exists at all. Table 4.1 presents the supporting data for these statements. Even when we break out various versions by category – by elderly men and women, for example – little consensus exists. (The numbers refer to the tale's constituent units cited above.)[2] All we really have is a chant centering around the phrase 'ko wutu, ko wutu'.

Table 4.1   The Tale of Wutu

Category	67% Consensus	75% Consensus	100% Consensus
Elderly men	6a	–	–
Elderly women	6a	6a	–
Most informed	3, 4, 5, 6a, 8, 9, 10, 12 14, 15, 15a	3, 4, 5, 6a, 12	6a
All males	3, 6a	6a	–
All females	6a	–	–
Total: all groups	6a	6a	–

Readers might perceive hope in the fact that informants in the most informed category – as ranked by Pukapukans – have a fairly comprehensive collective tale to tell. But two words of caution. First, the tale's shared constituent units sharply decline in this category when we move from a 67 per cent consensus level to a 75 per cent consensus level. (Or since this category involves 15 individuals, when we move from 10 to 12 informants.) And second, those deemed most informed (within the most informed category), did not tell the story in the same way in repeated tellings.

Table 4.2 indicates which parts of the tale did, and did not, vary in three different tellings by Molingi and Petelo (the two informants deemed by their peers to be most knowledgeable about such tales).

I hope readers will not see the tale of Wutu as somehow exceptional. On a relatively egalitarian Polynesian coral atoll, such as Pukapuka, I believe it to be fairly common – certainly with popular tales such as 'Wutu'.

Table 4.2   Repeated renditions of 'Wutu' by the same informants

Molingi	Unchanged constituent units:	1, 4, 5, 6a, 8, 10, 12
	Slightly changed constituent units:	3, 9
	Changed constituent units:	1a, 2, 6b, 10a, 11, 13, 14, 15, 15a
Petelo	Unchanged constituent units:	1, 3, 5, 8, 9, 10, 12, 13, 14
	Changed constituent units:	1a, 2, 4, 6a, 7, 10, 15, 15a

Let me return to implicit knowing. At least one reason so much flexibility appears to be accepted in various renditions of tales such as 'Wutu' is, perhaps, that the tales involve not only certain matters of content but also certain styles of presentation. The *act* of telling can be as critical as the *content* of the told (cf. R. Lakoff 1973; Grice 1975). The way Petelo and Molingi told 'Wutu', for instance, conveyed a sense of excitement. Independent of this or that detail, Petelo and Molingi knew how to make the tale come alive. The reason 6a became such a marker for the tale might well be because of the performative style that goes with it – a certain cadence and hand movement that animates the story. We need to ground such tales, in other words, in meaningful activity. (We need to situate them 'in the trajectories of participation in which it takes on its meaning', to quote Lave and Wenger (1991:121).) Which is to say, we need to take note of the implicit as well as the explicit understandings surrounding tale-telling.

In a way, we might suggest that the telling of 'Wutu' – or more generally, any cultural performance – is a creative act in a certain regard – as the teller adjusts her performance to a specific audience, as she includes this or that detail (depending on her emphasis or her memory). There is always a move beyond the habituated, beyond the repeated.

But here is the problem. If the tale is highly fluid – beyond a basic core – then it is not clear that Tai's 'creative' act was creative at all. There is really no set form for the tale. So how can we say his addition is 'novel'? It seems that each new telling of the tale is, in some sense, novel. Telling the story in an innovative way is part of the habituated routine, so to speak, which, if we follow what was said above, makes it not novel at all. It is just more of the same, simply business as usual. So where is the creativity?

THE POWER OF CONFORMITY

Let me leave this puzzle, for a moment, and add one more facet of the problem to complicate matters slightly further. Just as there is a context to storytelling, so there is a context to creativity. Cultural standards and expectations come into play in judging creativity. How should we describe Robert Mapplethorpe's image of an erect penis publicly displayed in Cincinnati, for example? Should we describe it as a creative work of art or as a morally indecent act?

Creativity cannot be too radical if it is to be viewed as such. Otherwise it is not seen – by others in the society – as creative; it is seen as something more akin to indecency, absurdity, or a violation of the law. Creativity, I am saying, constitutes an historically negotiated judgement. It is culturally defined, culturally framed. Whyte notes: 'the concept of creativity does not seem to be particularly important in Ugandan societies [in contrast to] ... European and American societ[ies where], ... originality is admired, genius is prized' (this volume).

The point helps to clarify an interesting contrast between Tai and myself. For Tai's 'creative' effort to pass muster with others, he could not really frame it as 'creative'. It would lack validity, authority. He had to deny his creativity – say his idea came from various elders – in order to be viewed as credible. I, on the other hand, needed to emphasize my creative efforts to be viewed as credible. If I wrote about Pukapukans in the same way that Pearl and Ernest Beaglehole, Andrew P. Vayda, and Julia Hecht did – the other anthropologists who conducted research on the island – my dissertation might not have been approved. At best, my work would have been seen as of poor quality; at worst, it would have been deemed plagiarizing. Even in this chapter, I am pressed to say something creative about creativity if I expect other scholars to read it.

Delineating creativity can be a complex matter. Much negotiation goes on – not everyone agrees, even on a small coral atoll such as Pukapuka. It is the same in America. Should those who put on the Mapplethorpe exhibition, for example, have been arrested for public indecency? Or was the exhibition a creative act of free speech? No consensus existed – in or out of Cincinnati – on these questions. That is why creativity takes on a political, negotiated quality. Sometimes, the courts have to define it.

But if one has to conform to a certain degree to be deemed creative – which is my basic point here – does this not bring us back to habituated routines? One is practising one's creativity in certain habituated, routine ways – nothing too dramatic, nothing too different. We come, again, to the point noted above. Being creative in structured ways involves a rather diminished sense of creativity.

CONCLUSION

Tai's addition to 'Wutu' – that the ghosts took the *kumete* to Te Aumaloa – was standard fare in Pukapuka. Pukapukans were continually trying to make sense of what they heard from others or recalled from times past and, in the process, were continually adding their own meanings disguised as recollections from others. In 'preserving' the past, they were constantly 'changing' it. Tai's addition was simply part of a larger cultural process.

There is a fluid quality to cultural understandings, cultural traditions, that at times gets lost in our efforts to write them down on paper, in our efforts to make 'culture' something concrete. The result is, as I note in *Making History*, that anthropologists over-structure cultural traditions in the process of recording them, they 'emphasize uniformity at the expense of diversity, stasis at the expense of change' (1987:2). To bring dynamism back to our analyses we often highlight, we often 'find', cultural creativity. Having excluded fluid understandings from our anthropological analyses, I am saying, we tend to bring them back by discussing cultural creativity. Creativity adds a vitalizing quality to our cultural analyses of other lands and other times. And – in a case of intellectual convergence – it becomes central to our identity in Western scholarship. (It symbolizes our modernity as Liep notes in the Introduction.)

Yet grasping creativity is like trying to catch the wind. Creativity is more gerund than noun – more a creating, a process, than a thing to be located. It is always in motion. The irony of creating is that it is always having to be born anew to be what it is. It always needs to change to deserve its appellation. We have discussed how creating moves beyond prototypes, beyond the habituated routines of life. And we have discussed how such movements become habituated in turn, leaving us with more creative appearance than substance. To be true to its name creating involves being on a treadmill – always having to be something new, to do something different from life's usual habits. It emphasizes a contradiction that goes to the heart of the anthropological project of understanding others to understand ourselves – how we define ourselves and others through the presence or absence of change.

Is not part of the answer to 'locating creativity' to realize how, once we have de-emphasized the fluid nature of others' cultural understandings, to recognize why we give creativity such importance? De-emphasizing others' fluid understandings, becomes a way to stress our modernity vis-à-vis others. ('We' change more than 'they'.) Embracing others' creativity – after de-emphasizing change – becomes a way to affirm others' humanity vis-à-vis ourselves. (All of 'us' possess a creative spirit.)

And is not part of the answer to realize – as in Robert Frost's 'The Gift Outright' – that creating often seems to be something all of us – in the West and the Rest – need to struggle with to make real? In its ambiguous reality is the reality of our own condition. We could not live a single day without creativity – no matter how much we habituate our approaches to the unexpected. There is always something more that needs to be coped with. (That is certainly true no matter how many times we drive the same route to work.) Creativity – the act of exploring, of coping, beyond the habituated – is basic to dealing with the unknown, the uncertain, in our lives. It is always being called upon. We need only pause – whisper its name, so to speak – to see it. But when we frame it, structure it, it tends to evaporate like the morning dew. It is a songbird that cannot be caged.

NOTES

1. See Rosch (for example, 1978), Rosch and Mervis (1975), Gibson (for example, 1979), Kosslyn (for example, 1988), Kosslyn et al. (1989), and Reber (for example, 1992).
2. For further details regarding the meaning and significance of the tables consult Borofsky (1994).

REFERENCES

Bergson, H. (1988) *Matter and Memory*. New York: Zone Books.
Borofsky, R. (1987) *Making History: Pukapukan and Anthropological Constructions of Knowledge*. New York: Cambridge University Press.
Borofsky, R. (1994) 'On the knowledge and knowing of cultural activities', in R. Borofsky (ed.) *Assessing Cultural Anthropology*. New York: McGraw-Hill.
Bourdieu, P. (1977) *Outline of a Theory of Practice*. New York: Cambridge University Press.
Donald, M. (1991) *Origins of the Modern Mind: Three Stages in the Evolution of Culture and Cognition*. Cambridge, Massachusetts: Harvard University Press.
Dreyfus, H. and Dreyfus, S. (1986) *Mind over Machine: The Power of Intuition and Expertise in the Era of the Computer*. New York: The Free Press.
Gibson, J. (1979) *The Ecological Approach to Visual Perception*. Boston: Houghton Mifflin.
Grice, H. P. (1975) 'Logic and conversation', in P. Cole and J. Morgan (eds) *Syntax and Semantics, vol. 3, Speech Acts*. New York: Academic Press.
Hasher, L. and Zacks, R.T. (1984) 'Automatic processing of fundamental information: the case of frequency of occurrence', *American Psychologist* 39(12):1372–88.
Hatch, E. (1973) *Theories of Man and Culture*. New York: Columbia University Press.
Keesing, R. (1982) *Kwaio Religion: The Living and the Dead in a Solomon Island Society*. New York: Columbia University Press.
Kosslyn, S. (1988) 'Aspects of a cognitive neuroscience of mental imagery', *Science* 240:1621–6.
Kosslyn, S., Koenig, O., Barrett, A., Cave, C.B., Tang, J. and Gabrieli, J. (1989) 'Evidence for two types of spatial representations: hemispheric specialization for categorical and coordinate relations', *Journal of Experimental Psychology: Human Perception and Performance* 15:723–35.
Lakoff, R. (1973) 'The logic of politeness: or, minding your P's and Q's', in C. Corum, T.C. Smith-Stark and A. Weiser (eds) *Papers from the Ninth Regional Meeting, Chicago Linguistic Society, April 13–17, 1973*. Chicago: Chicago Linguistic Society.
Lave, J. and Wenger, E. (1991) *Situated Learning*. New York: Cambridge University Press.
Lévi-Strauss, C. (1963) 'The structural study of myth', in *Structural Anthropology*. New York: Basic Books.
Mannheim, K. (1982) *Structures of Thinking*. London: Routledge and Kegan Paul.
Mauss, M. (1973) 'Techniques of the body', *Economy and Society* 2(1):70–88.
Reber, A. (1992) 'The cognitive unconscious: an evolutionary perspective', *Consciousness and Cognition* 1a:92–133.
—— (1993) *Implicit Learning and Tacit Knowledge: An Essay on the Cognitive Unconscious*. New York: Oxford University Press.
Rosch, E. (1978) 'Principles of categorization', in E. Rosch and B. Lloyd (eds) *Cognition and Categorization*. Hillsdale, New Jersey: Lawrence Erlbaum.
Rosch, E. and Mervis, C. (1975) 'Family resemblances: studies in the internal structure of categories', *Cognitive Psychology* 7:573–605.
Schacter, D. (1992) 'Understanding implicit memory: a cognitive neuroscience approach', *American Psychologist* 47(4):559–69.
Squire, L. (1992) 'Declarative and nondeclarative memory: multiple brain systems supporting learning and memory', *Journal of Cognitive Neuroscience* 4(3):232–43.

5 CELEBRATING CREATIVITY: ON THE SLANTING OF A CONCEPT[1]

Orvar Löfgren

THE AGE OF CREATIVITY?

Some years ago I did a study of the moral economy of the Swedish Christmas (Löfgren 1993). Wading through interviews, life histories, newspaper clippings and other mass-media products it seemed to me that one of the most important virtues of the modern Christmas was creativity: the ability to design your own personalized version of it.

There was a great seriousness surrounding this basic notion. Both in the individual interviews and in the mass-media advice there emerged a heavy stress on the importance of producing something authentic and genuine, of reworking and elaborating existing traditions. For many people, a home-made object took on a special magical power at Christmas. There was a profound significance about having made a Christmas present yourself, about having picked the cowberry sprigs in the forest rather than buying them at the market, or at least having made the wreath yourself. Preferably, each family should develop their own creative micro-culture of rituals and traditions. These normative and moral stances also mean that people devoted great energy relating to (and evaluating) other people's celebrations. Christmas had to be a celebration of personal creativity in order to be a good Christmas.

This made me think of the ways in which ideas of creativity have developed in popular usage as well as in academic studies and the ways in which they may be linked. The concept of creativity was not only found in discussions about Christmas; during the 1980s it had become increasingly popular in the media and public discourse. The virtues of creative solutions, creative people and creative attitudes were extolled in judgements of artistic and occupational success or failure, they were celebrated in career profiles and in high demand in recruitment ads. This fascination with creativity had its roots in the counter-cultures of the 1960s and 1970s, the interests in alternative lifestyles and pedagogics, as well as the democratization of artistic expression.

Creativity also worked its way into anthropological and ethnological texts (including my own), but here the concept mainly functioned as a counter-argument. Groups and settings which at first glance seemed characterized by passivity, simply reproducing dominant cultures or just doing nothing, were in the new studies coming out as culture builders and *bricoleurs*: busy reworking, elaborating, thickening their lives with new meanings and routines. In both popular and academic usage the basic attitude was that cultural creativity is good for you! (You simply can't have too much of it.)

To understand the ways in which cultural creativity has become such a central concept for many of us, I think we have to look specifically at the new types of cultural analysis of consumption which emerged during the 1980s in anthropology, European ethnology, sociology, media research, and above all in the very rapidly expanding interdisciplinary field of cultural studies. What I want to do in this chapter is to explore some of the ways in which this concept has become so central in studies of consumption, but also how it has come to be applied to some contexts more than to others. In the following I will explore a few aspects of the 'where, when, how, why and who' of everyday creativity in this interdisciplinary field. My aim is not to dismantle this perspective, but to discuss how its use has sometimes become too narrow, and finally to reflect on the possibilities of redressing the balance.

THE MAKING OF A COUNTER-ARGUMENT

In general the arts establishment connives to keep alive the myth of the special, creative artist holding out against passive mass consumerism, so helping to maintain a self-interested view of elite creativity.

   Against this we insist that there is a vibrant symbolic life and symbolic creativity in everyday life, everyday activity and expression – even if it is sometimes invisible, looked down on or spurned ... (Willis 1990:1)

This opening statement in Paul Willis's study *Common Culture: Symbolic Work at Play in the Everyday Cultures of the Young* is rather typical of the ways in which discussions of everyday creativity have become counter-arguments against the presupposition that creativity is an elite resource, a cultural capital of the gifted, of artists, writers, intellectuals etc., but also against the notion that consumption is a passifying, homogenizing force in people's lives. In many ways I find Willis's book stimulating and his aim important – my critique has more to do with the ways in which it becomes part of a genre in cultural studies which I mentioned earlier, the study of consumption as cultural creativity. Another aspect of this approach has to do with the theme of resistance:

The youths consumed images and space instead of commodities, a kind of sensuous consumption that did not create profits. The positive pleasure of parading up and down, of asserting their difference within, and different use of, the cathedral of consumerism became an oppositional cultural practice. (Fiske 1989a:17)

This is John Fiske describing the ways unemployed youths hang out at a local shopping mall, and his approach to popular culture is often used to exemplify the linking of creativity and resistance.

Some have argued that the interest in consumption studies was a way for disillusioned Marxists to develop new approaches to the study of hegemony and counter-hegemony, and above all a way to bring agency rather than structure back into cultural theory. One observer has illustrated this transformation by examining the individual research career of Paul Willis, from his *Learning to Labour* (1977) to his 1990 book *Common Culture* (see Laermans 1993). Similarly, David Harris's (1992) recent book on the history of the influential Birmingham cultural studies tradition bears the title *From Class Struggle to the Politics of Pleasure*. In many ways it is a rather one-dimensional argument Harris is pursuing, but there are some interesting aspects to it. He sees a heavy direct or indirect leaning on Gramsci's ideas of hegemony and resistance in the new kinds of cultural studies and studies of consumption that emerged in the 1980s: the consumer as the active subject, changing her/his world, consumption as 'collective resistance' in John Fiske's words (1989b). Consumers, in this perspective, became political actors 'voting with their wallets'.

Although this certainly is a very simplified way of writing academic history, I can recognize some of these Gramscian undertones in my own and other colleagues' work from the 1980s: an echo of a grand narrative of cultural resistance, with military (and masculine) metaphors of guerrilla warfare, raids, appropriations, seizing territories, etc. The theme of resistance through consumption has also been very marked in youth culture and working-class studies – and still is, in many cases. In this scenario it is rather obvious who are the guerilla warriors, but it is more difficult to locate the enemy: the who, where, how and why of dominance.

When consumption was redefined as 'cultural production' or 'symbolic production', creativity moved in to occupy a central position in this production process. It is only fair to underline, however, that this emphasis on cultural creativity as resistance must be seen as part of a pendulum swing in consumer theory, which I have discussed elsewhere (Löfgren 1990). The resistance scenario must be seen as a reaction against an earlier discourse on the seduction of mindless consumers: locked up in the iron cage that is held together by market forces.

The concept of cultural creativity can be seen as an attempt to redress the balance, to develop a more actor-oriented approach in studies of mass consumption. Creativity became, in some ways, the weapon of the weak – a positive strategy of resistance. More rarely, the concept was used to describe strategies of dominance and oppression: other terms were used for the imaginative and innovative ways of control and manipulation.

CREATIVE CULTURES

But let us return to Willis. From his focus on creativity as a force in everyday life he moves on to single out the group he is interested in:

> We are thinking of the extraordinary symbolic creativity of the multitude of ways in which young people use, humanize, decorate and invest with meanings their common and immediate life spaces and social practices – personal styles and choice of clothes; selective and active use of music, TV, magazines; decorations of bedrooms; the rituals of romance and subcultural styles; the style, banter and drama of friendship groups; music-making and dance. (Willis 1990:207)

Willis's interest in the cultural creativity of youth cultures is very typical of the ways in which studies of creative consumption have developed in cultural studies during the last decade. The result is that we now know quite a lot of the ways in which teenagers use consumption as a laboratory for identifying constructs: trying out styles, combining media activities, hanging out at the mall, experimenting with new hairstyles, choosing a disco, renting a video, playing with commodities and fashions, signalling group identity through styles and commodities. This is one specific focus on consumption, typical of a certain age group and emphasizing certain rather spectacular aspects: consumer activities with a high degree of visibility – and also consumption as fun.

The same tendencies may be found in other well-developed fields, such as the study of shopping, where over the years we have had a focus on the delights of daydreaming and desiring, the art of window-shopping and the skills of the *flâneur*. There is a tilt towards viewing consumption as symbolic production.

My argument is not that this focus is wrong. On the contrary, the research into fields like youth culture or the art of shopping and consumer fantasies has been very rewarding – it has really vitalized the general cultural analysis of consumption. My argument is rather that the focus on the spectacular and the symbolic tends to overshadow other, more mundane or seemingly trivial, aspects of consumption. In studies of teenagers, homemakers and shoppers you sometimes feel that you are drifting, gliding through a symbolic forest or an exhibition of meanings and messages. There is often very little body work in these discussions of cultural creativity. We need more blood and sweat in the analysis of creative consumption! What do people actually do with things? Not only do they look or gaze at them, read or contemplate them, but they may also touch, smell and taste them; people drag objects around, use, wear, tear, fix, repair and maintain them, grow tired of them, put them away, discard them and rediscover them.

The fact that cultural creativity in consumption studies has tended to become the same as symbolic production may also have had some consequences for what types of cultural production we tend to look for. Certain types of consumption become more explored than others, from life in shopping malls to soap operas, because they, in some ways, constitute 'easy reads' (cf. the discussion in Löfgren 1994b).

THE AESTHETICS OF EVERYDAY LIFE

One further narrowing down of the field of studies in creativity came with linking it to the aesthetic dimensions of life. Especially in the debate surrounding postmodernity, it has been argued that contemporary lifestyling contains a strong element of the aestheticization of everyday life (see for example Fredric Jameson 1993 [1988] and Mike Featherstone 1991).

The strong link between consumption, creativity and aestheticization has, I think, also to do with the ways in which cultural studies have developed in much closer contact with the classical aesthetic disciplines, such as the visual arts, literature, media studies etc. In anthropology the problems of aesthetics were for a long time limited to the sphere of 'primitive art', and there were very few attempts to develop an analysis of the aesthetics of everyday life.[2]

My main quarrel with this new focus, is its tendency to drift into an evolutionary perspective. Aesthetics is seen as much more important in contemporary everyday life than it ever was before. Before we accept such a statement (which might have a great deal of truth in it), we need to look critically at the ways in which we use the concept of aesthetics transhistorically and transculturally. What arenas, activities and actors are defined as having aesthetic dimensions in different historical and social settings?

In an ongoing project on changing forms of consumption in twentieth-century Sweden, I have been struck by the ways in which arenas for everyday creativity change over time. During the 1940s and 1950s the craze for hobbies swept over the country; later on home improvement became a focus for family life. Couples became engaged in questions about the scenography of the home: choosing wallpaper, furniture, decorations. People who would never have dreamt of visiting an art gallery or drawing a picture learned to feel fully competent to design their home and to choose colours and fabrics for the new living room. Homemaking became a safe arena of cultural creativity and also a joint project for the married couple. Men were drawn into the domestic sphere in new ways (cf. Löfgren 1994a).

The linking of creativity and aesthetics also raises a question about the ways in which contemporary skills of creative consumption and the staging of identity are gendered and class-based. Are women depicted as more creative than men or alternatively as developing different skills in the aestheticization of everyday life? Do men and women develop and express their creativity in different forms, situations and spaces? How does this focus on aesthetics rework or reinforce the division of labour between the sexes? In this process patterns of aesthetic authority, decision making and control of investments tended to differ among generations, but also among classes.

An ethnological study of working-class households in the small town of Asketorp (Rosengren 1985, 1991) identifies the home as a family project, where love, solidarity and care are materialized in the continuous ambitions of home improvements; but in comparison with middle-class families, gender and domestic life are organized differently. Women are very much in control of home and consumption – on some levels:

> ... the entire home is usually her creation, from the choice of wallpaper and furniture, to curtains, tablecloths, and flowers. But also the external appearance of the members of the family bears her mark. She chooses and buys clothes, not only for herself and her children, but also for her husband ... When the couple goes to a party on a Saturday evening or he goes to ice-hockey on a Tuesday evening, his outward looks are very much a creation of her ideas of how a man should look. If you visit him at home you will find him sitting and talking to you in clothes chosen by her, and in a surrounding created mostly with his money, but mainly through her ability, ideas, and wishes. (Rosengren 1985:84)

For the men, the garage and the car became an alternative arena for male creativity, but again we encounter marked class differences in this locating and gendering of creativity as the aestheticization of everyday life, for example in the willingness to experiment with new styles, fashions and imports.

During the later part of the twentieth century the art of the bricolage, the will to explore new combinations, the cult of flexibility has usually been typical of the intellectual wing of the middle class, which is also a group that shows a very marked degree of continuity in their way of life. They can afford to experiment with new forms of creative consumption because it in no way threatens their identity and basic values. Expressive and fluid lifestyles may thus hide a marked cultural stability on a more fundamental level (cf. the discussion in Frykman 1985).

LOCATING CREATIVITY

I have tried to sketch some of the roads along which the notion of cultural creativity has travelled in academia during the last decades. It is an example of a loose term which has drifted into cultural research – not as a sharp analytical tool but rather as a framing concept. In this process it has gained certain connotations and associations, as well as strong links with certain other concepts.

It has played a crucial role in the new types of consumption studies, which have vitalized the field of cultural studies and also influenced the work of anthropologists, European ethnologists and cultural sociologists. I have argued, however, that we should be a bit wary of the ways in which the 'when, where, how, why and who' of cultural creativity have been narrowed down in this process, and the close links between cultural studies and arts and media studies have produced certain paved roads: the tendency to over-research some aspects and arenas and overlook others.

What strikes me is that this slanting of the concept has not been a very conscious process. It started with the focus on consumption as creativity, a creativity focused mainly on symbolic production and expressive forms: this very selective emphasis was made more narrow by the marked concentration on youth culture settings, and the constant experimentation with identities and the reworking of mass-media and mass-consumption styles, images and commodities. These perspectives have tended to favour a 'reading of cultures', a focus on the symbolic and expressive, as well as the aesthetic dimensions of creativity.

Let us just imagine that the ethnographic materials had been taken from other fields. How would a study of cultural creativity among old-age pensioners or rural labourers look, what kinds of creativity do welfare families develop in their everyday skills of economizing? What if we looked at more mundane forms of creative consumption, or focused more on the trivialities and routines of everyday life?

We can observe similar processes of routinization and narrowing down in the works of anthropologists and European ethnologists. Here as well the concept of creativity has worked rather like a searchlight, illuminating some parts of the landscape, while others remain in the shade.

In this selective use the most striking thing is that cultural creativity becomes a very positive concept. It is seen as enrichening, elaborating, 'thickening' local lives, a process through which people make their everyday existence colourful, unique, specific, distinct and above all positive.

It is also a concept mainly for the age of modernity (and postmodernity); there is sometimes a compensatory ring to it: being creative is how we cope with the vicissitudes of modernity. Eighteenth-century peasants are seldom presented as practising cultural creativity: they are busy making a livelihood, producing crops, keeping home, carrying out rituals, fooling the landlord.

Finally it is often reserved for those defined as the underdogs of the modern world: consumers, workers, women, teenagers, colonial and post-colonial subjects, and this is where the concept is closely linked to ideas of counter-hegemony, to the tactics of resistance in the world of mass consumption or in post-colonial processes of globalization.

Amongst these various usages two major trends can be discerned. One focuses on creativity as the art of coping or surviving, compensating a lack of resources by resorting to local or personal ingenuity. The other aspect could be summarized as underdog tactics for 'beating the system'. This is creativity as the weapons of the weak (Scott 1985), the forms of guerilla warfare carried out by the dominated. In both cases the emphasis is on creativity as a special type of cultural competence, developed to compensate for a difficult situation.

A third clustering is found around the study of cultural innovators, brokers and *bricoleurs*: people in local settings who transcend cultural barriers, bend or break local rules, develop new cultural forms or fields of activity – in short very active and innovative culture builders. Here, creativity might sometimes be described as an artistic gift or a personal blessing and the creative person can often be defined as the outsider or the marginal woman or man.

There are other ways of illustrating this narrowing-down process. One is to look at the kinds of arena in which creativity is located and analysed in anthropological studies. The dominance of artistic life, religion and ritual is striking, as well as new forms of popular social movements, as for example in revitalization movements. Another has to do with the work in the cultural borderlands, creativity as the art of hybridity: mixing, blending, exploring different cultural traditions. (In the anthropological tradition cultural creativity has sometimes become a synonym for the more problematic concept of aesthetics.)

In the same way we can reflect on the verbs chosen to describe creative processes, words like improvise, innovate, invent, discover, explore, negotiate, enunciate, appropriate etc. Most of these are extremely active forms: doing something with culture. Again, these verbs echo the restless credo of hypermodernity, the constant need for change, improvement, flexibility and experimentation. In connection with this we also find a tendency to rationalize cultural activities – to invest them with purpose and direction: a teenage rebellion becomes an act of resistance, a play with cultural forms constitutes a process of learning, an improvisation is seen as an attempt to transcend cultural limitations through experiments, ambiguity as a subaltern strategy, etc.

So what are the lessons for us, who have enjoyed such a frequent use of the perspective of cultural creativity? Maybe that any research tradition will develop into routine and institutionalize certain approaches and perspectives – create fixed entries into a research field where we learn to follow fairly unconscious rules about how a project is to be packaged, organized and carried out. I am urging a greater use of back doors and tradesmen's entrances. We need to reflect constantly on the ways in which we pick up the topic of cultural creativity, delineate it, choose an approach, and, as an antidote, sometimes try to bring a bit of anarchy and experimentation into the research process. We need to look at what happens when the concept is used transculturally and transhistorically and try to identify the different polarities and counter-texts created in the process. What is a non-creative culture or actor?

I see, however, no need for us to discard a concept which has been used to redress several kinds of imbalance in the cultural analysis of everyday life – in many disciplines; but my main point is that we imported this concept into academia as rather an open one, and we should make sure that we are not narrowing it down. What kinds of activities, situations, actors tend to be overlooked in many of the current studies of cultural creativity? I think that European ethnologists and anthropologists constantly stressing their ability to move between different cultural settings and time periods have a heavy responsibility here to make sure that the concept is constantly widened to include other spheres, settings and epochs than those explored in the cultural studies of creative consumption.

NOTES

1. The chapter was written as part of an interdisciplinary research project on national and transnational cultural processes, financed by the Swedish Research Council for the Humanities and the Social Sciences (for a presentation of the project, see Hannerz and Löfgren 1994).
2. One exception is John Forrest's study (1988) of the everyday aesthetics of a fishing community in North Carolina. He starts off with an interesting discussion of the ways in which the field of aesthetics has been narrowed down in anthropological research, but his own attempt at an ethnography does not live up to the ambitions of his introduction.

REFERENCES

Featherstone, M. (1991) *Consumer Culture and Postmodernism*. London: Sage.
Fiske, J. (1989a) *Reading the Popular*. Boston: Unwin Hyman.
——— (1989b) *Understanding Popular Culture*. Boston: Unwyn Hyman.
Frykman, J. (1985) 'Ur medelklassens familjeliv', in B.-E. Andersson (ed.) *Familjebilder: Myter, verklighet, visioner*. Stockholm: Studieförbundet Näringsliv och Samhälle.
Forrest, J. (1988) *Lord I'm Coming Home: Everyday Aesthetics in Tidewater North Carolina*. Ithaca: Cornell University Press.
Hannerz, U. and Löfgren, O. (1994) 'The nation in the global village', *Cultural Studies* 8(2):198–207.
Harris, D. (1992) *From Class Struggle to the Politics of Pleasure: The Effects of Gramscianism on Cultural Studies*. London: Routledge.
Jameson, F. (1993 [1988]) 'Postmodernism and consumer society', in Baker, M. and Beezer, A. (eds) *Reading into Cultural Studies*. London: Routledge.
Laermans, R. (1993) 'Bringing the consumer back in', *Theory, Culture and Society* 10:153–61.
Löfgren, O. (1990) 'Consuming interests', *Culture and History*, 7:5–45. (Reprinted in J. Friedman (ed.) *Consumption and Cultural Identity*. London: Harwood.)
——— (1993) 'The great Christmas quarrel and other Swedish traditions', in D. Miller (ed.) *Unwrapping Christmas*. Oxford: Oxford University Press.
——— (1994a) 'The empire of good taste: everyday aesthetics and domestic creativity', in B. Klein and M. Widbom (eds) *Swedish Folk Art: All Tradition is Change*. New York: Harry Abrahams.
——— (1994b) 'En akademisk trettioårskris? Om rutiniseringen av Cultural Studies', *Kulturella perspektiv* 3(3):43–51.
——— (1997) 'Scenes from a troubled marriage. Swedish ethnology and material culture studies', *Journal of Material Culture* 2:95–114.
Rosengren, A. (1985) 'Contemporary Swedish family life through the eyes of an ethnologist', in J. Rogers and H. Norman (eds) *The Nordic Family: Perspectives on Family Research*, Uppsala Essays in Social Demographic History 4. Department of History, University of Uppsala.

—— (1991) *Två Barn och eget Hus: Om Kvinnors och Mäns Världar i Småsamhället.* Stockholm: Carlsson.

Scott, J.C. (1985) *Weapons of the Weak: Everyday Forms of Peasant Resistance.* New Haven: Yale University Press.

Willis, P. (1977) *Learning to Labour: How Working Class Kids Get Working Class Jobs.* London: Gower.

—— (1990) *Common Culture: Symbolic Work at Play in the Everyday Cultures of the Young.* London: Open University Press.

6 THE CONSTRUCTION OF AUTHENTICITY: THE CASE OF SUBCULTURES

Rolf Lindner

The traditional dilemma of anthropology as an account of the culturally different is contained in the postulate of authenticity which, explicitly or implicitly, underlies it. In this context the word 'postulate' should be taken quite literally: a moral demand is made of the group being investigated, that it keep as far away as possible from worldly influence, whether of an economic, social or cultural nature. Renato Rosaldo (1989) has drawn attention to the fact that for anthropologists, if they adhere to the classic norms, the groups possessing the most 'culture' are those that are in themselves coherent and homogeneous, and to the greatest degree untouched and unsullied by external influences. These anthropologists would prefer to abandon a whole investigation rather than reflect on change in and through their research. Rosaldo mentions the example of a German linguist who rejected the majority of his Galician informants because these had, in his opinion, been 'corrupted' by Castilian and therefore spoke an 'impure' Gallego-Portugese. The attitude of the linguist points to the collector's syndrome underlying the research activity. This is sustained by the idea that the culture being researched will inevitably vanish. The curt dismissal of the informants can therefore also be interpreted as an expression of the disappointment of a collector of disappearing cultures who came too late in the never-ending race against time.

In James Clifford's brilliant essay 'On collecting art and culture' (1988) cultures are described as ethnographic collections which are assembled according to the same criteria as art collections. What counts are authenticity, coherence and rarity; in this context, interventions from outside are necessarily regarded as 'interferences' and borrowings and appropriations as 'adulterations'. Very evident here, making the analogy between art and culture appear especially fruitful, is the pure gaze, unclouded by considerations of profit or use, which presupposes a break with everyday relationships to the world. The aesthetic attitude, which finds expression in the pure gaze, is characterized by the separation of the perceived object from its surroundings, by disregard for the historical context and, above all, by indifference to the existence of the object. It is the *image* of a dying culture that must be captured, not the culture itself. Just as the art collector, through the act of collecting and preserving, bestows lasting value on the chosen object, so the anthropologist, who 'records' customs and behaviour, becomes the true preserver of the culture at the moment of its disappearance. This results in the paradox that the decline of the culture is accompanied by the rise of the anthropologist. '*Welcome of Tears* is a beautiful book', writes Margaret Mead in a review, 'combining the stories of a vanishing people and the growth of an anthropologist' (quoted from Clifford 1986:109). The inversion of the traditional idea of 'culture', as the expression of and refuge for education and refinement, which is linked to the demand of cultural abstinence made of the research group, can be explained as follows: the concept of cultures in the plural proves to be related to the concept of culture in the singular, because both are shaped by the idea of totality. Put differently, it is only the cultivated gaze, shaped by culture in the narrow sense, that is able to comprehend, that is, produce, culture as an autonomous whole – culture, therefore, in the larger, anthropological sense.

Renato Rosaldo's argument also applies to research 'at home', above all where attention turns to subordinate groups – those which, in the eyes of the anthropologist, are especially filled with culture. The group under investigation should be culturally pure, without breaks and faults.

This socially conservationist viewpoint has been especially marked in research into working-class culture during the last two or three decades. For example, in the mid-1970s, Heinrich Breuer and the present writer carried out research into the significance of the football team in the mining districts of the Ruhr. The football player was described as a representative of the environment in which he originated, as someone who not only remains bound to it, but is bound to it as the source of his particular way of life: '... as a hero chosen by his own people and not by the media', we wrote at the time, 'demands are made of him. He did not dare put on the airs of a "star", in fact the very word "star" is an anachronism in relation to what the top players of the time [the 1950s, R.L.] meant to the public. To become superior, arrogant, self-satisfied, would have meant betraying those who had raised him up' (Lindner and Breuer 1978:64).

To be authentic – which the 'people's hero' (*Volksheld*) was in contrast to the media star – obviously means that one does not leave the environment of one's origin, one's own class.

In his study *Sincerity and Authenticity*, Lionel Trilling described this conception of authenticity as characteristic of the nineteenth-century English novel. The novelists of the period saw class position as the decisive condition of personal authenticity: 'His sentiment of being, his awareness of his discrete and personal existence derives from his sentiment of class' (Trilling 1972:115). This organistic conception implies that a person does not automatically become inauthentic through ascending the social ladder, as long as the feeling for class situation remains. Only through the *intellec- tual* surrender of origin, which is manifested in a loss of integrity, does he lose authenticity. 'To a certain degree the football player as local hero and public representative is similar to the working-class child, who was able to go to grammar school and perhaps even to university', we wrote in our analysis of football. Our organistic argument continued: 'If this child, despite university education, remained "natural", that is, if the child did not become arrogant, superior, if he did not forget where he came from, and retained his connection with his locality, then his ascent up the social ladder was not considered class treachery, but was a cause for pride among the extended family and in the neighbourhood of the mining settlement' (Lindner and Breuer 1978:64). What was demanded here, for the sake of authenticity, was the retention of the communal, collective ideals, which Raymond Williams viewed as the decisive difference between middle-class and working-class culture. 'The crucial distinction is between alternative ideas of social relationship ... We may now see what is properly meant by "working class culture". It is not proletarian art, or council houses, or a particular use of language; it is rather, the basic collective idea, and the insti- tutions, manners, habits of thought and intentions which proceed from this' (Williams 1975:312–13). Williams, a former scholarship boy, may be regarded as the doyen of researchers dealing with working-class culture, and it is those researchers, above all, who have remained loyal to this collective idea.

If, following Lionel Trilling, it is true that 'we understand a priori that the prescriptions of society pervert human existence and destroy its authentic- ity' (Trilling 1972:161) then the field of subcultures, that is of those formations which come about as critical responses to existing social conditions, is surely the field of authenticity par excellence. Indeed, it can be demonstrated that in this field all the participants are imbued with the *idea of the authentic*; the members of the subcultures, who hold to a strict code of subcultural authenticity, just as much as the subcultural researchers, who are looking for authentic experiences in the field. In subcultural research, the logic of cultural purity running through anthropological studies takes on features of a negative teleology. That is also true of Dick Hebdige's (1979) seminal analysis of subcultures. '*Subculture* is as much a celebration of the authentic moments in postwar youth subcultures, as it is an epitaph of their inevitable passing', write Jennifer Daryl Slack and Laurie Anne Whitt in their analysis of the ethical implications of Cultural Studies (Slack and Whitt 1992:578). Celebration and epitaph constitute the two poles of analytic con- siderations of authentic cultures: the researcher is here midwife and gravedigger in one.

For Hebdige, the existence of subcultures is unavoidably a life in the shadow of death. 'The cycle leading from opposition to diffusion, from resistance to incorporation encloses each successive subculture' (Hebdige 1979:96). In its course through genesis, flowering and decay, the subcultural cycle is reminiscent of the cultural philosophy of an Oswald Sprengler and the model of history of an Arnold Toynbee, and so adheres to the conventional pattern of cultural criticism. Inherent in this conventional form of argument is the myth of origin, which leaves the background of the subcultures in the mythical darkness of a grassroots movement, as well as the story of an all too certain end as yet another entertaining spectacle of the culture industry. The influence of the media and mass culture can only be thought of as a process of contamination, bringing about the death of the phenomenon – and with that the end of any concern with it. It is interesting – and of considerable (cultural) analytical significance – that *cultural contamination* replaces *physical infection* resulting from cultural contact as the source of the destruction of a 'tribe'. In both cases a group without powers of resistance, that is, one that is natural and innocent, is struck down and destroyed.

At this point it is worth returning once again to Clifford's analogy between art and cultures. Quite obviously, in the case of the original, 'genuine' subcultures, we are dealing with collector's items which fulfil the criteria, such as authenticity, coherence and singularity, applied to works of art. It is equally obvious that the incorporated subcultures, as fashion variants of the consumer industry, correspond to inauthentic artefacts characterized by reproduction and the commodity form. Therefore the cycle, whose stages I once summed up (Lindner 1981) as constitution/diffusion/incorporation, exemplifies a 'hierarchy of legitimacies' (Bourdieu 1981) declining over time. If, in analogy to art theory, we equate the phase of constitution with the creation of the original, diffusion with the copy and incorporation with print production, then it becomes evident that the stages of the life cycle conceal the various spheres of cultural practices, such as Bourdieu has elaborated in his theory of cultural legitimacy.

THE CASE OF SUBCULTURES

11 March 1979:
With infinite sadness I stare at the empty stage, which Eric Burdon, drunk and shattered, has just left.
But I love him, I love him, Eric Burdon, quite madly.
He is as honest as he always has been. (Jaenicke 1980)

Nowhere is it more manifest that the field of subcultures is imbued with the idea of the authentic than in the characteristic practice of genuine subculture members (which thereby demonstrates them to be genuine) of strictly distinguishing between originals and hangers-on. Each of the succeeding subcultures has continued to make this distinction in order to separate 'outsider' from 'insider', the 'follower of fashion' from the real 'freak'. 'Weekend pseudo-beats', 'weekend hippy', 'burrhead rasta', 'plastic punks'

– it's always a matter of defining the hangers-on from the point of view of the 'authentic people'. But where do the 'genuine' beats, hippies, punks obtain the criteria that allow them to make this distinction? Evidently the temporal dimension – 'weekend beats' – cannot be decisive here. Decisive, rather, is knowledge of the subcultural code whose elements – the specific argot, the attitude – form the 'philosophy' of the group. But where do the 'insiders' get their knowledge? The historic reconstruction of subcultures shows that each of these currents had its cult book, and hence a manual for self-interpretation. In the case of the beatnik movement this was undoubtedly Jack Kerouac's *On the Road* (1973), which became a kind of deviant travel guide.

In an account which links an autobiography with the history of the beatnik movement the author writes:

I had read this book by Jack Kerouac. I had devoured it in a single night, fallen in love with this crazy guy Dean Moriarty – this insanely fast, wild, tender life – life of the beatniks – on the road – which raced with all the force of longing through my head – you can't take it any more, you have to get out, get away – now this minute! I had read this book by Jack Kerouac. I was an apprentice at the Bavarian State Bank, and I didn't have a single day's holiday left and had already skipped work so often – but I *had* to get away – on the road – it didn't let go of me any more. To Scandinavia, where I had already been in the summer and where I had experienced a tiny bit of this road feeling on three weeks holiday. The relative freedom which I had experienced there, the parties, the beat and blues – very different from our discos at home – and the people wore quite different clothes, brightly coloured and made by themselves. Whereas at home only a few dared to grow their hair, to wear different clothes, little chains and headbands, in Denmark almost all the young people seemed to be like that ... I had read this book by Jack Kerouac, and now I was right in the middle of it myself ... None of the people whom I got to know there still lived with their parents, most didn't work, at least not regularly. Everything necessary for life was acquired with as little effort as possible, everything superfluous was done without. I was quite surprised at how much is superfluous! Yeah, they really did live with the same attitude as Kerouac's guys in 'On the Road' and of course they had all read it. Sometimes one of them pulled his copy from a Tuborg crate and read out a passage that he particularly liked. (Jaenicke 1980:31)

To mock the rapturous enthusiasm of these lines would be to miss the 'holy solemnity' accompanying the authentication of an attitude. The power of the imagination is evident, but that does not make an event any less real. In hardly any area is the inevitability of the Thomas theorem – 'If men define a situation as real, it is real in its consequences' – more familiar than in the area of subcultures (an altogether dark chapter of subcultural history when one remembers those that fell by the wayside).

The retrospective authentication of subcultures is not a recent phenomenon. A self-definition as a generation with reference to precursors, for example, did not begin with *Generation X*, nor even with the *Blank Generation* of the punk era. In Jack Kerouac's account of the origin of the *Beat*

Generation (1959) his reference point was the *Lost Generation* of the 1930s. In order to understand what I consider to be the peculiarity of the most recent developments, it is necessary to take into account the history of subcultural research itself, which begins after the Second World War. The 1960s saw the emergence of the first generation of students who were not only possibly members of a counter-cultural grouping (hippies, commune movement, yippees, etc.), but in addition were well-read in subcultural analysis and the sociology of deviance (Howard S. Becker's pioneering analysis *Outsiders* appeared in 1963). That, however, means that there is the possibility of a reflexive grounding of subcultures not only in literary discourse, but directly in social-scientific academic discourse.

As early as 1978, while the thesis of 'dole-queue rock' was still dominant, the British sociologist Simon Frith pointed out that what was happening in the punk scene 'is not the spontaneous confirmation of subcultural theory, but the deliberate use of subcultural ideology by young sophisticates who have read their Stan Cohen and Jock Young and understand deviancy theory as a neat form of legitimation' (Frith 1978:536).

One of these 'young sophisticates' was Malcolm McLaren, a former art student and creator of happenings who, together with friends from his art-school days, created, in the 'Sex Pistols', the original image of punk. According to Frith, it was McLaren's ambition 'to turn spectacle (the passively experienced structure of reality that we live with as consumers) into situation (the structure blown up, its rules made clear, the possibilities for action and desire exposed)' (ibid.:535). It is not hard to recognize in this conception the action-aesthetic programme of the Situationist International which, in the words of one of its founders, Jørgen Nash, aimed 'to provoke the public, to force it out of its passive consumerism, and persuade it to create its own environment and culture' (quoted from Hollstein 1969:84). Malcolm McLaren, who came in contact with situationist ideas during the May Days of 1968 in Paris while 'on the art school student's grand tour of Europe's rebel capitals' (Frith 1978:535), comprehended the action-aesthetic programme as the 'frame of reference' for the staging of punk. For the concrete realization of their programme, McLaren and his collaborators drew on the findings of labelling theory. As is well known, the central thesis of the labelling approach is that deviant behaviour is behaviour that people label as such. From this perspective, deviant behaviour is seen as the result of a transaction between a social group concerned with the laying down and enforcement of rules and a second group seen by the former as rule breakers. The collection of essays *The Manufacture of News* published in 1973 and edited by Stanley Cohen and Jock Young, became representative of this transactionist approach. Three themes are addressed in this volume: the selection of events as newsworthy, the presentation of these events as deviant, and the effect of this presentation on the perception of self and others by the actors.

In addition to case studies of the media presentation of the mentally ill, homosexuals, consumers of LSD, demonstrating students, etc., the volume also contains two sections from Stanley Cohen's study *Folk Devils and Moral Panics* (1973), which investigates the role of the media in the construction of mods and rockers as troublemakers in society. These sections read virtually like a script for the staging of punk. Apart from the processes of media prediction and media distortion, Cohen devotes particular attention to the media's production of symbols in relation to outsiders. In terms of ideal type, and formulated very briefly, this process runs through three stages. 'A word (Mod) becomes symbolic of a certain status (delinquent or deviant); objects (hairstyle, clothing) symbolize the word; the objects become symbolic of the status (and the emotions attached to the status)' (ibid.:40). This summary contains, almost as a set of instructions, all the ingredients that became necessary for the creation of punk: a word (punk) – used since the end of the nineteenth century in the United States to describe youthful idlers – symbolizes a delinquent status; objects (short, spiky hair, torn T-shirt) symbolize this word; the objects become symbols of this status (and the emotions that become attached to this status). At the end of the book Cohen predicted: 'More moral panics will be generated and other, as yet nameless folk devils will be created.' (ibid.:204). In punk his prediction came true, admittedly in an unforeseen way: as a self-fulfilling prophecy.

CONCLUSION

The more the social sciences progress and are disseminated through the media, the more we must be prepared, to paraphrase Bourdieu (1985:56), to encounter in the research object the sediments of preceding research. The apocryphal stories of African and North American Indian informants who, when questioned by anthropologists, consult the works of Meyer Fortes or Alfred Kroeber, have by now come true. The anthropologist must not only expect that the 'others', about whom he is writing, form part of his readership (as a rule critical, but occasionally also simply amused) but that it is also increasingly the case that academic works function as the archives of the cultural inheritance of the group described. It is therefore predictable that the Tewa Indian questioned in Hans-Peter Duerr's *Dreamtime* (1985) will respond that the University of Southern California is the best place to learn something about Kiva dances. With the help of anthropological texts, cultural interpretations and fictional and documentary information disseminated by the mass media, genealogies are drawn up, traditions reproduced, collective identities asserted and cultural self-interpretation practised.

Simon Frith has drawn attention to the fact that it is impossible to understand the punk subculture, for Dick Hebdige the example par excellence of a 'semiotic guerilla', without noting how many of the early punks had been students of Cultural Studies, 'and understood semiotics for example' (Frith 1992:182). According to Frith, Hebdige's book *Subculture*, written at a 'Faculty of Art and Design', reacted upon the phenomenon it describes. That does not necessarily make the phenomenon inauthentic; in view of the fit between discourse form and habitus form evident here, I am tempted to say, on the contrary. Moreover, Hebdige's interpretation of youth subcultures as a semiotic guerilla, which operates by subverting conventional meanings of signs and symbols, itself draws on a lecture by Umberto Eco, originally entitled 'For a semiological guerilla' (1972), given at the *Vision '67* congress of the International Centre for Communication, Art and Sciences in New York. In this lecture Eco predicted (against the background of contemporary movements like the hippies, which he interpreted as a rejection of the society of technological communication) the birth of a new subculture able to use the sign language of the media. This prediction also took shape in the subculture of punk – or rather, of its avant-garde, art school graduates familiar with sign theory, and susceptible to interpretations of the self and the world that derive from sign theory.

Such a process cannot be grasped in terms of the dualisms 'real' and 'unreal', 'true' and 'false'. Once the essentialist error, 'the search for the nature of things', has been left behind and cultural identity and ethnicity are understood as an inter-subjective construction, based on the deliberate utilization of cultural symbols, then no taboos with regard to the materials used are conceivable. Social scientific knowledge too can form a thick thread in the homespun web of meaning. That this penetration of everyday experience by ethnographic elements meets with the questioning of social and cultural givens, simultaneously throws light on the fundamental processes of social change. What is required of anthropology/ethnology is that it investigates these processes using the patient methods of the ethnographic approach, paying attention to detail, but above all by way of cultural comparison. It is precisely cultural comparison that will show that the appropriation of construction material is not arbitrary. Contrary to rumours asserting the opposite, we do not, to adopt a striking image of Philip Schlesinger (1993:8), find ourselves in a supermarket of cultures in which identities can be freely chosen. We have historical, social, cultural and biographical handicaps that make certain offers appear more attractive to us, others less so. The investigation of these elective affinities in the process of social transformation is a central task of cultural research. Here too the punk movement constitutes an altogether instructive example, since, quite in line with Orvar Löfgren's thesis (1989) of the 'nationalization' or, rather, national interruption of global developments, there was a usage of the cultural symbolism of punk appropriate to various national conditions. Out of the imitation of the punk movement imported into Western Germany there emerged a specific variant that had its own theme: not about social crisis ('no future') as in the UK, but about the State (*'null Bock'*/'zero interest'). The West German punks were the children of the post-1960s era of reform, whose conditions of socialization were characterized equally by the increased informality of standards of behaviour and by a pedagogic appropriation of free space. Seeing the state as a teacher was what the West German punks had in common with the GDR punks of the 1980s. Admittedly, the latter's slogan 'no fun' was aimed at an (over-)planned society, which seemed to guarantee social security but allowed no free space for youth cultural forms of expression, whose first and simplest message is still 'have fun'.

Translation by Martin Chalmers

REFERENCES

Becker, H.S. (1963) *Outsiders: Studies in the Sociology of Deviance*. New York: Free Press.
Bourdieu, P. (1981) 'Die gesellschaftliche Definition der Photographie', in Bourdieu, Boltanski, Castel et. al. (eds) *Eine illegitime Kunst*. Frankfurt a.M.
—— (1985) *Sozialer Raum und 'Klassen'. Leçon sur la Leçon*. Frankfurt a.M.
Clifford, J. (1986) 'On ethnographic allegory', in J. Clifford and G. Marcus (eds) *Writing Culture: the Poetics and Politics of Ethnography*. Berkeley: California University Press.
—— (1988) 'On collecting art and culture', in *The Predicament of Culture*. Cambridge, Massachusetts: Harvard University Press.
Cohen, S. (1973) *Folk Devils and Moral Panics: the Creation of the Mods and Rockers*. London.
Cohen, S. and Young, J. (eds) (1973) *The Manufacture of News: a Reader*. London: Sage.
Duerr, H.-P. (1985) *Dreamtime: Concerning the Boundary Between Wilderness and Civilization*. Oxford: Blackwell,
Eco, U. (1972) 'Towards a semiotic inquiry into the television image. Postscriptum: the possibility of a "Semiotic Guerilla Warfare"', in *Working Papers in Cultural Studies 1972*.
Frith, S. (1978) 'The Punk Bohemians', *New Society* March 9th: 535–6.
—— (1992) 'The cultural study of popular music', in L. Grossberg, C. Nelson and P. Treichler (eds) *Cultural Studies*. London: Routledge.
Hebdige, D. (1979) *Subculture: the Meaning of Style*. London: Methuen.
Hollstein, W. (1969) *Der Untergrund*. Berlin.
Jaenicke, D. (1980) *Bewegungen*. Berlin.
Kerouac, J. (1959) 'Beatific: on the origins of a generation', *Encounter* 13: 57–61.
—— (1973) *On the road*. Harmondsworth: Penguin Books.
Lindner, R. (1981) 'Jugendkultur und Subkultur als soziologische Konzepte', in M. Brake (ed.) *Soziologie der jugendlichen Subkulturen. Eine Einführung*. Frankfurt a.M. and New York.
Lindner, R. and Breuer, H.Th. (1978) *'Sind doch nicht alles Beckenbauers'. Zur Sozialgeschichte des Fußballs im Ruhrgebiet*. Frankfurt a.M.
Löfgren, O. (1989) 'The nationalization of culture', *Ethnologia Europaea* XIX: 5–23.
Rosaldo, R. (1989) *Culture and Truth: the Remaking of Social Analysis*. Boston: Beacon Press.
Schlesinger, P. (1993) 'Wishful thinking: cultural politics, media and collective identities in Europe', *Journal of Communication* 43: 6–17.
Slack, J.D. and Whitt, L.A. (1992) 'Ethics and Cultural Studies', in L. Grossberg, C. Nelson and P. Treichler *Cultural Studies*. London: Routledge.
Trilling, L. (1972) *Sincerity and Authenticity*. Cambridge, Massachusetts: Harvard University Press.
Williams, R. (1975) *Culture and Society, 1780 – 1950*. Harmondsworth: Penguin.

PART II

LOCALIZED CREATIVE PROCESSES

7 NATIONALISM, FOOTBALL AND POLO: TRADITION AND CREOLIZATION IN THE MAKING OF MODERN ARGENTINA

Eduardo P. Archetti

From the end of the nineteenth century and through the first three decades of the twentieth century, Argentina became integrated into the global scene of massive world commodity exchange, vast international migrations, rapid urbanization, new images of urban consumption, world sports competitions and circulation of mass cultural products. Between 1890 and 1914, Argentina became one of the great immigrant nations in the modern world. Buenos Aires grew dramatically from 286,000 inhabitants in 1880 to 1,576,000 in 1914. In 1914 almost half of the population of Buenos Aires were aliens. Spanish and Italian immigrants constituted the bulk of the immigration. The British with 30,000 immigrants represented less than 2 per cent of the total foreign population (Solberg 1970:33–61). By 1930 the city had almost 3 million inhabitants, one-third of whom were European immigrants.

Urban life in Buenos Aires was rapidly transformed during this period: luxury hotels, restaurants, bistros, hundreds of cafés, cabarets, dance halls, theatres and a world-famous opera were all built by European architects. This prompted changes in the use of leisure time and created a new public environment outside the home. This period is also characterized by the rapid expansion of sports and the building of many stadiums and social clubs. The making of a modern peripheral society was then dependent on the conditions of transnational relations and the export of agrarian products, the type and rate of migration, economic and occupational changes, the importance of ethnic diasporas and the development of European leisure activities (opera, cabaret, cinema, vaudeville, theatre and sport). In this context, it is possible to state, as Clifford does, that Buenos Aires was a multicultural sprawl and constituted a privileged space for the analysis of cultural creativity under conditions of increasing cultural and social complexity (1988:4).

Creolization is usually associated with the growth of hybrid cultural forms in contexts of complex immigration and emigration. Creole cities can produce creole persons. However, the concept can also refer to social processes in which things, meanings, cultural forms (with their codes, practices and symbols, all originating in different spaces) circulate and mix extensively in a given place and a concrete historical period. This second meaning can be associated with recent theories of globalization: massive migration or diasporas and the mix of ethnic groups are not central, because meanings circulate through commerce, consumption, tourism, political propaganda and media diffusion. Creole meanings can be conceived as extraterritorial. Thus, concrete creole spaces are not needed for the creation of creole persons.

In my analysis of cultural creativity in Buenos Aires, I will try to show, with reference to football and polo, how creolization was primarily defined as an appropriation of a cultural form created and exported from Britain and practised in Argentina mostly by the British, since the 1880s. In this process the two sports were transformed into something different, to constitute a tradition, a local style, a new way of doing things, as idioms through which issues of identity should be discussed and articulated. In this sense, creolization and tradition in the two sports can be seen as resembling cognitive processes, in spite of the fact that the social mechanisms involved in creating 'otherness' differed substantially. In the creole imagery of football, players of British origin were excluded, whereas in polo they were active in the production of a creole style. During the early decades of the twentieth century, football and polo gave Argentina access to emerging international arenas for displaying identities in sports events and ceremonies. This process makes possible an analysis of practices of identity production as well as their transformation in time. These practices, I will argue, can be better understood as constituting idioms of nationalism in the process of Argentinian modernization.

DEFENDING TRADITION: THE LANGUAGE OF NATIONALISM

By 1914 the positive image that European immigration had enjoyed among the Argentinian intellectual elite was tarnished. Foreign-born businessmen and foreign enterprises controlled a large share of the national economy. Urban foreign workers, especially in Buenos Aires, organized trade unions, went on strike continually and became highly militant. Moreover, from 1904 the Socialist party became one of the dominant political forces in Buenos Aires, where anarchists were also very active. Liberal values and cosmopolitanism had guided the generous Argentinian immigration policies since the 1850s. The modern Argentina had been imagined as the result of massive European immigration, rapid integration in the world market through foreign capital investment, technological change, increased local production and expanded consumption of foreign industrial goods. A rapid urbanization was expected to change rural traditional attitudes, *caudillismo* and political clientelism. The new economic policy of the state would provide immigrants and natives with possibilities for an increasing economic and social mobility, and the consolidation of national feelings would be highly dependent on the rapid development of schooling and literacy. This liberal conception put the accent on the freedom and the autonomy of the individual as constituting the limits of the sovereignty of the nation state. According to Alberdi, one of the fathers of the nineteenth-century modernist Argentinian project, the individual and his liberty were above the authority of the fatherland (1858). His vision of the impact of immigration was cosmopolitan: the new Argentina was going to be the product of the socio-economic and cultural impact of the immigrants. In this sense he rejected the idea that Argentinian culture was something fixed, a stock of existing meanings, symbols and practices. Argentinian society and culture were conceived of as something to be produced through a modernization process.

Regarding the status of the immigrants, Alberdi thought that Argentina should only guarantee citizenship and political rights. This image was consistent with the way of life of Argentinian cosmopolitans like himself. They were not bound by local habits (which many of them considered to be traditionalism and prejudices); they spoke many foreign languages and lived long periods of their lives in exile or as immigrants in Europe and the United States. Their life experiences, sensibilities and ideology made them perceive the immigrants in the same way as themselves. The immigrants were leaving their villages and cities, customs, food habits and local rituals, showing a great flexibility of mind and an open spirit. Following Friedman (1994:25), we can see that in this modernist imagery, nature was going to be conquered, domesticated and transformed into something new (grain and beef in the case of Argentina), and culture, defined as a set of traditions, ought to be radically transformed. The wild life of gauchos in the plains was going to be replaced by settled farming, private property, a world market, global culture (European theatre, music and opera), railways and modern agriculture.

Ibarguren, a prolific nationalist writer, reacted against this creed:

The struggle against the desert and the political barbarism of the gaucho led Alberdi to the contrary exaggeration, rejecting what was the authentic creole culture and trying to transform our country into a cosmopolitan conglomerate without national spirit and character ... Without any doubt, immigration has brought about great material benefits. But I must emphasize a trait typical of the immigrant which hinders his spiritual integration and solidarity in the building of a nation: his individualism ... He is free of tradition, which is always a constraint, sees freedom and social exchanges with the egoism and openness of mind of one who has broken all ties with his original community in order to find easily obtained economic wealth abroad. Therefore the immigrant is an intense individualist with a great difficulty in being integrated within a national coherent social group. (1934:152–5 [my translation])

Nationalism was the solution in order to protect the creole cultural heritage against the massive avalanche of extreme individualist, materialist and cosmopolitan immigrants.[2]

How should the ideas and sentiments of belonging to the Argentinian nation be transmitted to the sons of immigrants? One strategy was the adoption of obligatory conscription for the sons of immigrants who automatically became Argentinian citizens. Even a war against Brazil was thought of as an important step in creating national sentiments (see Gálvez 1910:78). The other strategy, which for most intellectuals was the most attractive, was the transformation of the elementary and secondary curricula into a nationalistic education emphasizing Argentinian history and geography, national civic duties and a morale based on the cult of Argentinian heroes, the Spanish language and Argentinian literature (see Solberg 1970:144–54; Escudé 1990:25–86).

Between 1880 and 1910, the expansion of the educational system in Argentina was extremely impressive. By 1910, the rate of illiteracy of the adult population was as low as 4 per cent (Prieto 1988:13). The 'nationalist restoration' of education produced a shift of emphasis in pedagogical theory which brought a change in the teaching of history, geography, national civic duties and morale, and Argentinian literature from 'positivism' into 'fiction'. By 1910, this nationalist project was hegemonic. In 1911, Bunge defended the idea that the teaching of history must not be limited to the transmission of proven and real facts, it must introduce 'tradition', a mixture of real events and fiction, and 'legends', stories telling impossible and marvellous events. In this perspective, traditions and legends had an important nationalist value. Thus what was defined as 'poetic and social fiction' was conceived as a key pedagogical instrument in creating a nation (see Escudé 1990:38–41).

By the First World War, the nationalists had found, in the gaucho, a symbol to represent the cultural heritage of the nation under the threat of immigration. In the cosmopolitan milieu, the gaucho, a free cowboy riding in the pampas, with an unstable family, hunting, gathering and working for a wage when needed, was the antithesis of civilization and culture: a symbol of rural social disorder, clientelism and political violence characteristic of early nineteenth-century Argentina. The nationalists revindicated the figure and the cultural meaning of the gaucho as 'the first symbolic type of the Argentine nationality' (Bunge 1911, quoted in Escudé 1990:41). Lugones, one of the paladins of the nationalist intellectual revival, emphasized the fact that the gaucho was the typical creole, the product of the mixture of Spanish and indigenous blood, permitting a smooth ethnic transition and separation from Spain. Moreover, he postulated, the gaucho during the civil wars of the nineteenth century joined the federal troops and the caudillos who represented tradition and fought the liberal wing who were trying to impose political change, economic modernization and 'so-called civilization'. Thus the gaucho was the origin of the basic traits of Argentina's national character: romanticism, musical sensibility, the cult of courage, elegance, compassion, loyalty, lack of consistency, boastfulness and generosity. He acknowledged that contemporary Argentinians were not gauchos, but he stressed that in spite of the fact that immigration had created an ethnic confusion, these attributes will remain as characteristics of the typical Argentinian (1961 [1916]:79–84).

In this context of nationalistic revival the epic poem *Martin Fierro*, written by José Hernández in 1872 in a style reproducing the language of the gauchos – a historical narrative of a gaucho struggling against state justice in order to keep his freedom – was transformed into an example of 'national literature'. This reinvention of tradition was made possible by the privileged place that the 'creole literature' had occupied in the popular urban and rural literary consumption since the 1880s. *Martin Fierro* was not the only epic hero. He was accompanied by other mythical figures like *Santos Vega* and *Juan Moreira*, both noble gauchos like himself, fighting for what they considered just and representing freedom and tradition. Prieto has shown that the 'creole literature' was also read in the cities and among European immigrants to whom the colourful rural iconography was the only expression of something national, local, Argentinian, in the middle of the 'generalized disorder produced by the cosmopolitan flood' (1988:98–9). The 'creole literature' created morally committed human characters struggling in situations of conflict and tension introduced by modernization and cosmopolitan values. They were men of honour and courage representing idealized aristocratic images. It is important to bear in mind that by 1910, Argentina did not have a consolidated and strong literary tradition with an accepted historical narrative. Thus tradition ought to be imagined and, in many cases, recovered from the past.

CREOLIZATION AND TRADITION IN THE SOCIAL WORLD OF FOOTBALL

The British immigrants brought not only capital and technology to Argentina. Their boarding schools, with their emphasis on practising the new sports, and their clubs, where leisure time was occupied with sports activities, have played a key role in the construction of identities in the making of modern Argentina. Many clubs were founded after 1880, and the majority of these sprang up from British schools. In 1883, Alexander Watson Hutton, founder of the Buenos Aires English School, was the first president of the Argentine Association Football League and the first 'national league' was organized in Buenos Aires. The board of the association was entirely composed of British citizens. The association kept English as the official meeting language until 1906. Not until 1934 was 'football' replaced by the Spanish 'fútbol', when the new and definitive association was created: Asociación de Fútbol Argentino (Scher and Palomino 1988:25).

Not only was the game an import from Britain, but so too were the standards and the quality of the play. In the first decade of the twentieth century and until the First World War, Argentinian football grew under the influence of the excellent English teams that came to play in Buenos Aires. Southampton, Nottingham Forest, Everton, Tottenham and Chelsea, all of them professional teams, visited Argentina with great success, winning all their matches. In a global landscape articulated through the visit of British teams, the myth of the invincibility of British football was created. The local clubs, Lomas Athletic Club and Alumni, with roots in the British boarding schools and players of British origin, dominated the national league. Thus a hegemonic local British football tradition was established. A new way of playing was to develop in relation to what was perceived as British style.

Football rapidly became very popular in Buenos Aires and all over Argentina. Since 1900, a great number of football clubs have been founded in Buenos Aires and surrounding industrial cities. The majority of the new clubs rapidly incorporated European immigrants and their sons, or were directly founded by them. It is possible to define the competition between British teams and the new 'mixed' clubs as a growth point for inventive creolization. The British were the founders of the game; they codified the rules, they developed a morality based on fair play, they constructed a style of playing and exported it all over the world. The native Argentinians and the immigrants accepted and incorporated football as an important physical leisure-time activity and as a ritual context for competition and the emotional display of loyalty and engagement. The social and cultural complexity of Buenos Aires at the beginning of the century created a setting conducive to creativity.

Sport became as legitimate an arena for the creation of identities as schools and military barracks. Popular and elite sports were not only a kind of inward mirror, they made it possible for Argentina to compete internationally and to be seen by others (see Archetti 1994 a, b). Through sport, Argentinian men of various classes and ethnic origins could become bearers of national values and traits. In the expansion of a global sports landscape, the Olympic games and regional international competitions played a substantial role. Moreover, in many relevant sports, identity creation was marked by the power and dominance of the British image of excellence, as in the cases of football and polo.

The turning point in creating a creole football was the victory of Racing Club in the national league in 1913. This victory was defined as the 'creole victory' and Racing Club was called and popularly perceived as 'the first great creole team'. In this context, 'creole' was associated with the fact that all the players had Spanish and Italian names. British names were absent and not a single player was a past or present student of one of the prestigious British boarding schools. Alumni, 'the great British team', was dissolved in 1912 and almost automatically became the symbol of the 'British period', a time without creolization. Creolization can be seen in this context as a successful appropriation of some practice which originally had been exclusively associated with the identity of a given social group. In the beginning, football was played by the 'British' and 'British teams' won the national league. This was normal and expected because this sport was a British creation. That the British who dominated the Argentinian national football team until 1915 were a second generation of immigrants back in the 1860s was not seen as 'creole'. The British were pure as was their practice of football; they played the British way.

In the inventive creolization, transformed later into an accepted historical narrative, non-British immigrants and sons of immigrants were seen not only as successful athletes: they contribute to the creation of something original in the 'new country' they emigrated to. They were not included in an existing tradition, native or British. Moreover, they adopted the practice of football jointly with the native population. The creators of the game were British and they, with their sons, remained for ever British. In the history of Argentinian football, the British remained profoundly alien to the creolization process. Through football, it was explicitly communicated that working- and lower-middle-class Spaniards, Italians and other nationalities and their sons could eventually become 'creole', creating different styles. They were, in many ways, free from tradition. How was this perceived and explained?

Firstly, it was necessary to construct (and to imagine) another style of playing, a style different from the way the British played football. In this narrative, the British style was seen as being based on solid collective work, high team morale, long passes, speed, physical strength and lack of individual dribbling. It was defined as an 'aerial style'. On the contrary, the 'creole style', called euphemistically 'creole foundation', was a 'terrestrial style' based on short passes, precision, the ball preferably on the ground, slower than the British and with an emphasis on creative dribbling (see Archetti 1994 a, b). Through this foundation, Argentinian football was liberated from the British cage and a new form was developed. Secondly, the transformative element of style was explicitly related to the environment, to the products and characteristics of a given territory which conditioned the immigrants and their sons: air, landscape, contact with the natives, food and drink. The product was not Italian or Spanish, it was 'creole', because the new form developed from sources of mixed origins.

The victory of Racing in 1913 almost coincided with the democratic changes, the extension of civil rights and voting, and the incorporation of the immigrants in political life brought about by the Radical party, which won the national elections in 1916 and stayed in power until 1930. The nationalist voices created a pastoral imagery of the nation based on roots and continuity of tradition. While focusing on the importance of football, sports journalism and the popular press articulated new images and representations based on creolization and the important contribution of the immigrants in defining a national style. This process was consolidated through the international victories of Argentinian clubs and the national teams during the 1920s. Argentinian football was not a local phenomenon, it was recognized as something different and very competitive. This was an important chapter in the global expansion of the game, with teams and players circulating in an increasingly international market. By the 1920s, Argentina not only exported beef and grain: the best local players emigrated to Europe and performed the new 'creole style'. This style, historically created in Argentina in opposition to the British, was in Europe simply perceived as a different style, as a way of playing a more artistic football (see Brera 1978:98; Papa and Panico 1993:158–63). For Argentinians, the Spanish and Italian styles were perceived as different but not in a systematic contraposition to their own style (Archetti 1995).

TRADITION AND CREOLIZATION IN THE SOCIAL WORLD OF POLO

Polo, an old Asian equestrian team sport, was first played in its modern form by the British military officer corps in India in the 1850s and was exported to Argentina in the 1870s. In 1875, the first polo match was played in Argentina. All the players were British (Laffaye 1989:23). The first polo club was founded in Buenos Aires in 1882. By the 1890s, polo was mostly played in the provinces of Buenos Aires and Santa Fe in *estancias* owned by landlords of British origin. In 1892, delegates of the existing British clubs founded the Polo Association of the River Plate in Buenos Aires. By the First World War, polo was rather exclusively practised by British ranchers and by some Argentinian cavalry officers. The first 'creole club', El Palomar, was founded in late 1915 (Laffaye 1989:54). After this, polo became a popular sport among the landed Argentinian elite. This process culminated in the foundation of an Argentinian polo association in 1921, the Federación Argentina de Polo. The old British polo association joined the new organization in 1922.

By 1890, the rise of organized equestrian sport in the pampas followed the demise of the gaucho and of his traditional contests and pastimes. The gauchos had a number of rugged and violent games, contests and plays which required a good deal of strength and courage in both man and horse, as well as great speed. Accidents were common in the course of these competitions. On the contrary, polo was considered to be a civilized spectator sport and a sign of modern times. The enthusiastic adoption of polo by the native landed aristocracy was seen as an expression of a well-achieved civilizing process (Slatta 1985).

Since 1896 the British landowners and polo players living in Argentina took part in the big tournaments in Britain with great success. Each participation implied an impressive mobilization of maritime resources: five or six players, the peons (called *petiseros*) and between 20 and 30 horses with all the fodder needed for crossing the Atlantic Ocean. Usually they embarked in Buenos Aires in February in order to be in good shape for the summer tournaments in Europe which began in May. Success and victory were also business because the best horses, very cheap in Argentina, were sold in Britain. It was common that the best players were the owners of the best horses and gradually Argentinian 'creole' horses gained international fame. Moreover, an international circuit developed and the good players were invited to play in different countries with teams organized by British and European aristocrats or American millionaires. Paradoxically, some of the best 'Argentinian' players in this transnational arena of the 1920s, like Juan Traill or Luis Lacey, were British and in this role were often invited to play with the British team in the US Open competition (Laffaye 1989:73–88). The fact that Argentina was unable to utilize these players in international competitions contributed to the 'nationalization' of polo. Traill and Lacey would not join the Argentinian team in the Olympic Games in Paris in 1924, the first great victory of the Argentinian team and the recognition of their different playing style.

In the Paris Olympics the Argentinian 'creole style of playing' was founded. The Argentinian team, consisting of three '*anglos*', Nelson, Keeny and Miles, and one '*criollo*', the captain Padilla, won the Olympic title defeating the favourite teams of Great Britain and the United States. Suddenly, the 'world discovered' a new way of playing. This style of polo had undoubtedly existed before and had been developed individually or collectively in some Argentinian club or estancia, but without its Argentinian character being recognized. A French newspaper described the victory in the following way:

The Argentinian players try to stick to the saddle in such a way that the men and the horses constitute a single body. The 35 horses of the team are pure-blood and Argentinian creoles, rather small ... They have been selected among a great variety of types and trained in order to develop a great speed and resistance. Ridden with great gentleness, just with one rein, the horses make marvellous movements and incredible pirouettes, giving the impression that they enjoy complete freedom. The players control the horses like tennis players handling a racquet ... The Argentinians surprise us with their great ability in the use of the stick. Less strong than the Americans, they practice a way of playing that is much freer and varied. Each player rides at a fantastic speed, giving the feeling that, at each moment, they know the position of each other in the field. (quoted in Laffaye 1989:96 [my translation])

The victorious team was received in the harbour of Buenos Aires by thousands of people: they had won against the two big economic world powers, they were champions of the world, as Olympic gold medallists were usually called, and they had amazed the sophisticated Parisians and the European aristocracy.

The image of an original 'creole style' came back to Argentina and confirmed, in many ways, the existing self-image. Argentinians players were not surprised by this victory, they were expecting it. In 1924, before the finals, Major Sierra, a cavalry officer and a good player, elaborated a theory on the superiority of 'creole polo players' (*El Gráfico*, 1924, 216:19). Sierra put special emphasis, as the French journalist did in his article, on the creole way of riding but he added a number of masculine virtues. In his perspective the 'creole polo players' had inherited gaucho qualities; they were, so to speak, modern gauchos but still 'savages'. Sierra reproduces the classic ideological barbarism–civilization antinomy, which in the past (and in the 1920s) had divided nationalists and liberal cosmopolitans. Civilization is European and barbarism, imagined in the gaucho fighting spirit, is a creole attribute.

A good creole player needs a good pony. The theoretical superiority of a polo player is highly dependent on the quality of the horses he rides. Sierra explains that the main difference between Argentinian and foreign ponies is related to the fact that Argentinian ponies enjoy a strong and free life in an open landscape while the foreign ponies are in an artificial environment, in small paddocks and inside boxes (ibid.). The nationalist discourse of Major Sierra imagines the creole style as a meaningful point of reference vis-à-vis the 'others'. Further, it applies *temporality* as a key dimension. The temporality of representation is not merely drawn from the tensions existing between past, present and future (the coming struggles in Paris) but is organized as a bridge between cultural heritage and new social processes. Sierra knew very well that polo was a civilizing dimension in the politics of modernization, a British reinvention exported to Argentina, and, in addition, that the majority of his fellow players were '*anglos*'. Sierra is reconstituting a tradition, related to the gauchos, the open and free landscape of the pampas and the heroism of the blood of the creole ponies. In this creative indigen-ization a 'creole style and way of playing' is born. Nationalist discourses have the miraculous capacity to capture the fluidity of cultural influences and social exchanges, being able to accommodate them in a kind of 'magic' syn-chronization of multiple traits and complex meanings with a single result: the 'national'. Sierra's discourse, like the discourse of football, reveals its basic dependence on 'otherness'; it is at the same time essentialist and relativist because it must recognize other styles.

Polo was, and still is, the sport of the Argentinian landed creole aristocracy. The victory of 1924 transformed polo into a 'popular' sport, at least among the middle-class spectators in Buenos Aires. Polo created and reproduced a pastoral imagery based on the importance of vernacularism, gaucho idealization and aristocratic standards. The private appropriation of the mythological pampas, populated in the past by the free gauchos, permitted the Argentinian landed class to export grain and beef to the world market and to accumulate substantial wealth. In permanent contact with the descendents of the gauchos, transformed into paid riders and rural labourers, they could imagine a mimetic relation with the gaucho riding tradition. They were able to produce marvellous horses and riders, to win over British aristocrats and American millionaires in prestigious polo tournaments, and to be fully accepted by them socially. They entered early into a global system of economic and social exchanges, and continued to accumulate wealth, trophies and glory.

CONCLUSION

In the period between 1880 and 1930, Argentina entered into a contradic-tory process of accommodating disparate economic, social and cultural influences. Moreover, Buenos Aires became a metropolis of a special type, outside the great traditions and orthodoxies of the European cities. Buenos Aires was an open, complex and mobile society affected not only by massive international immigration but also receiving the educated elite of the marginalized provinces. The great nationalist writers, Rojas, Lugones and Gálvez, were all born into traditional provincial lineages. They experienced a chaotic city, strangeness, alienation and a real cultural distance between the European immigrants and the traditional cultures and societies existing in the Argentinian hinterland.[3] They experienced the complexity, as well as the miscellaneousness of the great metropolis, both sources of the rise of modernism and of avant-garde movements in the European and American metropolis (see Williams 1989:37–63). Their response was a muscular and masculine national imagery where courage, the defence of honour, generosity and freedom as spiritual values were in contrast to the materialism of immigration and cosmopolitan capitalism. The gaucho became the symbol of the nation. In the search for roots and continuity, the re-creation of a rural tradition was a cultural strategy. National identity was closely associated with a virtual home, the wild and open space of the pampas, and a virtual man, the gaucho. The gaucho and the pampas were used as archaic *thematas* for explaining the differences of 'others' and for tackling the contradictions between unity and alterity (see Slatta 1983:180–92; 1985).

The power of this imagery is better understood at the moment polo is transformed into a 'national sport'. The explanation of the superiority of the Argentinian polo players must be seen as the invention of tradition, as the creative indigenization of a British sport in which the '*anglos*' representing the nation are imagined as gauchos because they ride like them, they have male virtues like courage and the spirit of sacrifice, and their horses are a genuine product of the pampas. The fascinating paradox is that a rural sport became transposed into one of the main symbols of the city of Buenos Aires. The landed aristocrats displayed their physical abilities on horses and with a stick in the babel where they lived like modern urbanites in their mansions. They represented historical continuity and were the guarantee of the survival of an original creole culture. The '*anglos*' were a part of the landed gentry and as such were socially accepted.

It was lower-middle-class and working-class immigrants, on the other hand, who creolized football, another British invention. The '*anglos*' abandoned the sport when it was appropriated by the immigrants and their sons. During the first two decades of the twentieth century, Buenos Aires was transformed into a world metropolis of football with her modern stadiums and prestigious clubs. Here, the language of creolization legitimized immigrants as Argentinians: they founded the creole style in contraposition to the British style. Before 1915 the '*anglos*' had represented the nation, but in the popular imagery constructed by the sons of immigrants, they continued to play like their ancestors. They were never transformed into real creoles.

The national discourses and images I have discussed can be seen as examples of class cultural strategies where the concept of 'creole' is used in an explicit way. In polo, 'creoleness' is claimed to have a direct link to the typical 'creole' of the gaucho (Spanish and Italian); while in football, 'creoleness' arises from a mixing of immigrants of different nations, and the link to the land seems more imaginary (air, landscape, food and drink). A fully developed national imagery would have to integrate the different types of 'creoleness', because it needs all the fragments, all the dislocated and mismatched identities that arise from the changing character of the groups which inhabit its territory. This has, however, not been totally achieved in Argentina. Argentina entered into modernity producing a series of identities and contradictory cultural tendencies that refused integration and containment within a single national imagery. My examples show that high and low culture, popular and elite, local and transnational visions were at work when Argentinian society entered into modernity. Argentinian cultural identity was highly dependent upon multiplicity (see Masiello 1992:165–200).

NOTES

1. For comments on a previous draft of this contribution, I am deeply grateful to John Liep, a real critical editor, and Signe Howell.
2. For a history of nationalism and an exhaustive presentation of the ideas of the different writers and political wings see Rock (1993).
3. Rojas described Buenos Aires in 1909 as an alienating city, rootless, without community feelings, with cosmopolitan values, with a decadent sensualist atmosphere, with a spoken Spanish polluted by the 'dialectical barbarism of the immigrants', very rich and opulent, and with an extreme influence over the Argentinian provinces and the rest of the country. He believed that owing to the dominant role of the city, the nationalist battle ought to be fought there (1909:88–90).

REFERENCES

Alberdi, J.B. (1858) *Organización de la Confederación Argentina*. Besancon: J. Jacquin.
Archetti, E.P. (1994a) 'Argentina and the World Cup: in search of national identity', in J. Sugden and A. Tomlinson (eds) *Host and Champions: Soccer Cultures, National Identities and the World Cup in the USA*. Aldershot, Hampshire: Arena.
—— (1994b) 'Masculinity and football: the formation of national identity in Argentina', in R. Giulianotti and J. Williams (eds) *Game Without Frontiers: Football, Identity and Modernity*. Aldershot, Hampshire: Arena.
—— (1995) 'Estilio y virtudes masculinas en *El Gráfico*: la creación del imaginario del fútbol argentino', *Desarolla Económico*, 35:419–42.
Brera, G. (1978) *Storia critica del calcio italiano*. Milano: Tascabili Bompiani.
Clifford, J. (1988) *The Predicament of Culture*. Cambridge, Massachusetts: Harvard University Press.
Escudé, C. (1990) *El fracaso del proyecto argentino: educación e ideología*. Buenos Aires: Instituto Torcuato Di Tella–Editorial Tesis.

Friedman, J. (1994) 'Modernitetens implosion: den förrädiska samtiden', in O. Hemer (ed.) *Kulturen i den globala byn.* Lund: Ægis forlag.

Gálvez, M. (1910) *El diario de Gabriel Quiroga: opiniones sobre la vida argentina.* Buenos Aires: Arnoldo Moen e Hno.

Ibarguren, C. (1934) *La inquietud de esta hora.* Buenos Aires: Roldán Editor.

Laffaye, H.A. (1989) *El polo internacional argentino.* Buenos Aires.

Lugones, L. (1961 [1916]) *El payador.* Buenos Aires: Ediciones Centurión.

Masiello, F. (1992) *Between Civilization and Barbarism: Women, Nation, and Literary Culture in Modern Argentina.* Lincoln: University of Nebraska Press.

Papa, A. and Panico, G. (1993) *Storia sociale del calcio in Italia.* Bologna: Il Mulino.

Prieto, A. (1988) *El discurso criollista en la formación de la Argentina moderna.* Buenos Aires: Editorial Sudamericana.

Rock, D. (1993) *La Argentina autoritaria: los nacionalistas, su historia y su influencia en la vida pública.* Buenos Aires: Ariel.

Rojas, R. (1909) *La restauración nacionalista.* Buenos Aires: Ministerio de Justicia e Instruccion Pública.

Scher, A. and Palomino, H. (1988) *Fútbol: pasión de multitudes y de elites.* Buenos Aires: CISEA.

Sierra, Major. (1924) *El Gráfico,* 216: 19.

Slatta, R.W. (1983) *Gauchos and the Vanishing Frontier.* Lincoln: University of Nebraska Press.

—— (1985) 'The gaucho in Argentina's quest for national identity', *Canadian Review of Studies in Nationalism* 12:99–122.

Solberg, C. (1970) *Immigration and Nationalism: Argentina and Chile, 1890–1914.* Austin: The University of Texas Press.

Williams, R. (1989) *The Politics of Modernism.* London: Verso.

8 THE 'PLAYING' OF MUSIC IN A STATE OF CRISIS: GENDER AND RAÏ MUSIC IN ALGERIA

Marc Schade-Poulsen

INTRODUCTION

In this contribution I assume that 'true' creativity involves the making of novelties. It is not the outcome of a quasi-divine inspiration found in certain artistic geniuses: 'the ones that create, that draw something out of nothing' (cf. Robert 1978). Rather, creativity means forming, giving shape to something; it is the outcome of combinations of new potentialities or new combinations of existing resources.

Creativity is closely linked to processes of appropriation. Novelties are nothing unless *accepted* and *worked* on as social facts. A 'social contract' has to be established between the creators and their surroundings in order to generate a common understanding of the novelty (cf. Passeron 1991:286).

True creativity must be distinguished from less radical creative forms such as virtuosity, variations and improvisations arising from sets of rules. Virtuosity consists in having eminent skill in generating forms based on established rules and resources rather than in creating new rules and forms. Variations or improvisations – the latter meaning the unexpected – occur on the basis of the expected and are thus part of an established set-up.

My point of departure here is that there seem to be certain moments when separate set-ups become connected. In these cases a change in the social surroundings of the agents seems to enable participants in diverse settings to establish new ways of interaction. In popular music this kind of innovation seems important and to have the character of play.[1] That is moments when rules are relaxed.

In the following pages I deal with a product – *raï* music – that took shape in Oran, Algeria, in the late 1970s/early 1980s. Through an analysis of the raï songs that were recorded on cassette tapes at that time, I intend to reach a qualitative understanding of the social significance of this creation. In order to do this it is necessary to describe the product historically and the social aspects of its production, distribution and consumption. As I have dealt extensively with this subject elsewhere (Schade-Poulsen 1994), I shall here take a further step and examine whether the product itself, that is, the recorded songs, contains elements that sum up its significance at the time as a wider societal factor.

Briefly stated, I shall consider raï as a game, and more specifically focus on the pleasure of 'crossing the border' and participating in the game of raï. I do this not only because the game concept has often proved useful in conceptualizations, models and metaphors of social life, and because games in many cases seem to be instructive and formative elements in social life (cf. Caillois 1958; Geertz 1973, 1983; Huizinga 1970; Turner 1988 etc.). Raï in fact contains several games that are interrelated, if we use the term, in a sense following Bourdieu, for an arbitrary and autonomous social construct played out in a certain 'field'. A game has '... explicit and definite rules ... and extraordinary time and space. Entry into the game takes the form of a quasi-contract, which is sometimes made explicit' (Bourdieu 1990:67).

I do not assume games to be *models of* or *models for* society in the strict sense that people in social life enact them as automatons. As Hoggart (1971), among others, established, people do not play games unreflexively, and social actors have multiple ways of relating to them. All the same, games are not played at random. People do prefer some above others. You might say that a game gives pleasures that are not found elsewhere and that some games give more pleasure than others.

This contribution starts with a description of the different elements in raï and their relation to ordinary life. This exercise should lead to an understanding of the interrelations between the elements of raï that constitute the overall game, the playing of which gives pleasure. Subsequently it should lead to an understanding of the significance of the raï novelty created in the early 1980s.

However, if we only analysed correlations and parallels between games and ordinary life, we would miss the point about the relationship between games and the world. The raw material of the game is found in or taken from ordinary life, but the tension, feeling and pleasure of the game result from a recomposition of these elements. In this sense, the pleasure of the game lies in the dissolving of the signifiers, of *signifiance*, rather than in the signified (cf. Barthes 1987; Middleton 1983).

In order to stay within the spirit of the game concept, in order not to reify or pacify the game, I shall not reach any 'significant statement' in the sense that the pleasure of playing raï will refer to precise objects, things, matters, etc. Games have reasons that reason does not at all perceive (cf. Bateson 1972a:134) as, at one and the same time, they deal with relations between their elements and with comments on the difference between game and non-game (cf. Bateson 1972b on play and non-play). In the following I shall limit myself to the male points of view in Algeria[2] and state that what it was that was given new form, in Algeria in the late 1970s, was *male pleasure in disinterested encounters with femininity*.

All in all, my statement is 'unreasonable' because it does not seek to essentialize the concepts of disinterestedness or femininity; but as the concepts are recognizable it still makes sense. Finally, the statement has the effect of creating an open-ended text to encompass the generalizations of the following sections.

RAÏ HISTORY

Electrified raï came into being as a new style of music in the numerous cabarets of Oran in the late 1970s. In these spaces for male amusement with professional female attendants the entertainment consisted of at least two orchestras, one playing rock and pop (Beatles, Johnny Halliday, etc.), the other Egyptian, Moroccan or *wahrani* styles (see below). In the late 1970s the Arab part of the programme seemed increasingly to be of the acoustic raï genre, instrumented in combinations of percussion and melodic instruments such as accordion, trumpet and violin.

Musicians report that the two groups would fuse together, simply for fun or when a musician was missing in one of them. They were a success (in terms of the number of people on the dance floor) that became the standard genre in the cabarets. The music was subsequently recorded on cassette tape and diffused to a wider audience. Through the 1980s it spread all over Algeria, to the rest of North Africa, to North African communities in the West, and also worldwide (cf. Schade-Poulsen 1994).

The success of raï cannot be understood without taking into account the local producers' access to new music technology (electric instruments, amplifiers, etc.) which spread worldwide in the 1970s, and the global changes in technologies of music diffusion such as the cassette tape and local commercial radio stations (cf. Wallis and Malm 1984).

Neither can raï be understood without considering the significant social changes that have taken place in Algeria since independence. These include a huge rural influx into the cities (and a corresponding change in the composition of the clientele of the cabarets), the more autonomous position of the conjugal family within the extended family of the cities, the democratization of the system of education in gender-mixed institutions and the lengthening of the period of youth. The emergence of raï coincided with the time when a first generation of Algerians appeared in independent Algerian institutions. It also coincided with a time when a huge number of wage-paying jobs had been created in the Algerian cities and with a period of relative surplus arising from the oil economy. This was however followed by a severe recession in the 1980s, leading to a catastrophic crisis of the economy. Among other things, this found political expression in the Islamist movement, which is much concerned with gender relations.[3] It is necessary to have these elements in mind in the following.

To sum up, raï can be said to be a novel game that was the outcome of two previous games with different rules coming together in 'playing for fun' in a specific milieu, the cabarets, and in a context of new resources as well as of changing social conditions. Furthermore, the enormous success that raï had in the early years *outside* any official channels shows that, in Algeria, a social contract had been established between producers and consumers. The creative moment in the cabarets was accepted as socially significant by the Algerian audience.[4] The correlations I have sketched do not, however, explain how raï 'works' and why recorded raï had such a success outside its initial sphere of origin. But this can be done by making a games analysis of the raï product.

THE FORM OF RAÏ AND ITS SPHERE OF ORIGIN

The basic form of raï has its roots in an oral, improvised performance, the original locations of which were wedding parties or spaces for male amusement (for example, the cabarets). Tuned to an ongoing dance rhythm, the singers choose a catchy key phrase to which they repeatedly return. They have a range of phrases at hand to keep the movement going, while displaying their inventive skill in improvising new phrases to move the audience.

The interaction between performers and audience cannot be isolated from the music and poetics. Dedications and song lines addressed to individuals are an integral part of the performance. As such, they are an element of the economic exchange taking place, inasmuch as people pay for the songs they want to hear.

At a male raï performance the two central figures are the singer and the *berraH*. The former sings what he is told to sing for money. The latter is a man supposed to have the power of words (*klâm*). He collects money from the guests and announces the sum of money offered, the name of the donor and the message that the donor wishes to accompany his gift. He often adds a shorter piece of poetry or a proverb to the message. Then follows the song requested by the donor – giving people the opportunity to dance. Frequently the entertainment has the character of a competition with people paying for a song in order to insult others present at the party. This leads to a counter-order, and increases the money invested in the orchestra. All this is done in fun, but sometimes, mainly in the cabarets, the game is taken seriously and may lead to fights.

While the *berraH* is in action, the relations between people present and absent are named, as if the social agents were evoked without distinction, as if no hierarchy was to be expressed. But at the same time, the competition involves an opposing trend which constitutes a counterpoint to the preference of equality. Thus, the person of the *berraH* and the game he instructs illustrate the social behaviour to be found in *public* male life in 'ordinary time', that is, ideals of equality among men, the art of strategic and political thinking, of using the right words at the right time, etc.

This was the performance that was transferred to the recording studios in the late 1970s, with the exception that only the singer's voice materialized in the studio. But the singer still offered dedications and song lines as if in a person-to-person relationship, sometimes joking and singing in an improvised mood of gaiety.

The themes of the songs were taken from the cabarets where the singers borrowed a part of their verbal stock from an older repertoire, that of the *shikhâtes* – female singers who entertain men at weddings, in brothels and pleasure parties. A number of song lines from this period dealt – sometimes crudely – with men's relationships with courtesans. Other themes were centred around the problems of maintaining a relationship with the courtesans, and a number ventured into descriptions of the problems of criminality and alcohol abuse, deploring the fact that the 'environment' led men away from their proper path in life. In this sense the songs were descriptive of what was going on in the cabarets where ordinary gender boundaries were crossed both by males and females – the latter displaying male behaviour such as drinking and smoking, the former expressing an obvious pleasure in the opposite sex not displayed elsewhere.

It was these themes, together with the raï performance and its musical accompaniment, that in the early 1980s achieved such a success outside their sphere of origin. Later, love songs came to predominate over songs of lust in the raï repertoire. Nevertheless, since its beginning, raï has provoked a debate in Algeria in which the socio-moral behaviour of the family has been at stake.

The notions of reason (`aql), respect (qder) and modesty (hashâm) are involved. Basically their observance consists in avoiding smoking, drinking and matters of love and sexuality in front of family members according to their position of power. The weaker thus display modesty in front of those with greater power: young men towards their fathers, wives in front of their husbands, sisters towards their brothers, etc. The possible exceptions are cases where sons deal with these matters in front of their mothers, who might make long-term investments in their son's virility through apparently disinterested acts of caring.

The socio-moral structure of the family tends to be situational, that is, what you do not do in one situation you might do in another. However, family behaviour is linked on a number of points to scriptural Muslim doctrines including notions of impurity and purity. In Algeria tension has been growing through the 1980s between the situational views on morality and scriptural Muslim doctrine, which in its Islamist version applies universally (that is, what you do not do in one situation, you should not do in any other). Raï has been at the centre of this controversy, but its consumption mainly takes place according to a situational logic, that is, within gender and age groups. Paradoxically, however, at weddings it is perfectly possible that family members listen to raï together.

THE WEDDING PARTY

The paradox has been explained on the grounds that wedding activities are institutionalized or framed and therefore judged using different criteria from those for everyday life.[5]

In Algeria it is obvious that the wedding is framed to denote that what occurs has to be judged using other criteria than those applying to non-wedding behaviour. For example, when processions set off to bring the bride or groom to the party there is noise – car horns, music, rhythm – not only to show 'how many we are', but also 'how happy we are', that is, here a party is taking place, celebrating a wedding.

At the wedding it is generally as if social values, ideologies and feelings are exposed in order to demonstrate the elements that make up the tissue of social life, primarily the relations between man and woman, husband and wife. Not only does the husband often arrive on a fiery horse with the shooting of guns, hiding his head in a cloak in order to avoid impotence brought about through the sorcery of jealous women; he also enters the bridal chamber to display his virility in what comes as close as possible to a *public* performance of the sexual act, that is, the defloration of his bride. After this object lesson in the social idea of the wedding contract, the importance of blood lineage is emphasized by publicly displaying the bride's blood-stained garment. Finally, the groom leaves the bridal chamber, demonstrating that male and female only come together in the (procreative) interests of the patriarchal family.

However, at a number of weddings in the early 1990s no blood-stained garment was publicly displayed – it was only shown to a few women. Other weddings took place *en famille*, which meant that a selected number of guests were invited and genders were not segregated. On several occasions, the bride joined the groom at the festivities after the sequence in the bridal chamber. In this sense the weddings reflected the social changes in the structure of a number of Algerian families (as mentioned above). I will return to this below.

Here, the main point is that the wedding party can be described as involving inversions of the daily moral and sexual norms of family life. But further insight into the consumption of raï at the wedding can be gained by comparing it to a third situation: that found in the cabarets.

The wedding party has an affinity with the raï performances in the cabarets. In both you find the same competitive game and exchange of words for money accompanying raï performances. In both, people 'lose their heads'. Both also feature sexuality, in cabarets through men's acquaintance with 'free women', at weddings through the consummation of the sexual contract.

Nonetheless there are significant differences. At weddings, the formal purpose of the money invested in the game of dedications is to share the expenses of the wedding. This is not the case in the cabarets. Furthermore, in the cabarets, one can hear dedications to women who are mentioned by name, whereas this is unheard of at weddings. The naming of women in public opens up vistas of uncontrolled sexuality, as it also exhibits women in public life. Thus, cabarets are spaces for competitions between men featuring unregulated leisure and lust, where male and female roles are also altered. The wedding party confirms male unity and features regulated sexuality where male and female roles are validated. As a result, when compared to the cabarets, the wedding is in no way transgressive.

PLAYING THE GAME OF RAÏ – LISTENING TO RECORDED SONGS

There are many levels on which to listen to a recorded raï song: that of the voice, the music, the social setting, the text, etc. It would lead too far to discuss this in depth (see Schade-Poulsen 1994 for details). Basically, a number of listeners tend to identify with the voice embodied in an imaginary figure, a singer in a sound space who expresses themes matching the socio-cultural reality of the listeners.

Thus, a recorded song conveys the image of a singer, a young man, dependent on his surroundings. Furthermore, the singer evokes reminiscences of male arenas where games of strategy and equality are played out through the exchange of poetic words.

However, this particular male type is not located in a context based solely on everyday male life. When listeners describe how they perceive raï songs, they tend to associate with the logic of the raï performances.

PRIMARY SCENES OF REFERENCE

In general, in mass-produced songs, there seems to be an (imaginary) relationship between performers and audiences referring to certain social spaces or settings. This may be found in all kinds of music: the folk music club in the early Bob Dylan records, the rock concert, etc. It does not need to be a live performance venue but may just as well be movies, as in Hindu pop, Turkish Arabesk and Egyptian popular music (see Danielson 1988; Manuel 1988; Stokes 1992), or when, for example, Mozart's Piano Concerto No. 21 can be heard in the film *Elvira Madigan* as well as in the concert hall. In raï, the relevant venues are not only the recording studios, but also wedding parties and cabarets.

Thus, in the game of raï a young male is situated in a wedding party or a cabaret: phenomena that are deeply embedded in Algerian cultural and moral fields of reproduction. In both these settings gender relations are a central focus, and in both they are the result of *intentional* encounters in everyday life. In the cabarets these are mediated by money, at the wedding by family arrangements. But the occasions themselves are also moments when gender boundaries are relaxed. Singers and audiences at these parties address these 'acts of transgression' rather than the intentional actions that motivated the parties.

Thus, raï is primarily associated with cabaret and the wedding party. To understand how the development of raï came to embrace a wider world of gender encounters, one must explore further aspects of the experience of raï.

EXPLORING A WIDER ARENA: RAÏ POETICS

The singer is not only located in a context of transgression, he also sings about it. Space does not permit a discussion of raï poetics in Algeria, but it is possible to show that the listeners are *seduced* into entering into an imaginary relationship with a singer *as if* he were describing social events.

The most important thing is to stress that the major part of raï *poetics* consists of love themes evoking the meeting of men and women *outside* the regulated family context and *outside* the unregulated spheres of the cabarets, that is, gender encounters in the public spheres of Algerian society.

Assignations and romances, etc., are an important concern of male youth in Algeria; but the outcome of gender encounters is described by a vast number of men – mostly those without significant consumption capacity – in extremely negative terms. Briefly stated, modern Algerian women are described in raï songs and in public male spheres in terms similar to the image of the cabaret courtesans, as women incapable of disinterested encounters with men, that is, as women interested only in men with purchasing power. These images are matched by stereotypes of the local 'bourgeois' men as becoming effeminate as a result of their possessions and conspicuous consumption – which again is equated to their becoming Westernized (Schade-Poulsen 1994).

In this stereotyping one may recognise the resentment which condemns others for possessing something that you want for yourself, and a description of class differences in terms of gender in which wealth is attributed to feminine traits when used for pleasure and luxury rather than when used as an instrument of power (cf. Bourdieu 1992:36–8). Further, the image of the courtesan is contrasted with two other female images. The first is a nostalgic image of the pure, true Muslim woman who is uninterested in the world outside the home and the world of consumption, and who obeys her family and husband. The second is the Western woman, the only one capable of pure love – one who uses her brain, is trustworthy and is uninterested in material matters.

These female categories – to which the modern Algerian woman is compared – are interesting. Firstly, because it seems that the image of the

European woman has changed in the 1980s from that of a woman to be seduced by men (cf. Dejeux 1989) – similar to the Algerian courtesan (that is, like her able to act on equal terms with men) – to a woman *in the power* of love who gives without asking anything in return. Secondly, because a number of Algerian men thus seem to naturalize their socio-cultural, economic conditions and perceptions of transnational relations of power in terms of gender and love. Thirdly, because the West, and displays of purchasing power in general, are given female rather than male traits by those without such power. Finally, the images are interesting because both these ideal female types are absent from public life in Algeria. The true Muslim woman stays at home and the Western woman has left Algeria. It means that the poetics of raï alludes to gender encounters, gender boundaries being suspended outside the family and outside the cabarets. But the meetings evoked are rarely accomplished.

However, if raï describes socially and economically dependent encounters in ordinary life, what it transmits is something beyond that. The words of raï are not spoken words, they are recomposed into lyrics: *sung* words that *express* a longing for love. Thus, in raï we have a young male in a wedding or cabaret situation, where gender boundaries are crossed, who also expresses a passion for a meeting with the female Other (cf. Rougemont 1956). These elements translate those concerns of Algerian youth that rarely achieve recognition in everyday life – and they are related to the musical fusion that came about in the early 1980s.

MUSIC IN RAÏ

One of the characteristics of music is its capacity to be suggestive of time (Langer 1953, Nattiez 1973). The sound of music, the interplay of instruments and the rhythm move people in fictive time periods to other spaces, and bring people together at the same time.

Raï is a rhythmical music of a heavily repetitive character including small songs, inspired by Mediterranean pop (see Schade-Poulsen 1994). It originated in rural areas, and was influenced by the *wahrâni*, another musical form, which originated in Oran in the 1940s and 1950s, and makes reference to Egyptian musicals, Latin-American rhythms, Spanish flamenco, paso doble, etc. Here the foundations were laid for the musical style of later forms of raï. After independence the rural raï format itself was altered by means, for example, of accordions, trumpets and wah-wah pedal guitars replacing the reed flutes.

In the late 1970s the fusion of the two musical groups, discussed above, took place by means of analogy. The 'Western' group took the role of 'the other', the acoustic raï group. But new instruments offer new sounds and technical possibilities which alter the rules of the game. For example, the electric bass can play a harmonic figure, where only drum beats were heard before. In the first recordings it was generally the guitar that introduced something qualitatively new. Having no acoustic instrument to replace, the guitar was used to play the upbeats of the rhythm, creating a feeling of reggae.

During the early 1980s the synthesizer and drum machine were introduced and the process of analogy was left to the keyboard player. It would lead too far to go into the details of studio work. Suffice to say that the instrumentation reflected the acoustic raï scheme as well as Latin American style, American disco, *wahrâni*, rock, Mediterranean pop, etc. Moreover the keyboard player frequently started improvising, using patterns or formulas he had heard on Western funk, rock, disco and sometimes jazz records.

One of the most interesting aspects of the studio work was the difference between the recordings made of the voice and those of the instruments. While the voice was being recorded the singer was accompanied by the drum machine and simple chords and replicas on the synthesizer. The singer kept to the tune; he did not use improvisations based on the harmonies played by the keyboard player. Thus, the overall effect was as if the singer was singing in the acoustic genre, as in the past, with a reed flute (or an accordion) together with percussion. The addition of the instrumental part seemed to add another world.

Another notable fact was that although the synthesizer and drum machine were at hand, the producers chose to keep one track in the recordings for the hand drum to 'fill the holes' left by the drum machine. Together with the voice, this instrument is the sole representative of the acoustic past. This reflects the importance of the relation between voice and rhythm in Arab and Algerian music. They cannot be dissociated from each other (cf. Hasnaoui 1990:7; Salvador-Daniel 1986:46; Rouanet 1920:2843; Vigreux 1985:17).

Thus the acoustic elements that have survived in raï recordings are voice and percussion. They again are representatives of the basic elements of raï music. They might be seen as the elements that within the rhythmical and tonal universe of raï sum up its historical continuity, which, in the course of its development, has kept in tune with the times through the addition of new instruments, harmonies, etc. The raï of the late 1970s (in which was embedded the story of earlier rural raï, the city of the 1950s, the Egyptian movies, etc.) might be said to have been brought up to date by means of electric instruments and musical motifs representing Western sound.

Berkaak (1993) noticed how metonymous references to imagined liminal spheres in the Third World are found in a number of Western rock recordings. It is furthermore acknowledged that Western youth groups in the 1950s and 1960s used musical references to groups with a history of oppression in order to express their search for the 'freedom to consume'.

With raï it is possible to say that the upbeats of the guitar, the electric sound, some riffs and musical formulas in the keyboard may refer to what is perceived as specific spheres of gender encounters in the West – parties, discos, etc. – which feature groups which are in possession of or have gained access to purchasing power. This is indicated by the labels of 'pop raï', 'disco raï' and 'raï reggae' given to the electric genre in Algeria.

Thus in the late 1970s non-verbal references to Western party contexts entered into raï. These appeared as spheres for encounters between men and women in a context not mediated by money or family interests. Here, it seems that men – together with women in the power of love – could be imagined as displaying a consumption pattern which as mentioned above is linked to female traits.

CONCLUSION

Evidently raï is neither consumed nor produced as if all its elements continually constitute significant messages. If a work of art necessarily involves a kind of social contract between producer and consumer it never totally succeeds in fulfilling this contract. It is important to note that the playing of raï is a voluntary pursuit (only for a minority has it become an addiction) that offers the audience opportunities for relations on many kinds of level.

However, everything in the analysis of raï seems to indicate that interrelated games are embedded in the recorded songs. Taken together they deal with events during which everyday gender boundaries are altered. In recomposing elements from everyday life, the raï product offers a space for encounters with a female Other where any systematic evaluation is excluded, and as such a space for what can be termed the male pleasures of *disinterested* encounters with femininity – pleasures rarely expressed in everyday life.

With the musical fusion in the cabarets of Oran in the late 1970s, this pleasure was in keeping with its time. The references in the music to Western party contexts were accepted as socially relevant by a large Algerian audience, and matched the changes in some of the wedding procedures focusing on the couple as a central unit, the change in the family structure found in the Algerian cities, the appearance of women in public places, and the concern of youth with gender encounters outside the cabarets and weddings in an urban milieu with intensified consumption of popular music.

The success of electric raï outside the cabarets must thus be attributed firstly to its new 'soundscape', and secondly to the multiple experiences and imaginations the recorded songs offered youth in its exploration of the alterations in gender encounters in the specific context of Algerian society.

NOTES

1. Berkaak has noted, for example, that the rock 'n' roll of Elvis Presley was not created while the red lights in the recording studios were on. It came into being when Elvis and his musicians were 'goofing around', playing *in between* the recordings (Berkaak 1993:176).

2. This contribution is based on fieldwork in Algeria and Paris carried out between 1990 and 1992 and financed by the Danish Research Council for the Humanities. The main context for fieldwork was the city, the music, musicians and male youth of Oran (*Wahran*). Fieldwork conditions did not allow for a quantitative perspective on raï and male youth. However, the vast majority in my 'sample' are Oranians, unmarried, 20 to 30 years of age and with few social, economic and educational resources at their disposal. I would like to thank John Liep for his fruitful comments on earlier versions of the chapter

3. An extreme example of this was expressed in the GIA's (Groupe Islamique Armé) threat at the beginning of the school year (1994) to burn schools if genders were not segregated and if music lessons and girl´s gymnastics were not abolished (*Libération* 7 September 1994:7). This was a threat that in effect treated the schools as if they were cabarets.

4. Later, raï was to be appropriated as 'genius artistry' by mainstream pop industry ideology, but that is another story (see Schade-Poulsen 1997).

5. Among those who have related music and poetry to social processes are Abu-Lughod 1986; Guignard 1975; Lortat-Jacob 1980; Yacine 1990.

REFERENCES

Abu-Lughod, L. (1986) *Veiled Sentiments: Honor and Poetry in a Bedouin Society.* Berkeley: University of California Press.

Barthes, R. (1987) *Image, Music, Text.* S. Heath (ed.). London: Fontana Press.

Bateson, G. (1972a) 'Style, grace, and information in primitive art', in *Steps to an Ecology of Mind.* New York: Ballantine Books.

—— (1972b) 'A theory of play and fantasy', in *Steps to an Ecology of Mind.* New York: Ballantine Books.

Berkaak, O.A. (1993) *Erfaringer fra Risikosonen: Opplevelse og Stilutvikling i Rock.* Oslo: Universitetsforlaget.

Bourdieu, P. (1990) *The Logic of Practice.* Cambridge: Polity Press.

—— (1992) *Les Règles de l'Art: Genèse et Structure du Champ Littéraire.* Paris: Seuil.

Caillois, R. (1958) *Les Jeux et les Hommes.* Paris: Gallimard.

Danielson, V. 1988. The Arab Middle East, in P. Manuel (ed.) *Popular Musics of the Non-Western World.* Oxford: Oxford University Press.

Déjeux, J. (1989) *L'Image de l'Étrangère.* Paris: La Boîte à Documents.

Geertz, C. (1973) 'Deep play: notes on the Balinese cockfight', in *The Interpretation of Culture.* New York: Basic Books.

—— (1983) 'Art as a cultural system', in *Local Knowledge.* New York: Basic Books.

Guignard, M. (1975) *Musique, Honneur et Plaisir au Sahara.* Paris: Geuthner.

Hasnaoui, M. (1990) *Les Principes fondamentaux de la Pensée musicale orientale.* Alger: Stencil.

Hoggart, R. (1971 [1957]) *The Uses of Literacy.* London: Chatto and Windus.

Huizinga, J. (1970 [1949]) *Homo Ludens.* London: Temple Smith.

Langer, S. (1953) *Feeling and Form.* New York: Charles Scribner's Sons.

Lortat-Jacob, B. (1980) *Musique et Fêtes au Haut-Atlas.* Paris, La Haye, New York: Mouton.

Manuel, P. (1988) 'Popular music in India: 1901–86', *Popular Music* 7(2):157–76.

Middleton, R. (1983) 'Play it again Sam: some notes on the productivity of repetition in popular music', in R. Middleton and D. Horn (eds) *Popular Music.* Cambridge: Cambridge University Press.

Nattiez, J.J. (1973) 'Analyse musicale et sémiologie: le structuralisme de Lévi- Strauss', *Musique en Jeu* 12:59–79.

Passeron, J.C. (1991) 'L'usage faible des images: enquêtes sur la réception de la peinture', in *Le Raisonnement Sociologique.* Paris: Editions Nathan.

118 *Locating Cultural Creativity*

Robert, P. (1978) *Dictionnaire alphabétique et analogique de la langue française*. Paris: LeRobert.

Rouanet, J. (1920) 'La musique arabe dans le Maghreb', in *Encyclopédie de la Musique et Dictionnaire du Conservatoire*. Paris: Librairie Delagrave.

Rougemont, D. de (1956) *L'Amour et l'Occident*. Paris: Union générale dédotions.

Salvador-Daniel, F. (1986) *Musique et Instrument de Musique du Maghreb*. Paris: La Boîte à Documents.

Schade-Poulsen, M. (1994) *Music and Men in Algeria: an Analysis of the Social Significance of Raï*. Ph.D. dissertation, Institute of Anthropology, University of Copenhagen.

—— (1997) 'Which world: on the diffusion of raï to the West', in K. Hastrup and K. Olwig (eds) *Siting Culture: the Shifting Anthropological Object*. London: Routledge. Stokes, M. (1992) *The Arabesk Debate: Music and Musicians in Modern Turkey*. Oxford: Clarendon Press.

Turner, V. (1988) *The Anthropology of Performance*. New York: Paj Publications.

Vigreux, P. (1985) *La Derbouka*. Aix-en-Provence: Édisud.

Wallis, R. and Malm, K. (1984) *Big Sounds from Small Peoples: the Music Industry in Small Countries*. London: Constable.

Yacine, T. (1990) *L'Izli ou l'Amour chanté en Kabyle*. Alger: Bouchène-Awal.

9 CREATIVE COMMODITIZATION: THE SOCIAL LIFE OF PHARMACEUTICALS

Susan Reynolds Whyte

In the dark days of 1985, when Uganda was still gripped by political insecurity and a sense of acute deterioration and loss, a group of experts published a collection of articles documenting the breakdown of health services in the country (Dodge and Wiebe 1985). The dean of the medical faculty at Makerere University wrote a foreword to the volume, in which he bravely hoped for a better future: Ugandans would build a new health system on the principle of people's participation. In the intervening decade this has indeed happened, though not as the experts would have wished. Uganda, like many African countries, has seen the growth of an informal market where people 'participate' in health care by buying pharmaceuticals in markets, small shops, storefront clinics and even in government health units. This pattern has been well established in most Asian and Latin American countries for several decades. What is unique about the Uganda case is simply the abruptness with which the country has moved from a relatively well functioning system where medicines were available free from trained government health workers to a seemingly chaotic situation where antibiotic capsules, syringes, injectables and a variety of pills move in unconventional ways.

Even the many critics of this situation recognize its vitality. 'Drug shops are mushrooming all over the country', wrote the commissioners for the government inquiry into health services in 1987, who deplored the uncontrolled growth of the business of selling medicines. Since then, the term mushrooming has been picked up in other reports as a metaphor for the efflorescence of this business of health. A student of culture is struck by the inventiveness and promise of the signboards nailed up in small trading centres: The Garden of Hope Drug Shop, The Life Chance Pharmacy, The Downhill Essential Drug Corner, The Cheap Saviour Drug Shop. Everywhere traders, nursing aides, medical assistants and midwives are creating a new pattern of health care as they convert tokens of hope and healing into a source of income.

Not only has the provision of pharmaceuticals assumed vigorous, and many would say uncontrolled, new forms, but the ways in which the users of these medicines administer them are often unconventional from the professional point of view. We find people drinking a vial of injectable chloroquine, taking a single capsule of tetracycline for stomach ache, mixing the contents of a sampling of capsules with a variety of crushed tablets. 'Double colours' (two-toned capsules) and *episyo* (hypodermic injections) are everyday household remedies. Even 'medicine' for motor vehicles can be converted for human use. I had heard of the virtues of *bulegi* ('brake') for treatment of open lesions, but did not realize how widespread this therapeutic practice was until I saw a large announcement from Agip Uganda Ltd in the national newspaper warning the public that the use of brake fluid for treatment of fresh wounds and skin rash may be dangerous to health.

These exotic ways of taking chemicals are so foreign to those of us influenced by the biomedical view of bodies and therapeutic substances that they may seem like an invention based on very Other cultural principles. In all fairness, however, most local ideas of how pharmaceuticals should be used are inspired by professional prescribing practices which simply get revised and adapted as they become popularized. Medicinal self-help through which pharmaceuticals have become folk medicine could be described as a process of creolization through which a metropolitan culture of biomedicine has been creatively reworked as popular culture (Whyte 1991, 1992; Whyte and van der Geest 1994). However, instead of pursuing the notion of creolization, which might be taken to imply a mixture of pure types, what I want to do here is to consider more specifically the actual unfolding of these processes.

I propose that Ugandans are engaged in creativity at two interconnected levels: a cultural one in which they are reworking the values of therapeutic commodities in innovative ways; and a social structural one in which they are transforming the social relations of healing. By calling these processes of change creative, I do not mean to imply that the present situation is a fruitful and happy one. But I want to draw attention to the issue of conventions, and the ways in which local solutions to difficult situations may challenge conventions, including biomedical ones. My analytical emphasis is twofold. First, I examine the social conditions in which this kind of inventiveness has occurred, with an eye to the politics of value and disjunction in the global cultural economy. Secondly, since creativity involves agency, I consider organizations and the perceptions and motives of rural actors.

THE SOCIAL LIFE OF PHARMACEUTICALS: AN EXPOSITION

In Uganda, drugs are funny. They're carried into the health centre in boxes, and then they grow legs and walk out the back door on their own. They crawl into people's pockets by themselves. You put them in a cupboard and they move out and disappear somewhere.

Such observations are common enough in Uganda to suggest that Appadurai's (1986) proposal to examine the social life of things is well suited as a perspective on the core technology of medical care. There, as in many developing countries, medicinal drugs have public and private lives; they have 'rational' jobs of work to do, and they also moonlight in the service of the imagination and of hope and worry and gain. In the course of their lives these ambulatory drugs move through a series of arenas that reflect what Appadurai (1990) later called 'disjuncture and difference in the global cultural economy'. Let us begin by thinking about the creative possibilities that might lie in the movement of things through disjunctive regimes of value.

No drugs are born in Uganda; the country has virtually no functioning pharmaceutical industry. Pharmaceuticals are all immigrants – some with permits and visas, some illegal. The biography of drugs begins in an international arena, and then moves into a national one when they enter Uganda and the state regulatory space and become suject to the conventions that in principle obtain there.

The major supplier of drugs to Uganda is the Uganda Essential Drugs Programme, funded by the Danish International Development Agency (Danida). Under this programme, generic drugs purchased on the world market are packed into kits in a warehouse in Copenhagen. The kits are shipped to Entebbe from whence they are distributed to over a thousand government and other non-profit health facilities. Other donors also supply drugs through various health programmes. The government purchases some drugs on its own and for a while it was bartering beans for medicines with Cuba. (This arrangement was dropped because both beans and pharmaceuticals were past their expiry dates by the time they reached their respective destinations.) These drugs too are meant for the government health care facilities which are supposed to provide treatment free or for a minimal fee.

Appadurai writes of things moving through regimes of value and so we must ask what kinds of value are being realized in these government and donor transactions of drugs. Sjaak van der Geest and his co-authors (1990), using an analytical framework of levels and disjuncture somewhat similar to Appadurai's, have pointed out that Third World governments need credibility and political support. Providing primary health care would seem to be a way of gaining support from citizens, but in practice its results are not immediately evident and the emphasis on preventive rather than curative care does not correspond with people's felt needs. Supplying drugs, on the other hand, is concrete and immediate; it is also an obvious task for government, in that local people have become dependent on a costly technology they can neither produce nor obtain themselves in sufficient quantity.

The government itself cannot afford to purchase drugs, so it turns to donors. They realize a variety of values in providing supplies of pharmaceuticals. Critics are quick to point out that drug aid supports the multinational drug companies. That is obvious but too simple. The donors are concerned not just to promote industrial and commercial interests, but to ensure that these interests do not exploit developing countries too blatantly. An essential drugs programme is a way of regulating market forces. Moreover, supplying pharmaceuticals to the government health facilities keeps them running and allows them to undertake basic health measures including preventive ones, which are high on the agenda of many donors. The donors are concerned about the use of drugs according to sound biomedical standards and responsible economic principles, concerns summed up in the phrase 'rational use of drugs'.

The same motives that move the government and donors also figure in the transaction of drugs through religious organizations. Drugs are exchanged for credibility and support; they are negotiated in terms of values of charity and humanitarianism and biomedical standards and policy interests. The possible conflicts of value are particularly evident here; religious institutions send shipments of drugs which are not needed or close to expiry date, but which indicate the charity of the giver. This problem is not limited to religious organizations. Central Medical Stores in Entebbe has literally tons of useless drugs provided by well-meaning donors. Lacking disposal facilities, they are forced to allocate more and more space to use as a 'drug cemetery'. They used to dump them in Lake Victoria, but environmental awareness no longer permits this solution.

In addition to the government and donor arena with its regime of value, there is a private profit-oriented arena through which drugs also enter the country. A parastatal and several private companies are licensed to import drugs for sale. Other unlicensed enterprises also bring in drugs and an unknown quantity are smuggled into the country, mainly from Kenya. It has proved impossible to get a reliable picture of the quantity and inventory of the international trade in pharmaceuticals. The value being realized in this arena is profit, but this too is probably too simple. Some of the larger, more established importers are playing by one set of rules, while others disregard them. I have heard it said that older Asian-owned pharmaceutical importers are finding it hard to compete on a market flooded by drugs that are cheap because they are stolen and smuggled in.

Whether a drug enters Uganda in a kit sealed in Copenhagen or is carried across the Kenyan border by head load or bicycle, it enters a space of hypothetical national control. The exchanges in its biography are subject to regulation; it is not meant to acquire pure commodity status. This restriction on free exchange is what Appadurai calls enclaving (1986:22ff). He points out that limits on the exchange of certain things are often in the interest of powerful groups and may be aspects of state control. The enclaving of drugs in Uganda is attempted in two ways: by legal regulation which classifies drugs and provides for the registration of those allowed to prescribe and dispense them; and by the training and supervision of health workers in the conventions that ensure the 'rational use of drugs' (Ministry of Health 1991, 1992).

The efforts by government and donors to regulate and channel the flow of drugs are based on their commitment to realizing the purposes for which the drugs were transacted. But more specifically, they share a common recognition about a certain kind of knowledge. Appadurai (1986:41–3) notes that different kinds of knowledge about things are pertinent at different phases in their biography and for different kinds of transaction. Knowledge about production of drugs is irrelevant in the Uganda setting. But the Ministry of Health, high-level professionals and the administrators of the donor programmes agree that biomedical knowledge about *consumption* of drugs is so important that their circulation must be controlled by those who have been initiated through training. Drugs are not like other commodities because they can be harmful if used improperly. Their value is such that they must not be bought and sold freely.

Igor Kopytoff describes the tension between enclaving and free circulation in terms of the cultural tendency to singularize some objects, to set them apart as having singular, not common value. He writes: 'In the sense that commoditization homogenizes value, while the essence of culture is discrimination, excessive commoditization is anti-cultural ...' (1986:73). One could also suggest, I suppose, that in the sense that singularizing or enclaving is a form of convention, commoditization, which entails the breaching of enclaves, represents the possibility of creativity.

Commoditization is in fact a dominant characteristic of the biography of drugs once they reach the local social arena in Uganda. Those drugs that are carried into the government health centres and aid posts are often exchanged for 'soap' or 'tea' in the form of a small discreet cash payment. With the recent introduction of 'cost sharing', a euphemism for user fees, payment has come out of the closet to become policy at the government units. It is still the case, however, that drugs in these units either disappear or get finished, so that people are referred to the mushrooming drug shops and private clinics often located in the vicinity of government health units. Others go directly to these small businesses where they can buy drugs directly in any desired quantity. Recent research (Adome et al. 1996) has shown that most drugs used in Uganda today are obtained as common commodities. Only a quarter of the pharmaceuticals in a large survey were prescribed and dispensed from the 'enclaves' of formally authorized medical institutions. The rest, including more than half of all chloroquine and antibiotics, were purchased like other daily wares in shops and markets.

There are private clinics and drug shops in every trading centre. Some are licensed and some are not. In many cases the license is given in one name, but the attendant is someone else. Near hospitals and health centres, the private facilities are more likely to be run by health workers as a second occupation. Farther away, they are operated by people with less training or experience in established health facilities. In rural areas, I doubt whether there are any drug shops at all that fully conform to the regulations of the Pharmacy and Drugs Act; they all sell prescription drugs over the counter.

Ordinary provision shops often sell drugs, including antibiotic capsules, together with sugar, salt and soap. All of these shops and clinics buy drugs as well as selling them. On several occasions, I have been sitting in shops when people came in with a small amount of drugs to offer for sale – drugs which had crawled into their pockets somehow. In markets they are sold more or less openly and hawkers with attaché cases sell them in bus and taxi parks. In any neighbourhood, there are people who sell drugs or give injections from their homes. Some work or have worked at a health institution; the untrained cadres of staff, nursing aides and watchmen are the community health workers of their neighbourhoods in the sense that they provide the accessible services that the community finds appropriate. Other 'village health workers' have access to drugs and to information about how to use them, through friends and relatives whose occupations admit them to the enclaves from which drugs can be channelled out.

What kinds of value are being realized here? Profit of course: this is about money. Ugandans complain that the days of free things are gone. People are very conscious of the degree to which health care has been commoditized, a process that has been enhanced by the very nature of pharmaceuticals as things manufactured for the market. Slipping, walking or crawling out of, or merely avoiding, their enclaves, they easily reassume their identity as profitable wares. But exchanges in the local arena are not only about money, as a closer look at some of these transactions reveals. Drugs are given as gifts, exchanged for favours, and shared with loved ones as tokens of affection. Health workers at government facilities are local residents and participants in local networks of relationship. Those who come from outside the area often obtain land locally for crop production or they may join in local business ventures. Those who come from nearby, which is common for trained staff and universal for untrained employees, are deeply entwined in relations of kinship, affinity, friendship and neighbourliness. The values embedded in these kinds of relationship are also involved in the exchange of drugs.

The last chapter in the biography of drugs is about how they are finally used. From the variety of sources I have described, they move to their destinations in the bodies of sick people. On the basis of advice from someone who knows, or simply on the basis of past experience and personal conviction, people are injected with chloroquine or penicillin, they swallow tablets or capsules, or put solutions, ointments, powders or *bulegi* onto their skin or into their bodily orifices. These final movements in personal arenas are also attempts to realize values, of course. The therapeutic value of medicines, and in particular of pharmaceuticals rather than herbal medicines, is enacted by sick people and their families. It is this value, after all, upon which the values of all the other arenas are predicated.

We can construct a biography along these line, but in reality pharmaceuticals do not have a social life. To pretend so is, as Appadurai says, a conceit. It is a method of exposition and not an explanation. Only people have a social life and the closer one comes to issues of value and knowledge, the more difficult it is to maintain the conceit. But Appadurai uses the notion of the social life of things to point to the politics of value revealed in the exchange of things:

What is political about this process is not just the fact that it signifies and constitutes relations of privilege and social control. What is political about it is the constant tension between the existing frameworks (of price, bargaining, and so forth) and the tendency of commodities to breach these frameworks. This tension itself has its sources in the fact that not all parties share the same *interests* in any specific regime of value, nor are the interests of any two parties in a given exchange identical. (1986:57)

The politics of value involved in the control, diversion, knowledge about, and transaction of pharmaceuticals is one of the central issues with which we are trying to grapple in our Uganda research. The notion of the rational use of drugs emanates from policy makers and professionals committed to the efficient and effective use of resources, to making a system function. The practices of diversion, commoditization, personalization of therapeutic relations, and self-medication are linked to health workers' interest in 'survival' and patients' desire for trustworthy help in moments of need.

With regard to creativity, it seems to me that the 'social life of things' perspective offers some useful reminders. The notion that things, as items for exchange, move through arenas of value, over geographical space and across disjunctures and differences in the global cultural economy helps us to be more specific about one mode of creolization. The point that relations of power and privilege are negotiated in attempts to singularize, enclave, divert and commoditize helps us to conceptualize the processes through which convention is challenged. The idea that different parties have diverging interests in any regime of value suggests a dynamic that we need to grasp if we are to conceive of cultural creativity as a process. Creativity in this perspective emerges as the capacity to realize interests and values by affecting the flow of things. The condition of creativity is the existence of distinct arenas of value in a global economy – arenas which are interconnected through the lives of things like ambulatory drugs.

THE MOTHER OF INVENTION: TOWARDS AN EXPLANATION

This still leaves us far from understanding the transformations in Ugandan health care however. Neither Appadurai, nor for that matter Hannerz (1992), is much concerned with the rather pedestrian question of the ecological, economic and institutional conditions under which creative commoditization or creolization might occur. The mother of invention is not just necessity, but also a constellation of social circumstances and availability of materials. Phenomena like the Cheap Saviour Drug Shop and the creative use of 'double colours' must be placed within a specific social context.

First of all, there is a sense of necessity arising out of the common experience of sickness and death. Malaria, the number one cause of mortality, needs medicine; everyone agrees about that. The frequent illness and death of children (see Barton and Wamai 1994) is associated in people's minds with a desperate need for treatment – the best and most powerful treatment. Over a million people in Uganda are HIV positive, and their illnesses create a strong demand for medicine. In this disease ecology, the deterioration of the formal biomedical health services adds to the sense of need.

The relatively good health delivery system of the 1950s and 1960s was severely disrupted by 15 years of war, looting, insecurity, international isolation, the ejection and flight of health professionals and the lack of medical supplies. After the accession of the National Resistance Movement (NRM) government and the advent of peace in 1986, resuscitation of health institutions began with the help of donors. But fundamental economic problems remained. A period of hyperinflation, the economic crisis of the state, and the demands for structural adjustment have reduced salaries for civil servants in Uganda to levels far below the actual cost of living. The payment of even those meagre salaries can be delayed for months. Instead of a living wage, government health workers receive what one of our colleagues calls a 'killing wage'. The necessity of finding other sources of income strangles morale and poisons efforts to improve government health services. 'Survival strategies' is the Ugandan term for creative ways of getting by on a killing wage. These include farming, beer brewing and trade. But for health workers the obvious possibilities involve using their institutional position to earn extra cash, for example by demanding under-the-table payments, or by treating patients or selling drugs on the side (van der Heijden and Jitta n.d.). A large proportion of the drug shops and storefront clinics have been established by people who were or still are employed in the government health services. When they are not behind the counters themselves, their relatives or trusted employees are there, providing user-friendly services for the patients whom the conventional system has failed. The keepers of convention, the supervisors whose task is to enforce the regulations about selling drugs and the standard treatment guidelines, seldom appear because there is no money for transport. In any case, they are preoccupied with their own survival strategies. The possibility for commoditizing the singularly valuable capsules and injectables, for diverting them from their intended enclave, arises because the gatekeeping functions of state institutions have been weakened.

It is notable however that the florescent period in which a thousand mushrooms bloomed occurred not when the need was greatest, during the dark years of breakdown, insecurity and shortages, but after the mid 1980s when peace was restored and the international community moved in to help rehabilitate Uganda. Uganda's formal health sector is now largely dependent on foreign aid. Donor efforts, like the Danida-supported Essential Drugs Programme, pour enormous resources into a health system that only survives because of these inputs, but that is incapable of functioning in the terms envisioned by the donors. The initiatives and exchanges meant by the donors to realize one set of values and interests are transformed into survival strategies by the enterprising recipients of the killing wage.

MISTRUST AND INGENUITY

Appadurai uses the concept of regimes of value to refer to the cultural contexts of commodities. He reminds us that the meanings and values that are realized in the exchange of a thing may be more or less fully shared by the parties to the exchange. In the field of health, researchers have pointed to the cultural gaps between providers and patients, the lack of shared values and meanings, a situation Lisbeth Sachs (1989) described in an article about elite Sinhalese doctors treating illiterate villagers, aptly titled 'Misunderstanding as therapy'. In Uganda such gaps of misunderstanding exist between national policy makers based in Kampala, and ordinary people, especially rural ones. But within local social arenas, regimes of value tend to be more deeply shared, at least in the sense that the parties to an exchange attend to each other's interests and evaluations.

We can see this in the cultural area of knowledge about consumption. Medical assistants are taught to use drugs according to standard treatment guidelines, as are other categories of trained staff, insofar as they are formally instructed at all in the use of drugs. As transactors of drugs they should value their utility in treating disease according to professional standards. However they often exchange drugs in terms of their economic and social utility; realizing these latter two values means recognizing the desires and knowledge of the consumers of drugs – satisfying the customer or pleasing an esteemed person, friend or relative. Thoughtful health workers sometimes speak of 'treating people psychologically' when they give drugs that are not useful according to standard treatment guidelines – such as antibiotic injections for herpes zoster, which is painful and known to trained health workers as a sign of AIDS.

Users of drugs are also attentive to the values and knowledge that providers impute to drug transactions. Particular types of medicine come to embody meanings through the way they are given by providers; these meanings stick with the drugs through transactions in different settings. I believe that the high value placed on antibiotic capsules and injections by consumers arises not from some magic value attributed by naive laymen, but rather from an appreciation of the meaning biomedical providers impute to them. Likewise users have learned that the value of chloroquine has declined; some know the term 'resistance'. Therefore requests are made either for a mixture of chloroquine and antibiotics or for some other anti-malarial.

Appadurai speaks of values being embodied in commodities, and of the way that values are imbued by exchange, rather than exchange being based on innate value. But his methodological decision to focus on things and their careers means that many aspects of their context and of the people who exchange them are neglected. In examining people's exchanges of drugs in Uganda, one comes directly up against issues of risk and trust which require that one attend to the cultural life of people rather than to the social life of things.

Let me give some examples. Complaints about government health institutions are common; people say that the service is poor, that the health workers are corrupt, that they steal or dilute the medicines, that they demand money unfairly, that they are rude and that they do not care about the patients. They say that if you want good treatment at an institution, you must go through someone you know. People sometimes travel to more distant health facilities, because they have a friend or relative working there. On the other hand, there is a strong faith in medicines themselves, as is evidenced by the high level of self-medication and exchange of medicines through non-institutional channels.

One of the striking findings from recent studies of pharmaceuticals in Uganda is the high prevalence of injection use. In a survey by Birungi (1994), between 25 and 30 per cent of households had used at least one injection over a confined two-week period. Most of these were administered outside of government institutions. Moreover, the majority of households (63 per cent in Eastern Uganda and 83 per cent in Western Uganda) owned a needle and syringe, despite the Pharmacy and Drugs Act of 1970 which declares this a criminal offence. They either bought injectables and got someone they knew to administer them, or they brought their own equipment to a government health facility. Partly this is for convenience and economy; families with many children often have one member who gives them injections when they are ill. But it is also related to perceptions of risk.

In Uganda AIDS has been represented as a man-made risk to which people expose themselves through contact with contaminated blood and through certain kinds of sexual behaviour. Part of the AIDS message mentions the dangers of injections. This is probably not a very significant route of infection in a population without intravenous drug use. But this message fits with a mistrust of formal health institutions and also with a general tendency to require patients to supply their own equipment and drugs. Birungi spoke with many families, and even health workers, who refused to receive an injection from institutional syringes, despite assurances that they had been sterilized for 20 minutes. At the same time, they saw no risk in using a syringe and needle kept at home, uncapped, in a dirty piece of plastic, for an injection of chloroquine bought in the market given by a neighbour.

Thus mistrust is one of the moods and motivations that moves people to seek control over their treatment by personalizing therapeutic relations or by assuming the role of customer rather than patient. They do not want to be dependent on a system that has failed them in the past, that presents risks and that does not respond to the needs they experience. So they are well disposed to the shops and small clinics and to the private treatment offered by health workers, their wives, hospital cleaners and other informal providers of drugs. A common comment is, 'these people are helping us'. The District Medical Officers, who should be enforcing the professional, regulated monopoly on prescription-only pharmaceuticals, say that it would be politically very difficult to close down the informal sector, even if they had the means to do so, as long as the government facilities are functioning poorly and are so widely mistrusted.

What about the providers, the diverters who commoditize those singular items? Here I am concerned not with the big operators, who cause whole shipments of drugs to disappear from Central Medical Stores in Entebbe, nor even those District Medical Officers who are suspected of selling off a kit or two of the essential drugs meant for rural health centres. I am thinking of the midwives and medical assistants, the dressers and nursing aides, the retired drivers and storekeepers who in various ways commoditize health by selling drugs.

'Surviving' is one response to the question of what they think they are doing. In Ugandan English, survival is a rich term that refers not only to escaping death but to the management of life in continuing situations of difficulty and scarcity. 'How are things?' 'We're surviving.' The reply refers to our common understanding that we do not just passively endure, but actively adapt. Neither the government, which cannot afford to pay civil servants, nor the donors, who are reluctant to assume responsibility for recurrent costs, have addressed the problem of survival for government health workers. That is left to them to figure out. The nursing supervisor sells moonshine gin in her staff house in the evening. The driver hires out the ambulance to transport rice from the swamps to the mill. A nursing aide has a food stall across the road selling porridge to the relatives of patients. A dispenser sets his wife up in a little drug shop. The luckiest ones get connected to a donor programme where they can collect allowances that are many times the size of their nominal salaries.

The common awareness of the need to survive gives rise to both grudging admiration and suspicion of ingenious solutions. This is part of a general attitude towards corruption. Stories of clever schemes are recounted like folk tales as examples of the fertility and agility of the human mind in the struggle with circumstances. At the same time, the consciousness of such cunning leads to an exaggerated mistrust. A friend of ours was laughing about the regulations intended to prevent theft of injectables by health personnel. Empty vials were to be returned to the stores to show that the contents had in fact been used to treat the patients in the health unit. Our friend told how people went to work with empty vials in their pockets. They recorded that a patient had been given an injection, pocketed the penicillin, and delivered their own empty vial to the medical store. 'We Ugandans are too clever', explained a nurse. 'We can always find a way.' Suspicion flourishes. If so much can be commoditized, what can be trusted? Laboratory tests are often viewed with cynicism. Stories circulate about AIDS testing, available in towns. When the Church of Uganda began to require AIDS tests before marriage, people said that certificates could easily be bought. One friend remarked recently that if someone came waving a test result showing he or she was HIV negative, you could be sure they were positive. Otherwise there would be no need to get such a paper. The people who work in labs are thought to survive by selling test results.

The valuable side of ingenuity is that initiatives are taken that provide services and solve problems, albeit in unconventional ways. A trained midwife, working at a health centre, was asked by UNICEF to teach several groups of 'traditional birth attendants' about principles of maternity care and home delivery. She picked out one of the brightest of her pupils and set her up in a mud-walled shop selling medicines and giving injections as well as delivering mothers who came to this little clinic. The midwife supplied the medicines, supervised her and took a portion of the earnings. Later, when the midwife was transferred, the 'traditional birth attendant' continued the business on her own. This went quite against the intentions and the conventions of the donor and the Ministry of Health. Traditional birth attendants are not supposed to administer injections or sell antibiotics. But many people in the neighbourhood appreciated the initiative of both the trained midwife and her protégée since it made them less dependent on the government hospital and provided a convenient local source of drugs.

In describing the attitudes and motives of the people who are popularizing pharmaceuticals in Uganda, I emphasize the role of institutions because I think that many of the discussions of creolization and even of the global cultural economy tend to pass them over. Perhaps institutions like schools, hospitals and courts are too sociological for the current paradigms in anthropology. But if we are going to think about how processes of change actually occur we cannot neglect the means by which citizens relate to the state. The institutions of biomedicine brought drugs into local settings in the first place. As they were weakened, their gatekeeping ability was undermined. Growing mistrust and the challenge of survival gave rise to commoditization of pharmaceuticals that breached the frameworks of biomedical convention.

WHOSE CREATIVITY?

Is this creativity? I don't think most Ugandans would call it so. Indeed the concept of creativity does not seem to be particularly important in Ugandan society. In European and American society, the control of inventiveness in art, science and manufacturing is a basis of power. Creativity is a marked category; originality is admired, genius is prized. Inventiveness is fundamental in marketing and we even talk about creative consumption. In Uganda, people are intrigued with new things and there are certainly Ugandan artists whose creative gifts are recognized. But the personal qualities that are remarked upon, and that have led to new social and cultural forms, are ingenuity and cleverness in problem solving. Smart people challenged by circumstance have reformed institutional patterns and infused something new into popular culture.

Creativity must fit with prevailing structures in order to be recognized as such. It must be seen as positive in a particular way. Challenges to convention can be creative but they can also be mad or criminal or dangerous or stupid or simply irrelevant. The analytical issue is to identify the arbiters of creativity and the standards by which it is measured. The case I have described here is particularly illustrative of this point. Donors and policy makers speak a discourse about community participation and community responsibility. They call for grassroots initiatives and underline the importance of tailoring programmes to local realities. However, they regard the flowering of small medicine businesses not as a grassroots movement but as an insidious tendency – insofar as they regard it all. Such unplanned responses do not easily fit into a cosmology that assumes that development is a planned process for which authorities design strategies. Creativity can only exist in its assigned place.

Doctors see the challenge to medical convention, the breaching of sacred enclaves, as dangerous and, in Kopytoff's terms, anti-cultural in that a singularity enshrined in values is made common through commoditization. The culture of biomedicine is such that challenges to its conventions are usually defined as unscientific. They are only creative under very special circumstances.

It is left to anthropologists to interpret as creative such processes as the indigenization of pharmaceuticals. If I use the term it is because I see the commoditization of health care as a bringing into being of new relations and social forms within local arenas and across global ones. The ability of drugs as things to move through different contexts connects regimes of value in ways that generate change. Using the word creativity puts a positive accent on these processes. Many see commoditization as purely negative. By calling it creative I draw attention to the wishes of many Ugandans to gain access to those singular valuables.

REFERENCES

Adome, R.O., Whyte, S.R. and Hardon, A. (1996) *Popular Pills: Community Drug Use in Uganda*. Amsterdam: Het Spinhuis.
Appadurai, A. (1986) 'Introduction: commodities and the politics of value', in A. Appadurai (ed.) *The Social Life of Things: Commodities in Cultural Perspective*. Cambridge: Cambridge University Press.
—— (1990) 'Disjuncture and difference in the global cultural economy', *Theory, Culture and Society* 7:295–310.
Barton, T. and Wamai, G. (1994) *Equity and Vulnerability: a Situation Analysis of Women, Adolescents and Children in Uganda*. Kampala: Uganda National Council for Children.

Birungi, H., Assiimwe, D. and Whyte, S.R. (1994) *Injection Use and Practices in Uganda*. WHO/DAP/94.18. Geneva: WHO.

Dodge, C.P. and Wiebe, P.D. (eds) (1985) *Crisis in Uganda: the Breakdown of Health Services*. Oxford: Pergamon Press.

Hannerz, U. (1992) *Cultural Complexity: Studies in the Social Organization of Meaning*. New York: Columbia University Press.

Kopytoff, I. (1986) 'The cultural biography of things: commoditization as process', in A. Appadurai (ed.) *The Social Life of Things: Commodities in Cultural Perspective*. Cambridge: Cambridge University Press.

Ministry of Health, Republic of Uganda (1991) *Uganda Essential Drugs Manual*. Second edition Ministry of Health, Republic of Uganda.

—— (1992) *National Standard Treatment Guideline*. First edition Entebbe: Uganda Essential Drugs Management Programme.

Sachs, L. (1989) 'Misunderstanding as therapy: doctors, patients and medicines in a rural clinic in Sri Lanka', *Culture, Medicine and Psychiatry* 13:335–49.

van der Geest, S., Speckman, J.D. and Streefland, P.H. (1990) 'Primary health care in a multi-level perspective: towards a research agenda', *Social Science and Medicine* 30:1025–34.

van der Heijden, T. and Jitta, J. (n.d.) 'Economic survival strategies of health workers in Uganda'. Kampala: Child Health and Development Centre. Unpublished manuscript 1993.

Whyte, S.R. (1991) 'Medicines and self-help: the privatization of health care in Eastern Uganda', in H.B. Hansen and M. Twaddle (eds) *Changing Uganda: the Dilemmas of Structural Adjustment and Revolutionary Change*. London: James Currey.

—— (1992) 'Pharmaceuticals as folk medicine: transformations in the social relations of health care in Uganda', *Culture, Medicine and Psychiatry* 16:163–86.

Whyte, S.R. and van der Geest, S. (1994) 'Injections: issues and methods for anthropological research', in N. Etkin and M. Tan (eds) *Medicines: Meanings and Contexts*. Manila: Health Action International Network.

10 ESCAPING CULTURES: THE PARADOX OF CULTURAL CREATIVITY

David Parkin

IDENTIFYING THE PARADOX

I take the paradox to be globally widespread. Consumers or, more commonly, spectators of others' consumerism, see commodities replaced one after another by new ones. Yet, despite being new, each such commodity may sometimes be regarded as representing tradition and as having originated from inside the society rather than having been imported or affected by external influences. For example, local artists and craftsmen may think they know what foreign tourists want, but in fact find that their art works are bought by local people as much as and even more than by outsiders. This unexpected outcome is not always something we recognize in the culturally creative production of new objects, and shows how difficult it is for local producers to plan a consumerist strategy. It also shows that, when people consciously define something as indigenous and traditional, they presuppose external expectations which paradoxically prompt them to depart from tradition while proclaiming it.

I wish to reorder this as a phenomenological process. Producers or artists do sometimes create objects which they see as traditional or as bridging tradition and modernity. But they sometimes also abandon the production of objects which evoke only a moribund past in favour of those which evoke a past which speaks to the present. This selectivity arises from the producers' or artists' perception of what tourists seek rather than from any intrinsic features of the objects. Such selectivity also implies renouncing objects, or aspects of them, which are seen to be dead but uninteresting (and perhaps shameful in the eyes of foreign tourists) and substituting those which are old but invigorated by new tourist fashions and interests. This renunciation, sometimes amounting to denunciation, entails a kind of constant escape from a reified notion of traditional culture as elements of it are discarded, yet is coupled by a reaffirmation of other features. The escape from the unacceptable is thus also the position from which artists create images of past and present ethnic genius deemed to be acceptable to tourists. Whatever their skills and capacities, artists producing work for tourists, that is, for the 'other', cannot avoid this idiomatic play of ethnicity and race.

An unacknowledged strand in the current interest in 'cultural creativity' can be traced back to work on political ethnicity in the 1960s, particularly that of Abner Cohen (1969; and later 1974) and Barth (1969). While Barth saw ethnic identity as a negotiable resource to be manipulated creatively, Cohen analysed the tendency of ethnic groups under pressure to re-emphasize elements of their cultural traditions, even to invent them. The 'invention' or 'reinvention' of culture, and the question of indigenous claims for cultural 'authenticity' became thereafter a recurrent theme in anthropology. Still later, there were attempts to lessen the essentialism implicit in such a reified concept of culture by pointing out, for instance, that 'ethnogenesis' (see Fardon 1989) was an ongoing process by which different groups picked out from among their cultural diversity common elements which became foundational in their reconstitution as a single grouping with a common history.

A seemingly quite separate strand in the (re)birth of cultural creativity as a process worth studying is what we may broadly call the performative. This includes work on language, semantic categories and tropes, in particular that of metaphor (for example, Ortony 1979; Sapir and Crocker 1977; Lakoff and Johnson 1980; Fernandez 1986). If, like Sperber (1975), we also link a sense of smell to that of symbolic and tropic creativity (for smells evoke memories and judgements as powerfully as ironic situations and icons), the performative falls within the broader exercise of social taste or distinction (Bourdieu (1986[1979]), and hence the aesthetic (and see also, much earlier, della Volpe 1978 [1960]). From the aesthetic, which, according to Eagleton (1990), draws on a post-Enlightenment celebration of the human body, we move to bodily spectacle and theatre as familiar but now renewed areas of anthropological interest.

A theoretical Brechtian would subject the performative to the critical concerns of the political: s/he would make the audience see the roles they never expected their cherished models to play (catching everyday emperors without clothes) and expose as unhelpful mystification the emotional collusion between audience and players which is characteristic of orthodox theatre. Here the performative is used as a medium for political expression.

There is however an inverse possibility, which is when the political loses the clarity of its expressive force under a welter of over-performativeness. This happens, for instance, when people engage in performances which accommodate so many diverse cultural contacts and emotional ploys that their politically ethnic voice loses its distinctiveness (so buried is it in a self-conscious plurality of 'otherness'). At the same time they proclaim their distinctiveness. That is to say, the people of the ethnic group recognize themselves as such but speak, sometimes passionately, through a myriad of inventions and images, some of which they say belong to others.

Nowhere is this truer than in indigenous artistic fronts provided for tourists in much of Africa and Asia, where, as is well known, artists, dancers and musicians present or are persuaded by promoters to present versions of their traditions judged as most likely to appeal to the visitors. That the indigenous presenters may themselves come to believe in the authenticity of that which they have invented is at the heart of much so-called globally homogenizing consumerism.

However, and despite claims for their authenticity, the touristic artistic fronts are often numerous and fleeting. Any tendency to global homogenization is thus always being subverted by such proliferation, which includes the way in which artists constantly make use of new materials and styles as they become available. Moreover, this paradoxical inventiveness, that is to say presenting as authentic that which is constantly recombined and incorporated, seems inevitably to be accompanied by a tendency to renounce the familiar. If something new comes on the scene, its perceived predecessor is considered to be out of date or no longer appropriate. What, then, must remain for there to be at least a family resemblance between early and late versions of a tradition?

In Zanzibar, I believe I have witnessed something of this tendency partially to escape one's own culture while promulgating its timelessness and, in due course, to adopt and then discard others' cultural preferences, as part of the continuing drive to satisfy new waves of tourists. What is perhaps unusual is the rapidity of this process in Zanzibar, for tourism on any scale (and it is still not extensive) began only a few years ago, when the socialist revolutionary government moved closer to capitalism and deemed tourism the most likely new industry to generate foreign exchange.

To speak of an escape from, say, indigenous to 'Western' culture, and vice versa, is of course to essentialize the concept of culture, and it will be part of my task to redefine this process of escape. The escape is in fact only partial and obtains mainly in the area of pictorial art, for, otherwise, Zanzibar has a strictly Muslim population, a small number of whom have embraced radical or fundamentalist Islam. The role of Islam is indeed important here.

Thus, in this chapter I discuss two artistic domains which coexist in contemporary Zanzibar. While recent forms of pictorial art escape conventional Muslim standards of artistic expression, traditional wood-carving variations are generally kept within such conventional limits. As I shall show, the two domains exemplify two types of cultural creativity.

In non-Muslim areas of the East African coast which have fallen under the sway of tourism, it is dance and dress (often together) which commonly blend Western and indigenous perceptions in performance. In 'orthodox' Muslim society, dance seems much less likely to offer this possibility (for it involves the perceived sensuality of body movement (Parkin 1994)). Since it is not normally danced, the famous *taarab* music and song style in Zanzibar undergoes changes which are not challenged by Islamic clergy. It has been affected by a blend of Arab, Indian and Swahili-African influences rather than by Western ones, thus pointing more to a process of 'intra-globaliza-tion' within the smaller world of Islam and the Indian Ocean complex (Topp 1994). However, it is pictorial representation which is the one art form which is contantly changing and yet is potentially in conflict with Islamic theodicy.

THE ISLAMIC PROHIBITION ON THE REPRESENTATION OF LIVING THINGS: THE CASE OF ZANZIBAR

Pictorial and sculptural art in an orthodox Sunni Muslim society conflict with the widely believed Islamic prohibition on the representation of humans, animals and plants, that is, living creatures. In practice, this prohibition has been largely ignored in the great Islamic art of Persia and the Moghul empire, and is by no means absolutely held elsewhere, including Zanzibar. In fact, scholars of Islam generally agree that it is hard to argue that this prohibition stems directly from the Koran or Traditions (though many unconvincing constructions have been offered). Some say that it may have arisen out of the concern that mortals should never attempt to equate themselves with God in Its power alone to represent and, by breathing life into them, create living things. Or there is Grabar's view (1987:72–94) that Islam could only compete with Christianity's pre-eminence in representing living things by developing its own distinctive non-representational visual symbols and prohibiting others. In any event, belief in the sacred origin of the prohibition is sufficient in many if not most areas of Islam to constrain what may be regarded by clerics as representational activities.

The prohibition on the representation of living things, whatever its origin, may in due course have become an extension of the condemnation of *shirk*, namely the worship of many gods, and the commandment to worship only the one God, Allah. God, after all, first created living things and gave them the breath of life. They are thus refractions of God Itself. For humans to depict or mould such living things is to create likenesses of God and approaches the vain attempt to imitate God and give them the breath of life. How, then, do the modern local artists in Zanzibar who paint pictures for and about tourists get away with it?

We first have to recognize that the prohibition, as mentioned above, has never been absolutely applied in Zanzibar except with regard to mosque architecture and ornamentation. In other spheres, there have been limited conventions which appear to have been accepted.

At this point, it is worth attempting to apply a distinction. Before the 'modern' period of tourism, artistic creativity tended to be rule-governed, much like linguistic creativity (Parkin 1980), in which underlying rules impose limits on grammatical, morphological, syntactic, lexical and phono-logical licence. Depictions tended to be variations on acceptable themes. In more recent years, though perhaps in Zanzibar beginning in the later days of British colonialism, the rules appear at first sight to have been broken: paintings of women, some of them scantily dressed tourists, have been appearing for sale in large numbers. In each period, the different performative and artistic proclivities and constraints are politically informed and turn on issues of what we may translate as ethnicity.

Let me first treat rule-governed creativity (alternatively called transformational creativity). As an example, Zanzibar has for generations been famous for the magnificently carved wooden doors of its major stone houses. According to J.J. Adie (1946–47), who seems also partially to draw on Barton (1924), the Zanzibari doors were used to indicte the social status of its Arab and Indian householders by having their monogram and the date of the house carved into the lintel. Some doors were imported ready-made from India during the nineteenth and even early twentieth century, especially under the influence of Sultan Seyyid Bargash (1870–88) whose interest in major building works extended to elaborate floral designs. But, thereafter, increasing numbers of doors were carved in Zanzibar by Muslim Indian and Swahili craftsmen (though Barton regarded the indigenous art of carving as 'fast dying out in 1912 ' with very few skilled craftsmen surviving (ibid.). Zanzibar no longer imports but has for the last couple of generations actually exported its doors, an industry that has proliferated since the island's political thaw in the late 1980s. Most major houses in Zanzibar's Old Town still have their original doors, which might have been the starting-point for construction around which the rest of the house was built (as in the procedure for mud-and-wattle house building).

The right half of the door is called male and the left female, each half being decorated with brass bosses. The motifs carved into the wood of these older doors (which used to be made out of the termite-proof teak, sesame or jackfruit trees) are a lotus flower, a rosette (regarded as derived from the lotus), a fish, a metal chain, and patterns based on frankincense trees and date palms. A Koranic verse is also carved into the lintel.

Different parts of the door carry different motifs. The frames or uprights might have a fish design surmounting wavy lines (the sea) at their base. In the door's central panel is likely to be a more deeply carved lotus and bosses emerging from rosettes or other geometrical designs, surmounting and surmounted by patterns reminiscent of fish scales.

Adie suggests the following symbolism: the lotus derives from Egypt and denotes reproductive power; the fish may have come from the Syrian fish-goddess, Atargatis, and also represents fertility and, additionally, protectiveness; the chain indicates security; the frankincense tree suggests wealth and the date palm abundance. It is of course difficult to know whether there was such explicit symbolism in the minds of door carvers and owners (and whether this interpretation is correct) or whether, as seem more likely, the motifs were justified as no more than habitual forms of decoration. Nevertheless, a further observation by Adie is particularly interesting. He notes that the representations of fish take a number of forms (single-tailed;

scaleless; double-tailed; squamous; herringboned), and that they can meta-morphose into pineapples and, later, into vases of flowers.

The transformative use of fish scales is found elsewhere. Persian thirteenth-century porcelain plates are sometimes decorated with fish scales which merge with or shade into bird feathers and plants (probably of Chinese influence, given also the anthropomorphic depiction of oriental eyes and faces – examples can be seen in the Gulbenkian Museum in Lisbon). Bio-genetically, of course, scales, feathers and hair (the latter not perhaps represented in such art) are evolutionary transformations or variations of each other. We cannot go so far as to posit such evolutionary insights for the decorations of Zanzibari doors. But they do seem to indicate a parameter-bound creativity. They manage not to overstep the Islamic prohibition by broadly emphasizing the transformational geometry and symmetry of organic design (a geometry at times echoing ornamental Arabic calligraphy), so avoiding 'realistic' representations of animals and plants as discrete and discontinuous. Some of the same transformational organic symmetry of design is found in the carvings on the famous Zanzibar 'Arab' chests, and in some other examples of furniture.

Adopting the inevitable orientalist mode of his time, Barton identifies different styles ethnically by distinguishing early twentieth-century doors as of local 'Indian' workmanship and 'easily distinguished' from 'Arab and Swahili work by their more florid but less dignified style of decorative carving, also by the fact that doors made and carved by Indians almost invariably have arched tops', whereas 'Zanzibar Arab doors are rectangular without exception' (ibid.). Yet, with regard to the three main designs carved into the door, the derivatives of the lotus, the rosette and either the frankincense tree or the date palm, he links them to fish-like objects and scales, indicating that ethnic differences are still subsumed within a single transformational field of geometry and symmetry of organic design.

Modern tourism has encouraged the manufacture and export of such doors, chests and furniture. But while ornamental organic symmetry is retained, this is no longer in order to satisfy the constraints imposed by the prohibition on the representation of living things. It is simply what is regarded as customary, and what sells. Numerous small carpentry and joinery workshops have been set up in Zanzibar to this end.

Insofar as they continue to be works of art, albeit commoditized, the products are made without regard for religious rules. One or two more adventurous designs (for example, wardrobes carrying carvings of a palm tree set against sunrays and therefore vaguely reminiscent of a beach scene) indicate that carvers are evidently free to enter a more liberal world of rep-resentation according to their own and their customers' aesthetic tastes. But at present such realism in furniture carving is limited. Perhaps it is relatively difficult to depict real-life objects and scenes in detail. Or perhaps the aesthetics of furniture draw more on a combination of exterior form, consti-tutive balance, wood type and surface, than on inscribed depictions.

Symmetrically carved designs are therefore likely to continue to predominate, so causing no problem for the Islamic prohibition.

However, detailed, realistic representations are of course very much easier on canvas or even, say, batik. Moreover, their detail and pictoriality can be preserved through a range of impressionist, expressionist and realist art genres. Switching between, and experimentation within, genres is both easier and more rapid with brush, paint and surface, which therefore present a greater threat to the prohibition, through the representational creativity they invite. The circulation of paintings and drawings and the rapidity with which they can be created is nowadays seemingly greater than with other art forms. In any event, it is these pictorial art works which most vividly depict the paradox of apparent cultural escape: they preserve indigenous Islamic concerns but juxtapose them with unfamilar ones. They create new images, most of which ignore the old geometric designs and a concern with symmetry as an aesthetic end in itself. They instead depend heavily on the representation of people, animals and plants. In short their creative expression derives more from breaking than from following or transforming rules.

TWO GENRES OF ART IN ZANZIBAR

It may be possible to identify a number of different painting and drawing genres on Zanzibar. I simplify by selecting two at the present time. First, there are the roughly drawn and printed posters placed in Stone Town by the young Islamic fundamentalists.

These posters are stuck to walls at various key points in Stone Town, for example near one of the few hotels allowed to sell alcoholic liquor, which caters for visiting non-Muslims and is called 'The Bottoms Up Hotel' – a title unsubtly combining drinking and sexual innuendo. One set of drawings has pictures of men drinking from a bottle and smoking hashish and cocaine (*bangi* and *unga* (flour)) and evidently suffering the effects, with written warnings against this deviant behaviour. A second set simply shows a man praying (desirably pious behaviour) alongside another being carried off on a funeral cart, with the suggestion that virtuous habits and regular prayer are the best protection against death, and accompanied by a caption urging that it is better to pray than to be prayed for (that is, at a funeral). A third set strikingly contrasts a long-haired, very short-skirted European tourist, her upper as well as lower body scantily covered, with a Zanzibari woman covered everywhere except the eyes by the *hijab*, including a face veil. The tourist is referred to as the Devil's whore, an unbeliever who walks naked (*huyu ni kahba shetani, mwenda uchi kafiri*; note the Arabic-derived *kahba* (prostitute) instead of the more usual *malaya* – *kahba* is little used outside the main Swahili-speaking centres like Zanzibar, Mombasa and Lamu). By contrast, the Zanzibari woman is referred to as one of pious virtue, who covers her Muslim body (*kujisitiri mwili wake muislamu*) and whose clothes indicate her self-respect (*kujiheshima*). Given their setting, the visual messages cannot be lost on European tourists. But the Swahili phrases cannot be understood by them and are clearly aimed at the Zanzibaris themselves, with the implication either that Zanzibari women can become whores as a result of malevolent Western influence or that tourism begets prostitution practised and organized by outsiders. Indeed a few months previously an Italian-owned hotel had been raided and closed after disclosures that it had acted as a venue for mainland non-Muslim prostitutes and drug-dealing.

These 'politico-religious' posters are, it is claimed by their originators, immune to the Islamic prohibition on depicting people since they are created in order to protect Islam. Yet their expression of protest is very much in the tradition of pictorially represented political tracts used in other, secular world political movements. Drawn and printed in black on white, the caricatures of men and women are dramatic and shockingly effective, almost in the style of 'loud' expressionist cartoons. They attack the threatening 'ugliness' of Western decadence and so completely depart from earlier kinds of pictorial representation found in Zanzibar, which aimed at an aesthetic harmony of form and colour celebrating the peace of God. These latter took a number of forms and the following remark by Judith Miller indicates one such. Talking about the famous Zanzibari artist, Ali Darwish (1936–), she says, 'Islamic art which permits no figures and has its own type of patterns, is definitely an influence on ... his works (which) are composed of complex layers of textured patterns. The central image may be, perhaps, a tree, superimposed with a rich detail composed of touches of gold paint and sometimes Arabic or Kufic writing' (Miller 1975:16–17). Nothing could be further from the modern protest posters.

The second genre of modern painting contextualized in Zanzibar tourism does refrain from deliberate shock effect and the use of judgemental captions. But its artists all insist that each of their paintings carries a socio-religious message which, rather than protesting against tourism, stresses human unity. Their explicit appeal is to the injunction made by senior clerics defending tourism. They say that Islam encourages travel as a means of learning wisdom so that, just as a Muslim voyager discovers more of God's greatness as s/he walks the world, so an infidel tourist in Zanzibar will benefit from exposure to the wonders of Islam.

Typical of these ecumenical paintings are scenes of streets and houses, and even of a mosque paired with a church, in Zanzibar Stone Town. They also include boats at sea (motorized as well as with traditional sails) and beaches, often with white tourists, including bikini-clad women, represented alongside, say, Muslim Swahili fishermen or fully-covered women. Muslim and non-Muslim evidently coexist without conflict, though set at a slight distance from each other and not in obvious interaction.

I knew of two groups of painters of this genre. One consisted of some members of an extended family who had never received formal art training but had been instructed by elder brothers or cousins, fathers and grandfathers, these latter having allegedly learned to paint at missionary or government school in colonial times. It is clear, however, that much of the skill came from an East African modern tradition of painting which has in effect been indigenous for some time.

Members of this group blended inventiveness with practical constraints. One man had learned how to write shop signs and also designed and painted cloth school badges to be worn on pupils' clothes. But he also painted beach scenes and bowls of fruit on large polystyrene plates, creating an extraordinary juxtaposition of materials and brightly coloured images which sold more to local Zanzibaris than to the tourists for whom they were intended. His cousin painted similar, brightly coloured but more detailed Zanzibari street, house, sea and beach scenes on large, rectangular canvases and framed and displayed them in hotels which would accept them. His clients were roughly divided between tourists and locals, the latter being described as wealthy Zanzibaris, newly returned (following the political thaw), who wished to decorate their recently bought old but renovated houses in and around Stone Town.

Members of this first group see themselves as apart and perhaps excluded from a second group, a co-operative of ten artists, who regularly exhibit their paintings at an enterprise called Zanzibar Roots, this title having been chosen to evoke the representational authenticity of Zanzibar that this group of painters claim for their paintings. Since these display much the same range of themes aimed at tourist tastes as those of the first group, there is a sense in which they are indeed an 'authentic' representation of the modern (rather than 'pre-modern') issues concerning the co-existence of the races, of rich and poor, of religions, and the contrasting expectations of the behaviour of women and of men within and outside of Islam. The pictures are of Old Town, the countryside, palm trees, women carrying pots or loads, or working and talking, men walking or talking, and with a few including female white tourists in brief shorts, a sight that in reality is precisely what is condemned by the Islamic radicals. One man explained the 'symbolism' (using the English term in the Swahili conversation) of one of his paintings. It consisted of a Swahili man leaning over a hedge of microscopic palm trees, against a background of four spires: two, over his left shoulder, belonging to churches (Anglican and Catholic) and, to his right, one belonging to a mosque and the other to the House of Wonders (the former Sultan's palace). The painter claimed that these elements represented Christians, Muslims, white tourists, Omani and other Arabs, and ordinary Swahili as making up modern Zanzibar.

Members of this Zanzibar Roots co-operative, too, have learned to paint from older men in their families who had been taught the craft at school before the Zanzibar revolution of 1964, after which the subject was no longer available. What is particularly distinctive of this second group, however, is that they now paint exclusively on batik material and that the technique for doing so had been taught to them by an apparently well-known Japanese artist, Atsuko Morita, who came to Zanzibar for two years between 1987 and 1989.

Both groups of artists, the informal family-based one and the co-operative, are motivated by commercial as well as aesthetic concerns. Their intended social messages indicate acceptance of ethnic, racial and wealth differences and the celebration of existing features of life and landscape on Zanzibar. Let us call them both the ecumenicals. By contrast the radical Muslims aim to expose what they see as conflicts of politico-religious interest and use the most jarringly effective visual medium available to them, a kind of harshly expressionist cartoon.

In their different ways, both the ecumenicals and the radicals ignore the prohibition on representing humans and other living things in their pictures. The self-consciously geometric designs and symmetry in the early Zanzibar door carvings of plants and fish amount to an acknowledgement of the prohibition, for the abstract patterns had (and still have in modern furniture) priority over lifelike representations. They are worked within the rules, while the creativity of the new artists and makers of posters breaks these rules, in one case precisely to safeguard Islam and in the other in order to pursue the commercial opportunities offered by tourism, a development which is in fact condemned by radical Muslims.

CONCLUSION

In this proliferation of new representational styles, messages and media, there is no evidence of a 'traditional' Swahili-Islamic culture. The aesthetics are made up using numerous borrowings, many of indefinite provenance. Or, in the eagerness to appeal to tourists in the one case, or to warn against them in the other, perhaps the various new elements are attempts to escape Swahili-Islamic culture and to communicate in a more worldly idiom. However, what would such a culture be? Insofar as we may be aware of overlapping elements or family resemblances in the make-up of the artefacts, craft goods, customs, language and behavioural styles of the Swahili-speaking peoples living along the East African coast, we are conscious of something which we may call a Swahili cultural field. It is not therefore an essentialized culture but rather one according to which different communities, especially those distant from each other, may be similar in only one or two respects but contrast in many others.

Perhaps this differential borrowing and rejection from both inside and outside, alongside a retention of some existing elements, has always characterized a Swahili cultural field that is subject after all to an enormous number of Indian Ocean, European and mainland African influences. It is a cultural field whose constraints people constantly escape or deny, only to put in place new ones as they confront and absorb waves of migrants and ideas from overseas and inland. It is always both new and old.

I suggest that this process of escape, denial and replacement, all in the name of preserving the authentic, is more globally widespread. We locate cultural creativity by observing the conditions under which people transcend previous heavily held rules yet retain public belief in the cultural authenticity of what they are doing, as in the case of the Zanzibari artists and radical Muslims.

REFERENCES

Adie, J.J. (1946–47) 'Zanzibar doors', *East African Journal*.
Barth, F. (1969) *Ethnic Groups and Boundaries*. London: Allen and Unwin.
Barton, F.R. (1924) 'Zanzibar doors', *Man* 24(6):81–3.
Bourdieu, P. (1986 [1979] *Distinction: a Social Critique of the Judgement of Taste*. London: Routledge and Kegan Paul.
Cohen, A. (1969) *Custom and Politics in Urban Africa*. London: Routledge and Kegan Paul.
—— (1974) *Two-Dimensional Man*. London: Routledge and Kegan Paul.
Eagleton, T. (1990) *The Ideology of the Aesthetic*. Oxford: Blackwell.
Fardon, R. (1989) '"African ethnogenesis": limits to the comparability of ethnic phenomena', in L. Holy (ed.) *Comparative Anthropology*. Oxford: Blackwell.
Fernandez, J. (1986) *Persuasions and Performances: the Play of Tropes in Culture*. Bloomington: University of Indiana Press.
Grabar, O. (1987) *The Formation of Islamic Art*. New Haven: Yale University Press.
Lakoff, G. and Johnson, M. (eds) (1980) *Metaphors We Live By*. Chicago: University Press.
Miller, J. (1975) *Art in East Africa*. London: Frederick Muller; Nairobi: Africa Book Services (East Africa).
Ortony, A. (ed.) (1979) *Metaphor and Thought*. Cambridge: Cambridge University Press.
Parkin, D. (1980) 'The creativity of abuse', *Man* 15:45–64.
—— (1994) '*Maulidi*: Wahabism, *bida* and other mind–body dualisms in Islam', in S. Heald and A. Deluz (eds) *Anthropology and Psychoanalysis*. London: Routledge.
Sapir, D. and Crocker, C. (eds) (1977) *The Social Use of Metaphor*. Philadelphia: Pennsylvania University Press.
Sperber, D. (1975) *Rethinking Symbolism*. Cambridge: Cambridge University Press.
Topp, J. (1994) 'A history of *taarab* music in Zanzibar: a process of Africanisation', in D. Parkin (ed.) *Continuity and Autonomy in Swahili Communities*. Vienna: Institut für Afrikanistik. University of Vienna.
Volpe, G. della (1978 [1960]) *Critique of Taste*. London: New Left Books.

11 RECONTEXTUALIZING TRADITION: 'RELIGION', 'STATE' AND 'TRADITION' AS COEXISTING MODES OF SOCIALITY AMONG THE NORTHERN LIO OF INDONESIA

Signe Howell

Following independence in 1949, the new nation state of Indonesia faced the formidable task of uniting a population scattered over several thousand islands and consisting of several hundred distinct cultural groupings – each with its own language and cultural practices. The new motto became 'unity through diversity' and the national charter emphasized democracy, social justice and the belief in 'the unique Godhead'. Indonesian law recognizes five monotheistic world religions and has made the adherence to one of these a legal requirement. Moreover, Indonesian (*bahasa Indonesia*) was declared the national language, to be employed in schools everywhere and as the language of state and local government (see for example Hooker 1993).

Drawing upon fieldwork among the northern Lio people of the island of Flores in eastern Indonesia, I shall examine some results of activities by the Indonesian State in its effort to implement its national goals upon a remote part of Indonesia. Previous to this, the Dutch colonial government had adopted its particular strategies to gain control over the population. I shall argue that the cultural solutions to empowered culture contact – by which I mean that those contacted have no power to reject the initiating parties and their demands – need not necessarily be those of syncretism or creolization. Rather, when groups of people are subjected to strong, potentially dislocating social and cultural change, the effects are not predictable. Certainly, processes of creolization may, and in many cases do, occur. But new discourses may affect existing ones in ways that recontextualize them rather than hybridizing them. While new discourses challenge existing ones, none need necessarily emerge triumphant to the exclusion of the others. Rather, new and old may coexist, each discourse activating different discursive practices and different modes of sociality, each predicated upon different frames of reference. Moreover, those subjected to change, as well as the more powerful perpetrators of change, may adopt strategies that allow adaptations in their cultural orientations and practices without an accompanying loss of the overall thrust of their aims and values. Thus each is reconstituted, as it were, through interactions with the others, while maintaining its own respective identities and goals.

It is a truism to state that social and cultural institutions are constantly in flux; that creativity and imagination are part and parcel of human existence. While culturally significant creative moments and actions do occur as part of social processes, new ideas can have no cultural impact if members of the same interpretative community (Howell 1994) do not accept them – if there is no cultural resonance (Howell 1995b). For new practices to be adopted, those involved must – however implicitly – be partners in their formation and execution.

In the Introduction to this volume, Liep suggests a broad definition of cultural creativity as 'activity that produces something new through the recombination and transformation of existing cultural practices and forms'. While this certainly isolates one process of cultural creativity, it is not the only one. Based on my experiences with the northern Lio,[1] I shall seek to elucidate a process whereby an adoption of new ideas and practices has taken place among the indigenous population, but which has led to the establishment of coexisting discursive practices rather than to a transformation of the existing ones. My suggestion is that this has occurred as the result partly of a national policy that encourages separate socio-cultural domains (see below), and partly of the Lio leaders' use of this policy to recreate old categories in a new form through recontextualizing them. I shall elaborate these points while focusing both on long-term strategies developed at a higher level by the parties concerned, and on local-level tactics adopted in situations of actual interaction. While the various discourses may be operationalized as separate and delineated domains, they are nevertheless not static. The very fact of positing boundaries provokes continuous dialogic relationships (cf. Bakhtin 1986) with the other significant discourses. The task for the anthropologist becomes that of elucidating both alteration and continuity.

'RELIGION', 'TRADITION' AND 'GOVERNMENT': CATEGORIES OF THE INDONESIAN NATION STATE

I shall explore some of the above ideas in relation to actual instances observed during my fieldwork. They are all instances directly attributable to particular historical sets of circumstances which have dramatically affected the life of northern Lio communities, confronting them with challenges to the constituting principles of their social institutions and values. I will suggest that the northern Lio people have managed to reconcile the challenges, and ensuing contradictions, by creatively embracing the tripartite categorization of socio-political life introduced by the Indonesian nation state, namely those of 'religion' (*agama*), 'government' or 'state' (*pemerintah*), and 'tradition' (*adat*). The degree to which this tripartite classification of public life is operative varies across Indonesia.[2] The Lio leaders have used it to good effect, creating space as it were for the Catholic Church and the State to establish their domains according to their own criteria while, at the same time, insisting on the continuation of their own time-honoured values and practices, albeit in a somewhat restricted form. On a national level, representatives of both Church and State have pursued a strategy that seeks to render indigenous discourses harmless by referring to them as 'tradition' (*adat*), and by seeking to relegate them into a folkloristic category. This has not been successful in Lioland (cf. Acciaioli 1985 for a different response on Sulawesi).[3] Although all seek to promote their own position, the representatives of each group have chosen to adopt a path of pragmatic caution. Religious leaders – and to a much lesser extent the government (see below) – have developed long-term strategies in order to fight for acceptance. The leaders of *adat* have done so in order to fight for survival. In this chapter I am primarily concerned with the strategies adopted by the leaders of Lio adat, and my suggestion is that their relative success can be traced to a recontextualizing of adat in the life of the community. Amongst the general population one may observe a pragmatic, everyday creativity which allows them to attend to the three domains while at the same time keeping them separate.

Most Lio not only render to Caesar that which is Caesar's, and to God that which is God's, but also continue to render to the ancestors that which is the ancestors'. These have emerged as separate, but viable, coexisting discursive domains, each constituted upon different values, activating different modes of sociality. Although the vast majority of the Lio today are Catholic, it is still the third of these relationships that existentially makes life meaningful. It is *adat* which constitutes their sense of self in a world of 'significant others', and which the communities have taken measures to protect. But relationships with Church and State are realities which cannot be ignored and, in many ways, they are regarded as positive additions to adat. The point I wish to stress is that rather than a straightforward transformation of previous Lio categories through the incorporation of alien concepts, we witness a viable continuation of adat ones. In recontextualizing adat in relation to religion and government, both additions and subtractions have occurred, but not transformation. This in itself may also be interpreted as a form of cultural resistance: I return to this point towards the end. But Lio leaders could not have achieved this on their own. Their partners have been ordinary Lio men and women, as well as representatives of Church and State, all with their own reasons for cooperating.

Having established that the tripartite division of socio-cultural life is viable, it does not follow that the daily operation of these relationships is an easy task. Conflicts constantly arise. I wish to explore some of the tensions that have arisen out of the attempts both to maintain, and to negate, separate moral and political domains. My overall argument is that the northern Lio people with whom I came in contact handle the inevitable with imagination and pragmatic creativity each according to their particular social position. What is beyond doubt is that the demands of the Catholic Church and the State have provided profound challenges to the previously undisputed cosmologically-based epistemology and social organization of the northern Lio.

THE NORTHERN LIO

Until the first half of the twentieth century, the northern Lio people lived in a relatively well-defined universe. Theirs was a bounded social world in which it would be meaningless to divide social and cultural life into separate areas of concern. I will consider some effects of the introduction of Catholicism, primary education and the Indonesian language, and the intrusion of the State. These were all more or less forced upon the Lio, and today, depending on who one talks to, attitudes to their presence vary enormously. While those previously without access to power now find new opportunities, those accustomed to wield encompassing power feel threatened. The picture is therefore complex.

Until the Dutch subjected the northern Lio to a semblance of colonial control at the beginning of the twentieth century, they lived in scattered villages built on the steep hillsides high up in the mountains, where they practised a precarious form of swidden agriculture. It was a difficult terrain to travel through, both due to the topography and to the inhabitants' hostility to outsiders. People lived in small villages and hamlets which were socially and ritually focused on a core village controlling the larger domain. There was no authority above the level of the village domain and each core village with its satellites constituted a self-contained and bounded area of authority. The population of each village domain is made up of two categories of people: the nobles and the commoners. Before colonial control there were also large numbers of slaves. The nobles are constituted through named Houses and in named patri-groups (Howell 1995a). Until the arrival of the Dutch and the subsequent establishment of the Indonesian nation state, each village domain was controlled by a council of seven male priest-leaders, each of whom had a special title and special duties to perform. Today, the priest-leaders still exercise authority over people's lives, but no longer exclusively so, having to share with both Church and State. Accession to the office of priest-leader is through descent in the patriline and each male priest-leader is complemented by a female one, ideally his wife in the person of his mother's brother's daughter. The point is that the criteria for being 'licensed' orchestrators of social and ritual life, the guardians of truth, are embedded in a clear understanding about the past and people's place in it through descent and marriage. The central sacrificial, burial and ritual dancing space of a core village is bounded by the named ceremonial houses and a temple. Together this space and these buildings constitute a sacred domain where sacred time is anchored in the present, predicating the future. Lio ancestors are part of Lio daily life and relationship with them is integral to Lio moral order (Howell 1989, 1991, 1995a). Although necessary participants in the overall social and moral order, the commoners are excluded from direct interaction with the sacred and are in awe of all its manifestations.

OUTSIDE FORCES 1: TACTICS OF 'RELIGION'

Dutch Catholic missionaries accompanied the Dutch soldiers and adminis-trators to Flores. Dutch control was superficial among the northern Lio, whom the Dutch found extremely difficult (Dietrich 1989). Catholicism and education were first introduced during the 1920s, to be consolidated by the building of a church and the appointment of a Dutch priest in 1936 (Father J. Smeets, personal communication). The Indonesian government expanded the schools and introduced the Indonesian language to the region during the 1950s and 1960s. Due to the hard work of only a handful of foreign priests during this whole period, virtually all Lio individuals under the age of 50 designate themselves as Catholics, and most of those under 40 are literate. Most speak Indonesian fluently.

I now want to examine some consequences of these dramatic changes upon adat village life. My examples are all taken from Kanganara, a village domain which I know well. It is one of the main ritual centres of the region.

Colonial policy was to obtain young sons of the nobles, to be educated, converted and given Christian names; the intention was that they would influence their fathers upon returning home (Prior 1988). I wish to suggest that both Church and Lio leaders displayed a fair amount of ingenuity in the establishment and performance of their relationship. This has meant that one may now observe a high degree of compromise on both sides which allows for a relatively peaceful coexistence of 'religion' and 'tradition'.

Certain individuals may be seen to personify the Lio compromise and act as exemplars for others. One such is Martinus Kebe, a recently retired school-teacher. He was taken to Catholic schools before the Second World War, and as the first teacher in the village was instrumental in easing Catholicism into people's lives. He is also a senior priest-leader, having inherited the title from his pagan father. Kebe is a man who is very knowledgeable about Lio precepts and practices, their adat, and takes his various priest-leader duties very seriously. He is highly respected by the whole community, a man whose opinions are listened to. He is respected because he holds and wields high adat as well as government office (as teacher) and participates actively and with authority in the fora where adat, Church or government constitute the mode of sociality. The other senior priest-leaders are mostly 'pagans' – in fact or practice. At difficult moments Kebe emerges as a mediator between Church, state and adat, and in so doing, he is scrupulous in maintaining the boundaries between them. To many Lio he demonstrates the viability of the coexistence of the discourses.

Adat cosmology is well articulated and it permeates social, political and cultural life. The body of seven priest-leaders still exercises authority in most matters pertaining to village life. With the exception of schoolteachers and local government employees, who receive adequate salaries, the rest of the Lio farm for their living, as do those government representatives in the villages, the headman and his assistants, who receive stipends only for limited periods. Agriculture is precarious, it is an activity predicated upon myth and performed within cosmologically informed rituals. The annual planting and harvesting ceremonies are large-scale, profoundly serious, life-promoting activities vital for survival from one year to the next. These are moments when the priest-leaders orchestrate the relationship with the ancestors – the true owners of the land – on behalf of the rest of the community. Every farmer, man and woman, participates. It is an undisputed action; the past, the present and the future merge into one total social phenomenon.

Recent years have seen a new trend in the Catholic Church on Flores towards a policy of 'inculturation' – defined as 'the creative and dynamic relationship between the Christian message and a culture' (Barnes 1993:1). In its theoretical deliberations, the notion of inculturation as developed on Flores certainly qualifies as creative action. However, the effects of inculturation are not immediately obvious in the northern Lio region. Its implementation is dependent upon the inclination of the local priests, none of whom is Lio, and who therefore have varying degrees of understanding of, or tolerance for, Lio traditional perceptions.[4] On the whole, the clergy have adopted a tactic of maintaining a parallel discourse, thus inadvertently mirroring the policy of the Lio nobles. The ultimate aim, however, is to eradicate adat in all but its more colourful folkloristic manifestations.

It is interesting to note the cultural domains that the Church actively seeks to influence or replace. When I went on a reconnaissance tour of Flores before deciding upon an actual fieldwork site, I was struck by the large and looming churches on hilltops overlooking some villages. However, I could see no graveyards and asked a German priest why this was so. With some embarrassment he replied that, so far, they had left matters of death and burial alone because these were very important to the people and it was felt that, for the time being, the old practices should be allowed to continue. Instead, the Church had concentrated on baptism and marriage. The latter institution is thought extremely important, family life being the foundation of Christian sociality. The clergy object to 'cousin marriages' and to the practice of large 'marriage payments'. Instead, they advocate marriage based on unencumbered free choice and mutual love, not indigenous Lio notions.[5] Whereas most couples today go through a wedding ceremony in church as part of the long-drawn-out process, the marriage exchanges are far from eradicated. If anything they are more elaborate than ever (see also Prior 1988). Lio social organization is predicated upon the principle of exchange, and the relationship between wife-giving and wife-taking groups involves much more than just the event of a marriage. The wife-takers and wife-givers

orchestrate each other's flow of life across the generations (Howell 1989).
So we find that both sides continue to demand and exchange the prescribed
objects and services at times of birth, marriage and death of members of each
other's groups.[6]

While Lio notions of an afterworld are fairly hazy, it is important to make
sure that the dead are transformed into proper ancestors who will look after
the living benevolently. It is the responsibility of the living – kin and affines
under guidance of priest-leaders – to ensure this transformation. Graves are
close to the house of the deceased. Neither the Church nor the State
interferes, but 'religion' is often brought to bear on the proceedings. For
example, a schoolteacher with special responsibilities for teaching religion
may ask to say a prayer after the grave is closed. Permission is usually
granted, and some relatives may join in the prayer. While plates of cooked
food, together with cloth and gold or money, are placed on the grave by kin
and affines, accompanied by invocations to the ancestors, others may be
making a small crucifix to place on the grave. Both 'religion' and 'tradition'
are thus involved. As in the case of the marriage process, the priest-leaders
have ceded a limited space to accommodate 'religion' while core practices of
adat are maintained.

By contrast, Easter, the main festival celebrated by the Catholic Church
on Flores, is dominated by 'religion'. The Church encourages local villages
to put on a passion play, or enact the stations of the cross. I observed one
such enactment in 1989. On the night, the atmosphere was electric. The
actors were all adults. Elaborate costumes had been made, emulating those
seen in religious pictures. The event took place after dark. The young man
who played Christ carried a life-size crucifix past the twelve stations up to
the chapel. Here it was erected with the man tied on to it. He wore a crown
of thorns and, with his head on the side and body slumped, he gave a
remarkable performance. The crowd by this time was dense and excited. The
three Marys were crying, the apostles viewing from afar were grave, and the
Roman guards were hustling the crowd. Suddenly a rumpus broke out and
several people were shrieking. It turned out to be the father and senior
agnates of the Christ. They felt that he was being pulled too far into the role
and that the ancestors would react angrily. They demanded that the Church
representatives, local teachers, assist in a sacrifice to amend any offence. The
teachers agreed, and the following morning, a teacher brought a chicken to
the ceremonial house of the man's patri-group where the priest-leader
performed the sacrifice.

These examples demonstrate both the parallel discursive practices as well
as the tenuousness of the relationship between them. The participants and
audience at the Easter ceremony did not include the priest-leaders and their
close families. The latter did not, however, try to interfere, and they established
their own authority when insisting on the need to appease the ancestors.

Certain attempts at inculturation may, however, be observed. For
example, from the beginning of Catholic proselytizing, certain key terms were

translated into the Lio language. The word for God was taken from a local name for a major deity amongst the southern Lio. However, this name was not in use in the north so, as far as the people there are concerned, to pray to Du'a Ngga'e in church does not merge Catholic and adat deities. More recently, priests may try to copy what they see as clear-cut adat practices. Thanksgiving services have been introduced in some chapels and churches at harvest times. This is not receiving much support; agricultural fertility is the concern of the ancestors, not of the Catholic God. When a new church is consecrated, one or two buffaloes may be slaughtered and the whole population invited to a feast. This is a deliberate attempt to merge church and temple into each other as sacred buildings of the same order. The culmination of the rebuilding of a Lio temple is the sacrifice of a large buffalo in front of the building, when its blood is ritually applied to the main beams and pillars. This is the most sacred and inclusive of all Lio rituals, and it attracts the participation of far-flung village members, including highly educated Lio who occupy senior positions in nearby towns. The Church strongly disapproves, but refrains from condemning the ritual. On the occasion of a recent rebuilding, a foreign priest who was a strong advocate of inculturation heard about the event and came from afar in order to perform Holy Communion on the sacred space. He erected a small altar and prayed for the well-being of the villagers. Though no one objected outright, the priest-leaders were outraged and others were of the opinion that this was not right, because 'the temple is different from the church'. Similarly, in their preaching, some priests try to fuse the ancestors with the saints, the cosmogonic Lio brother–sister pair with Adam and Eve, the pre-social time at the sacred mountain top with the Garden of Eden and so on. So far, there is little indication that the Lio are ready for this kind of syncretism, preferring instead to maintain the two domains in parallel.[7]

While the Church has the long-term goal of eradicating adat except as folklore, the priest-leaders have more to lose and are eager to maintain co-existing modes. While the clergy and the guardians of adat outwardly show a desire to respect each other, they are at the same time waging a silent battle. Neither party condemns each other's beliefs and practices outright. Rather, as far as possible, both carry on largely as if the other did not exist, maintaining their separate discursive practices. It is my conviction that the two parties have only a superficial understanding of the principles of each other's cosmologies, and that they – primarily the clergy – at times make *ad hoc* and decontextualized selections of what they regard as central to the others' world-view.

The Church has moved slowly and carefully into the various personal aspects of people's lives. I suggest that the key to their relative success is precisely the restraint they have shown, and continue to show, in relation to the deep 'traditional' convictions of the Lio, while at the same time seeking to encompass adat practices within the Catholic mode.

OUTSIDE FORCES 2: TACTICS OF THE STATE

The 'government' experiences fewer scruples than the Church. Its power base is also much more secure.[8] Its influence in village life is manifest in schools, language, appointed headmen and their assistants, as well as in travelling minor local government officials (*pegawi*). Again, the main pro- tagonists are the priest-leaders. Unlike the conflict with the Church whose representatives are either foreigners or outsiders, most of the representatives of the State come from within the communities themselves, thus making conflicts more personal. What is emerging within Lio villages is a new artic- ulation of the old social categories of nobles and commoners in a new and often antagonistic mode. It is a noticeable fact that the commoners, and the less central members of noble patri-groups, have taken advantage of the opportunities that followed in the wake of State and Church presence. They eagerly seek education, regarding it as a commodity which can be transformed into salaried jobs. Thus, while the nobles have been seeking to entrench and confirm the cosmological basis of their authority, many commoners have sought an alternative path to authority. However, in Lioland, as in many parts of South-East Asia, power traditionally cannot be achieved, but is conferred automatically as a birthright. The process has been that inherent power attracts wealth. Educated commoners in the employ of the new State are seeking to reverse this process and make newly acquired wealth attract power. Here lies potential for real tensions.

Language and Education

Although primary education is obligatory in Indonesia, in the villages on Flores there is a very high drop-out rate due primarily to poverty (Prior 1988). But most children stay long enough to achieve a basic level of literacy and to learn Indonesian. All formal teaching, and all teaching material, is in the Indonesian language. In my experience, the teachers are without exception Lio and, unlike the headmen and minor civil servants, are often the children of priest-leaders and are posted in or near their village of origin. This means that their first language is Lio, which is therefore not totally banished from the schools. A lot of songs, for example, are in Lio and draw on Lio imagery. Interestingly, teachers do not take advantage of the right to teach up to 20 per cent of the timetable in the local language and about local adat. At first sight this seems surprising. On second thoughts, however, it may be explained in terms of the predominant Lio practice of maintaining the tripartite separation of significant social domains. The teachers choose to confine matters of education to matters of 'modernity', i.e. of State and religion. A prime task of the teachers is to instil in children a sense of being Indonesian, to give them a meaningful idea of the history and function of the modern Indonesian nation state, as well as to teach Catholic dogma. To bring the Lio language and adat into the classroom would be an unacceptable mixing of categories. Language is similarly used to mark the different discourses. Indonesian is the medium of matters pertaining both to religion and government, while Lio is that of adat matters and daily interaction. According to context and topic of conversation, most people switch between the two languages with no apparent difficulty.

Politics

All villages are incorporated into the region's local government schema with its different levels of control and influence. Each village domain (*desa*) has an appointed representative in the village headman, a local man who is appointed for a fixed period. His job is to be the mediator between the regional capital and the local population. He keeps demographic records, collects the small annual taxation levied on farm land, animals and crops, and distributes subsidies and information. He plays the host to more specialized government employees who come to give advice about health, agricultural practices, etc.

The headman's roles are clearly in opposition to those of the priest-leaders. Before independence, priest-leaders were the mediators with the outside world and the Dutch bestowed titles upon them. They, however, did not truly acknowledge any authority above their own. Dutch demands for labour and taxes were complied with because of superior military strength, not because they were expected to give any benefits to the villages. The post-independence State, on the other hand, employs a rhetoric of being in the service of the villagers, not the other way round. This has little real meaning for people – just as the clergy's teaching about a general human responsibility towards all other humans is met with incomprehension. The office of headman is perceived by holder and population alike as a prime means for enriching oneself and one's kin group, not the whole community.

In the northern Lio villages an uneasy division of labour has been established between the headman and the priest-leaders. Although there is clearly competition between them, I rarely observed any direct outbreak of hostilities. The headman hardly ever came from a major priest-leader patriline, but was usually a commoner with some secondary education. From a descent point of view he could not aspire to the authority of a priest-leader. The opportunities offered by the new regime became an attractive option for such men. Just as it irks many of them that the priest-leaders keep asserting their authority in matters outside the narrow official definition of adat, the priest-leaders are aggrieved at the headmen's interference. Priest-leaders acknowledge publicly the tripartite division of social life, but continually assert their own wide definition of adat sociality. Headmen, on the other hand, may disagree about the boundaries, and try to extend the parameters of their authority. They may, for example, turn up at various adat ritual events and make (unwelcome) speeches in the name of the government. Most headmen show prudence, but circumstances may promote conflict, as the following two examples show.

OUTSIDE FORCES 3: LIO STRATEGIES

The village of Kanganara has a very impressive central sacred space with a large temple and many ceremonial houses. This of course is adat domain par excellence. Government policy to make adat in Indonesia into art and folklore – and hence peripheral – has led to the appointment of guards for the adat buildings in certain particularly well-endowed villages. On my visit in 1993, I was informed by outraged priest-leaders that such a guard had been appointed there. The man was a commoner with no legitimate right to concern himself with adat matters. The priest-leaders did not dare to complain officially to the regional capital, but they never missed an opportunity to make loud allusions to the preposterousness of such interference which they knew the man would either hear or be told about. They also managed from time to time to bring the situation to a head, and exploited this to the full and with the support of the population. It is the duty of the priest-leaders to make sure that the villagers keep the sacred spaces and buildings tidy. This means cutting the grass and weeding the central space. When I arrived, this looked a mess. The priest-leaders complained to me, saying that if the newly appointed man really was the government's representative he should keep the space neat. 'What does he get paid for?' I was asked. They – and he – knew that they would never allow him to touch the space or the buildings without permission. He did not dare ask. They did not offer. There was clearly a stalemate. A big ceremonial event was due. The priest-leaders insisted that they could not start while the grass was so high. Yet, 'Why should we cut it when someone else gets paid for the job?' they asked, and claimed that the ceremonies would have to be postponed. Eventually, they ordered the villagers to clear the space, which they did, and the ceremony was performed.

Some time later, a group of students arrived from a regional university. They came with the express purpose of examining the adat buildings. Being on official business, they approached the headman and the adat guard, who received them politely and fed them, but did not dare to accompany them to the sacred spot. The headman's tentative approach to the priest-leaders was met with refusal to cooperate. The priest-leaders were annoyed that the visitors had not gone directly to them, the true guardians of the adat. They were also annoyed that the headman and the guard had pretended that they had authority. When approached by the students, they claimed that the only priest-leader with the right to take outsiders into the temple was living in a different village. The students sent a message to this man, asking him to attend. He had been forewarned and was not at home. Messages were left for him, but he never arrived. Although not Lio themselves, the students understood the severity of unauthorized entry into sacred buildings. The temple and the ceremonial houses were clearly not museum pieces, but living potent symbols of power. They were too frightened by the possible ancestral repercussions to make a forced entry and, after two more days, they returned with their business unaccomplished.

Throughout these proceedings, Kebe emerged as a central figure. Without officially committing himself fully to any group, his line of argument, which was adopted by many locals, was that the situation had arisen because of a collapse of the demarcated areas of state and adat. The whole village was in turmoil. There is no doubt that on both these occasions *adat* was confirmed as a viable autonomous discourse. All the described incidents involving issues of religion, government and adat exemplify the pragmatic, everyday creativity of all Lio concerned. They attend to all three domains and keep them separate. The teachers, and particularly Kebe, demonstrate this most successfully.

CONCLUDING REMARKS

While most Lio appear to have incorporated Catholicism and 'Indonesian-ism' into their personal and social identities, I argue that these are subordinated to their sense of being Lio, as this is predicated upon adat.

From the examples given, it can be seen that potentially highly disruptive attempts to forge social change were defused, and the various parties involved reached a kind of tacit understanding about the need to compromise. The official Indonesian division between religion, tradition and government met a cultural resonance among the Lio. The adat leaders adopted it most enthusiastically and this allowed them to reach the current compromises. Perhaps the old Lio practice of dividing the differentiated tasks of leadership between priest-leaders provided a model which made the modern division of social functions amenable to them and the commoners. Whatever the reason, they were able to make creative use of old and new concepts and practices. Both Church and State also chose to employ the three categories as part of their short-term tactics towards their final goal of encompassing adat. So I wish to argue that there is enough evidence to suggest that, for the time being at any rate, the significant actors in northern Lioland – insiders and outsiders – participated in operationalizing three modes of sociality: one for the Church, one for the State, and one for adat. I am not suggesting that they deliberately worked this out between them, but that, for different reasons, all parties concerned decided that they could gain most in this way. Church and State understood the need to tread carefully. They regard this as short-term tactics, while seeking to impose an order defined by themselves for the traditional order the adat leaders were working to maintain.

From this ethnographic example it is possible to isolate three levels of cultural creativity: that performed by the adat leaders, by the Catholic

Church (and to a lesser extent the State), and by the Lio populace generally. Löfgren (this volume) discusses how creativity can be used as a 'weapon of the weak'. This argument can be applied to the northern Lio priest-leaders who, in the face of powerful outside forces, insisted on the separate viability of adat. But the 'weapons of the strong' can also be creative. Liep points out (in the Introduction to this volume) that creative destruction of whole ways of life has occurred in the wake of colonialism and the spread of capitalism. 'It would be naive', he warns us, 'to be blind to the fact that creativity may also be employed in schemes and projects of seduction, control and domination.' The approach of the Catholic Church on Flores may be interpreted in this way. By initially turning a blind eye to some unacceptable practices in the hope that they would disappear in time, then by adopting a more aggressive line of inculturation, the Church has worked in conformity with long-term strategic plans. Local government officials are more forthright in their ambition to 'modernize' the Lio. In each case, this means abandoning adat discursive practices. The strategies of Church and State alike have been to acclaim the tripartite division of social life, while at the same time to make adat peripheral to daily life by folklorizing it.

However one chooses to view the situation, it is clear that operating three separate discursive practices leads to a reduction in the political and religious autonomy of the Lio village domains. Uniformity of perceptions about reality has been lost. However, recontextualizing adat rather than creolizing it, means that it continues to wield profound influence. At the same time, much has been gained from the powerful presences of religion and government.[9] Caught, as it were, between demands from three powerful groups, each with its own discourse, the Lio commoners have developed their own version of cultural creativity. In daily life they pragmatically attend to each domain, and take care to keep them separate.

Can the impact of Church and State on the pre-colonial Lio institutions and values be thought of as analogous to that argued by John Berger about the impact of cubism on European art, namely that it 'changed the nature of the relationship between the painted image and reality, and by so doing expressed a new relationship between man and reality'? (1972:145). My tentative answer is that it probably can, but only from a certain perspective. Any rapid change that affects a cosmology must necessarily affect people's orientation in their world and thereby their relationship to the world and to each other. Dramatic challenges from outside have meant that many details in adat itself have altered more rapidly than might otherwise have been the case. Nevertheless, underlying traditional principles continue to mould practice and constitute existential meaning for the Lio people. Adat is recontextualized, not creolized. The cultural creativity performed by the various social categories of the Lio people has been, precisely, to find a viable balance between renouncement, readjustment and continuation of values and practices.

My example is not presented as a unique instance of cultural creativity by weak and strong groups respectively. Rather, I wish to suggest that it may exemplify a more general social phenomenon, namely that in situations of rapid social change, different motivations generate different strategies within, and among, the groups involved.

NOTES

1. Fieldwork with the northern Lio has been conducted on five occasions between 1982 and 1993. It was carried out under the auspices of the Indonesian Academy for Science (LIPI) and with the sponsorship of the Universitas Nusa Cendana. Earlier versions of this work were commented upon by J. Smeets SVD, and presented at the Research School for Pacific Studies, University of Canberra. Special thanks are due to Eduardo Archetti who showed me how to cut some Gordian knots. Without the unrelenting constructive critical comments by John Liep, this final version would have remained more unresolved than it is now.
2. In Java, for example, Islam has been the dominant religion for more than 500 years.
3. This interference has also provoked a degree of reflexivity concerning local values and practices in all cases but, not surprisingly, particularly amongst the Lio.
4. Until recently all priests were foreign. The seminary on Flores trains Indonesian priests. In order to maintain impartiality in their dealings with parishioners, it has been Church policy not to send local priests to work in their own natal region. While several foreign priests have profound knowledge of, and respect for, Lio language and *adat*, the majority of the Indonesian ones have no interest in such matters. Ironically, this fact might assist the survival of *adat* as an alternative moral discourse.
5. The Lio adhere to an ideology of classificatory prescriptive cross-cousin marriage. The missionaries failed to pick up the subtlety of the system. Priest-leader couples who, for ritual reasons, should be sisters' sons married to brothers' daughters, are ingenious in explaining the kin status of prospective spouses.
6. With the population today in flux, kin relationships are more unstable. Often young people find spouses outside the village. To insist on the mutuality that is embedded in alliance exchanges may be one way to negate some of the potential disruptive effects of distant marriages.
7. Only once have I come across *adat* leaders appropriating Christian images. This was when, in a long list of ancestral addressees, the names of Adam and Eve were included. While in itself a feeble attempt at incorporating Christianity into *adat*, it nevertheless shows an awareness on the part of Lio priest-leaders of Church tactics.
8. Although Catholicism is the dominant religion on Flores, it is embraced by only a small minority in Indonesia as a whole, the vast majority of the population being Muslim. Christianity is also associated with colonialism. The Church has to tread carefully in its dealings with the State.
9. Most Lio individuals appreciate the benefits of education, modern medicines and irrigation. Many have a real affection for the foreign priests who have devoted their lives to bettering the quality of life for the villagers.

REFERENCES

Acciaioli, G. (1985) 'Culture as art: from practice to spectacle in Indonesia', *Canberra Anthropology* 8:148–72.
Bakhtin, M.M. (1986) *Speech Genres and Other Late Essays*. Austin: University of Texas Press.
Barnes, R.H. (1993) 'Local expressions of Christianity in a Catholic region of Eastern Flores'. Unpubl. manuscript.

Berger, J. (1972) *Ways of Seeing.* (Based on the BBC Television Series.) London: British Broadcasting Corporation and Penguin Books.

Dietrich, S. (1989) *Kolonialismus und Mission auf Flores (ca. 1900–1942).* Hohenschaflarn: Klaus Renner.

Hooker, V.M. (ed.) (1993) *Culture and Society in New Order Indonesia.* Singapore: Oxford University Press.

Howell, S. (1989) 'Of persons and things: exchange and valuables among the Lio of eastern Indonesia', *Man* 24(3):419–38.

—— (1991) 'Access to the ancestors: reconstructions of the past in a non-literate society', in R. Grønhaug, G. Haaland and G. Henriksen (eds) *The Ecology of Choice and Symbol: Essays in Honor of Fredrik Barth.* Bergen: Alma Mater.

—— (1994) 'Singing with the spirits and praying to the ancestors', *L'Homme* 132:15–34.

—— (1995a) 'The Lio house: building, category, idea, value', in J. Carsten and S. Hugh-Jones (eds) *About the House: Lévi-Strauss and beyond.* Cambridge: Cambridge University Press.

—— (1995b) 'Whose knowledge and whose power? A new perspective on cultural diffusion', in R. Fardon (ed.) *Counterworks: Managing the Diversity of Knowledge.* London: Routledge.

Prior, J. M. (1988) *Church and Marriage in an Indonesian Village.* Frankfurt: Peter Lang.

12   KULA AND KABISAWALI: CONTEXTS OF CREATIVITY IN THE TROBRIAND ISLANDS

John Liep

Some 25 years ago I wrote a popular article about the *kula* exchange system for a Danish magazine and needed some illustrations. I therefore asked the American anthropologist Jerry Leach, who had worked in the Trobriands in the early 1970s, for a selection of photographs. Among those he forwarded was one taken in 1973 showing baskets of highly decorated kula armshells on a platform outside a house built of local materials on the main island, Kiriwina. The scene would have been redolent of the 'kula tradition' had it not, unfortunately, been marred by incongruous intrusions of modernity. It was bad enough that on the wall in the background hung a calendar from Ela Motors in Port Moresby with a picture of a man in a crash helmet racing a Yamaha motorcycle. Far worse, further back, through an opening in the wall, there appeared the dim visage of a bearded man with a grave face framed by long hair and a beret. It was a poster of Che Guevara. At that time this spectre was an embarrassment to me: how could I illustrate the 'kula tradition' with a picture containing such dissonant elements? It seems to be a sign of the times that today I appreciate the same picture quite differently. Now it presents a striking juxtaposition of 'local' and 'global' images. In fact, it inspired the following discussion of two contexts of cultural complexity and creativity in the Trobriand Islands.

In the present era the impact of global forces on local culture is causing much concern and debate. This is also the case in anthropology. World-system theorists have argued that local cultural processes everywhere are being shaped by the penetration of the capitalist system. They have been opposed by 'culturalists' who insist on the resilience of local cultural structures. In Pacific studies the two best-known protagonists used to be Marshall Sahlins and Jonathan Friedman. Sahlins argued for the local cultural specificity of historical process. The expansion of capitalism was shaped in each society of the Pacific according to the existing local cultural order. Thus, capitalist forces everywhere were realized in exotic cultural logics (Sahlins 1985). Against this Friedman argued for the primacy of the world system in determining the conditions of local reproduction. Moreover Friedman located structure not at the level of culture but at the level of social practice, for which cultural schemes were representations after the fact, so to speak (Friedman 1988). An intermediate position was taken by Nick Thomas (1991, 1993), who used such terms as 'entanglement' and 'hybridization' to describe transcultural transactions between Europeans and islanders.

More recently Sahlins and Friedman have converged, or come close to having exchanged positions. Sahlins acknowledges that there is a 'complicated intercultural zone where ... cultural differences are worked through ... in creolized languages' (1993:13). Friedman, on the other hand, asserts that external circumstances are *assimilated* through localizing strategies (1997). Friedman, however, still locates continuity at the level of practice while Sahlins sticks to the cultural order.

At issue is, I think, first, the distinction between the levels of determinant relations. On the one hand, there is the level of the systemic forces of the world system. On the other, the level of the local field of practice and of meaning. Seen from one point of view, the global forces everywhere encompass local fields of action. Seen from within, the external influences are enveloped in local practice (ibid.). It is the conceptualization of the *inter-penetration* of external and internal determinations and effects that is the problem. Secondly, the issue is about how much integration should be assumed in the local field of relationships. Both Sahlins and Friedman draw upon structuralism, but whereas Sahlins privileges the practice of structure, Friedman insists upon the structure of practice. Both perspectives, in my view, imply too much structural closure at the local level. But we are not much better served by conceptualizing the field of tension between the external and internal as an 'intercultural zone' characterized by 'creoliza-tion' or 'hybridization'. Rather, social action and cultural production should be seen to take place in a *multi-centered field of interference* where conflicting strategies and disparate cultural models are negotiated. And it is here, where new localizing strategies are tried out, that improvisation and creativity come into play. Here, models must be reinvented, schemes reconstituted and values condensed and symbolized in new ways in attempts to construct webs of meaning and forms of practice to cope with complexity. In one of the cases to be discussed here this process was successful; in the other it failed.[1]

ACCOMMODATING TRADITION: THE KULA

The kula is a vast complex of practices connecting a number of island societies in the Massim. The reciprocal circulation of armshells and necklaces in the kula ring is an early example of a transcultural institution uniting populations with differing languages and conceptions.

The kula is also the jewel in the anthropological crown: the cherished case of natives defying the doctrines of Western economics because they insist on the pursuit of prestige rather than material profit. The kula is the archetype of a project of 'Otherness'. In Malinowski's exposition (1922) it had to be thus, because he depicted the kula as a static and closed system circulating a fixed fund of valuables through stable partnerships in perpetuity. Later research has shown that the kula is a much more dynamic and complex phenomenon (Leach and Leach 1983, Weiner 1988, Keesing 1990). Firstly, the kula takes place in a transcultural and multi-centered field. It is an aggregate product of multiple decentralized strategies. This lends an instability to the system, as any change influencing decisions in a local environment has repercussions on the whole. Secondly, kula objects are also employed in a variety of local projects such as kinship exchanges, purchases of pigs and payments for land rights. A kula participant must continually adjust his strategies to the demands of his home community. Thus the kula is not an insulated circuit. Kula players must strategically steer their valuables between the sometimes conflicting, sometimes reinforcing goals of expanding prestige in the kula and social influence in the home community. Therefore kula objects are continually leaving and entering the ring as they are invested in internal exchanges or reinserted into the kula. Likewise, partnerships are frequently broken and new alliances formed through competition among overseas kula players. The kula is therefore particularly responsive to changing practices in its overall environment.

In fact, the kula *has* been transformed in major ways during the last 150 years. Colonial pacification allowed the pattern of regular inter-island expeditions described by Malinowski, where exchange was earlier interrupted by fighting. Already from the 1830s the kula had become a channel of distribution for large numbers of iron tools from whalers and from a short-lived mission establishment on Woodlark, 150 km east of the Trobriands. Greenstone quarries on the same island were abandoned and stone axes disappeared from the kula before the end of the nineteenth century. The same happened with pig-tusk ornaments, which had formerly been much coveted. Large numbers of kula armshells were bartered with whalers and European visitors or collectors. On the other hand, European traders in various places manufactured or imported a considerable number of the necklaces circulating in the kula.[2]

Malinowski argued that: '[i]n an institution having the importance and traditional tenacity which we find in the Kula, there can be no question of the interference of fashion to bring about changes' (1922:357). But fashion of a sort has in fact played a role in the changing variety and even the appearance of kula valuables. They now appear as 'creolized objects', quite different from the photos in *Argonauts* (ibid. Pl. XVI, XVIII, compare Pl. 5, 7 in Leach and Leach 1983). Armshells are now furnished with rope loops and are heavily decorated with egg-cowries (ovula). Large pearl-shell crescents have been attached to the necklaces. Both valuables have been profusely embellished with trade beads, seeds and pieces of shell, plastic, money, etc. (Campbell 1983). This decorative accretion of kula valuables has been rather played down by contemporary anthropologists who seem to regard it as vulgar. But it reflects the synthetic aesthetics of a changing environment of value production including the cash sale of marine resources (pearl shells, coins), industrial imports (plastic), as well as traditional evocations of rank (ovula).[3]

There have been other major changes in the context of the kula. The associated trade of foodstuffs, craft goods, pigs and canoes, which some have seen as the real basis of the kula, has largely been disengaged from kula exchange. However, an advanced position in the kula demands considerable control of resources in the form of garden crops, pigs and money to extend hospitality, finance expeditions and solicit kula gifts. Thus, the pursuit of fame in this 'traditional' sphere also presupposes involvement in the 'modern' cash sector. Kula visits are often made by means of modern trawlers or motor launches. Information about the departure and arrival of kula expeditions is announced on the provincial radio station now called 'The voice of the kula' (Jens Kofod, personal communication).

It could, however, be argued that these changes in the stuff and context of the kula merely relate to outward form, leaving the 'essential' kula, the honourable game of prestige-building through reciprocal gift exchange, with its associated cultural values and 'mental attitude', largely unaffected. There is though one indication that a considerable change in the conception of possession and the corresponding conduct of social relationships is taking place. The concept of *kitoum* has recently led to some debate (see, for example, Munn 1977, Gregory 1982, Leach and Leach 1983, Weiner 1988). It was unknown to early researchers (Malinowski 1922, Fortune 1932) but has gained much currency since. Briefly, a *kitoum* is a kula valuable that a man has acquired outside the kula and owns as a personal possession. If he invests it in the kula, he claims an ownership right to any kula valuable exchanged for it, or the right to take it back if it is not properly reciprocated. It has been argued (especially by Gregory 1982:197) that *kitoums* are evidence of the inalienability of gifts. On the contrary, I argue that the increasing importance of the concept of *kitoum* is a sign of the expanding adoption of *private property* notions among kula participants and in the area generally. This 'privatization' of kula objects as well as subjects means that people feel less strongly bound in their relationship to kula partners, more autonomous in their decisions about what to do with their possessions. The concomitant effects are a decreasing stability of partnerships and of the flow patterns of kula valuables (see also Liep 1990).

I contend that the kula has been transformed through the historical interaction of its communities and participants with the technology, goods and ideas of the European intruders during colonialism. Does this mean that the kula is now a 'creolized' or 'hybrid' cultural form? I think the question is wrongly posed. There is no doubt that the contexts and conduct of the kula have changed in major ways during the last century, but it is still experienced as a consuming passion by a large number of men in the communities involved. And it is also now, I believe, appreciated as an example of vital 'tradition' in contrast to modern 'business' activities. It is not possible to point to specific creative acts in the long historical transformation of the kula. We are concerned with diffuse and elusive processes which may only be suggested. But there seems to be no doubt that myriad creative actions have taken place through the ongoing practices of people – mainly islanders, but Europeans were indirectly involved – in taking new opportunities and overcoming new obstacles to carry on the kula. This has involved giving up some kinds of wealth and appropriating other kinds, shifting the routes of kula flow, accommodating an increased number of participants and trying out new ideas of property and strategies of the kula. Through this process of creative appropriation kula men have changed the shape of the kula, transporting it into the conditions of a contemporary post-colonial state as a vital regional institution. It is a different kula but it is still kula.

WHEN CREATIVITY FAILS: THE KABISAWALI MOVEMENT

I shall now return to the Che Guevara poster on a Trobriand house wall during the 1970s. Indeed, this revolutionary icon was not an anachronism at the time. The waves of revolution and protest movements which swept the world in the late 1960s and early 1970s had repercussions even in these islands (see Leach 1982 on which this analysis is largely based).

The early 1970s were a time of great political change in Papua New Guinea. The national elections in 1972 resulted in the formation of a coalition government committed to self-government which followed in December 1973. In 1975 the nation gained independence. The period was one of heated debate about constitutional issues, and political movements in Papua, New Britain and Bougainville voiced separatist programmes. There was thus considerable political ferment throughout the country.

In early 1972 a young Trobriand student at the University of Papua New Guinea, who was the most promising writer in the country at the time, John Kasaipwalova, was the main speaker at a number of public meetings on the main island of the Trobriands. His activities led to the formation of a political movement, the Kabisawali ('to search'). It was founded by himself, his father and his mother's brother, the chief of a village in north-eastern Kiriwina and a man having an outstanding kula career. John K, as he was called by most Trobrianders, had embraced radical student politics while studying at the University of Queensland where his involvement in the New Left movement had prevented him from renewing his scholarship. '[D]ressed theatrically in African nationalist style' he urged that Trobrianders should now take control of their own affairs (ibid.: 265). Through the efforts of its members the movement would run trade stores, transport services and a tourist business.

Although the large audiences attending these meetings were at first ambivalent they eventually agreed that 'creative experimentation was the Trobriand way of doing things' (ibid.: 266). A Kabisawali fund was raised with support from a number of important chiefs and contributions from village supporters. During 1972 and early 1973 nearly 40 village stores opened. Later, the movement bought a large Toyota truck with the help of a Development Bank loan. With KABISAWALI painted on it in large letters, it busily transported members around the island and became a powerful symbol of the movement. In 1973 the movement engaged in tourism, building a large rest house, and in 1974 it registered as a commercial company in which capacity it traded artefacts through an outlet in the capital. In the same year plans were made for a tourist hotel, an arts centre and a museum. A small trading vessel was also bought. At a later stage the company diversified its activities in Port Moresby, engaging in various ambitious schemes such as a restaurant, a bank, a computer service, super-markets and an international hotel (ibid.: 288–9). But before this stage the movement had already shown signs of mounting crisis. The system of village stores had collapsed as early as in 1973. In 1976 Kasaipwalova was charged with the embezzlement of funds from the National Cultural Council, for con-struction of the cultural centre. After serving nine months of a gaol sentence he won an appeal and was released. In 1977 the company went bankrupt.

The movement had from the start been opposed to the government-sponsored Local Government Council whose president was Waibadi, the heir apparent of the 'paramount' chief of Omarakana. In early 1973 an incident in which the new Kabisawali truck was slightly damaged by a council vehicle resulted in a march by Kabisawali supporters on the government centre, Losouia. Riot police were flown in from Port Moresby, the crowd was dispersed using tear gas and John K was briefly arrested. The news of these riots made headlines in the national media and in Australia. After consul-tation with representatives of the new national government the situation was defused and the police withdrawn. Later the same year Kabisawali took part in the LGC election, won a number of seats, and managed to dissolve the council in 1974. During this period, opposition to the movement was mounting and this resulted in the formation of a rival organization, the Tonenei Kamokwita ('search for truth') movement, with Waibadi as one of the leading members. The TK programme included development schemes similar to those of Kabisawali (see May 1982). By the late 1970s the development ventures of the two movements, both of which had received central government funding, were moribund (Weiner 1982, 1988:23–4). In 1980 Kasaipwalova bought a small island copra plantation in the area and in the same year he was successful in the kula (Weiner 1982).

As Leach makes clear, these political conflicts reflected certain divisions of Trobriand society. Before colonialism the political centre of the main island was in the fertile garden lands of the north-eastern district of Kiriwina. It was here, in Omarakana, that the most powerful chief of the highest ranking lineage, the Tabalu, controlled a fund of wealth in yams and an important position in the kula. With colonialism, however, the political–economic centre of the island shifted to the area of the north-western lagoon, with its safe anchorage for European vessels. The government, missions and traders established their headquarters and services here. A 'beach' zone arose and the lagoon area became the chief beneficiary of cash incomes, job opportunities and medical and educational services. The population here became more receptive to mission influence. They were increasingly involved in the cash economy and abandoned the kula. The former centre, on the other hand, became a peripheral zone in terms of modern development. Opposition developed between a new modernized centre, which saw itself as sophisticated and Europeanized, and a 'traditional' hinterland that resented this change but prided itself on possessing the highest-ranking chiefs and the heritage of ancestral ways (Leach 1982:249ff.; see also Malinowski 1922:468). It was in this deprived peripheral area that the Kabisawali movement arose and won greatest support.

When the Local Government Council was formed in 1966 the chiefs were indignant that the council allowed them no official position. Although Waibadi later became council president, other chiefs, who were not elected, opposed the council. For the first years of its existence the tax money collected by the council was spent in building the council centre, also located in the lagoon area. Thus it was felt that the council was dominated by the lagoon centre and only reinforced the unequal distribution of development on the island.

The emergence of the Kabisawali movement and its opposition was also influenced by long-standing rivalries between Trobriand chiefs. Among the leaders of the movement were John K's mother's brother, a chief of the Kwainama lineage, who are traditional affines and rivals of the Tabalu of Omarakana, the 'paramount' chief. Another Kabisawali chief represented the traditional enemy of Omarakana. A third chief, from a district near the lagoon, was from a branch of the Tabalu that opposed the right to preeminence of the Omarakana chief (Leach 1982:269; Powell 1960:130; Seligman 1910:694ff.). The 'paramount' chief Vanoi was ambivalent in his attitude towards the movement and shifted allegiance repeatedly during the conflict. His heir and competitor, Waibadi, the council president, was throughout opposed to the Kabisawali revolution against the established political body of the LGC. Apart from Waibadi, the TK opposition was led and supported by chiefs and villages from the lagoon side of the island. Thus, the political division of the island reflected the opposition between those who supported the established system, which had benefited them most, and those who wanted to create a new structure that would give them access to government funds and development. Further, this division cut across entrenched 'traditional' rivalries between important chiefs.

At first sight the activities and projects of the Kabisawali movement appear as a mixture of 'modern' and 'traditional' elements. Trade stores, truck transport, a cargo vessel and tourist facilities were elements of modern 'development'. But a reinvigoration of traditional gardening and the kula were also on the movement's programme. Pride in and enhancement of Trobriand cultural values were important elements in the attitude of the movement.

While the political crisis unfolded several events were subject to a 'traditional' interpretation or were themselves 'traditional' ways of political action. Thus, a collective and competitive scheme, similar to the traditional *kayasa*, was employed to collect money to repay the Development Bank loan for the Kabisawali truck (Leach 1982:268). A drought during late 1972 was widely believed to have been caused by weather magic wielded by Vanoi, the 'paramount' chief. As a result during the yam harvest of 1973, the Kabisawali villages among Vanoi's affines offered him only a pitiful token tribute of 20 baskets of yams, whereas all the chiefs belonging to Kabisawali had large, new yam houses built and filled by their supporters (ibid.: 270–1; 275). In October 1980 I visited one of the former Kabisawali chiefs who during the crisis had sequestrated the council building that stood on land traditionally belonging to him. He was living in this large brickwork building but adjacent to it loomed an imposing yam house filled to the roof with sprouting yams, whereas Vanoi's yamhouse in Omarakana was empty.

However, the contrasting of 'modern' and 'traditional' elements may be a superficial reading of heterogeneity into the movement. It is all too easy to label a truck 'modern' and a yam house 'traditional' – but Trobrianders have lived with both for generations. It was not that the people were unused to stores, trucks or trawlers. They had been part of the Trobriand environment for many years. What they wanted was to appropriate and control these things fully, making them part of Trobriand life. The Kabisawali truck transported copra to buyers, women to mortuary feasts and young people to gatherings at the lagoon centre (ibid.:268). It became a vehicle for a range of pursuits embracing both the 'modern' and the 'traditional'. What the movement sought was a modernized Trobriand existence incorporating a range of indigenous activities.

The complexity of the context in which the Kabisawali movement developed should, I believe, be explained by considering, not concrete cultural elements, but more general processes, those which interact while having their centres of gravity in different but overlapping spaces. If the Trobriand Islands is one such space, we can see how a colonial process of much wider scope penetrated the Trobriand space and produced a restructuring of it, resulting in the division between a modernized centre and a traditional periphery.

Another feature of complexity is the interaction between John Kasaipwalova, the charismatic leader of the movement, and the other leaders and supporters. Quite different environments had contributed to the formation of the habitus of this leader and that of his supporters. John K's fertile mind was informed by ideas and incentives from radical student circles, university education and urban contexts. His perspectives and horizon differed greatly from those of the villagers. For John K, the liberation of his people from subservience to the Europeans was a primary issue, and his personal attitude was strongly resentful of the whites and the government. For the other leaders and the village supporters, however, a redistribution of real benefits was the concern, and they wanted to assert themselves in relation to the new centre at the lagoon (ibid.: 284). Kasaipwalova brought to the leadership some knowledge of Tanzanian *ujamaa* socialism, as well as of the Mataungan Association of New Britain, another protest movement (ibid.: 283,n.1). He also had connections with people influential with the new localized national government, and some familiarity with legal procedures. He had considerable ability in communicating his views to the media, which paid the movement much attention.[4]

The creativity of the movement resulted first and foremost from the genius of Kasaipwalova, who incessantly turned out plans and projects. But collective creativity was involved in the formation of the movement as a novel political organization based on a steering committee of five (which included John K and another university student as well as influential chiefs), a larger group of over 70 representatives from the villages supporting the movement, and mass meetings of the rank-and-file supporters, where programmes and tactics were debated and decided. Thus, creativity evolved as a social process in which experienced local leaders screened John K's output of ideas and tempered his anti-white radicalism. Confrontational tactics inspired by protest movements elsewhere were combined with Trobriand forms of mobilization of support. A programme was developed which included business initiatives as well as the support of cherished indigenous institutions. The project of a combined tourist hotel and cultural centre is the best example of how an income- and employment-generating enterprise was joined to an institution for the advancement of Trobriand culture. With growing enthusiasm, the movement initiated a number of projects and had some initial success, first in resisting police and government interference and later in defeating the LGC and exploiting the development funds established by the new national government. Later, when the stores and other local enterprises had failed, Kasaipwalova spent increasing amounts of time in Port Moresby, involving the movement in the series of abortive investments mentioned above. In this phase he seems to have become estranged from the grassroots objectives of the villages, and opposition was mounting within the movement itself (ibid.: 288–9).

Again, we see how the course of the movement was shaped through the interference of processes in internal and external spheres. Conditions for development initiatives changed rapidly during this period. The new national government was favourable towards regional development and new funds became available for such projects. Self-government in 1973 led to a massive localization of administration. Kasaipwalova's urban contacts in the new elite took on a new strategic value. He was increasingly drawn by the political and economic resources and opportunities of the capital. Thus, although the movement was originally concerned with internal Trobriand development, its mushrooming activities followed the vectors of the larger system beyond the Trobriand scene.

Seen from a rational economic point of view the collapse of the movement was of course due to a lack of management experience. Technical and business skills in storekeeping, truck repair and investment policy were largely absent. In another vein one may argue (Friedman, personal communication) that sound business operation on the basis of cost-benefit calculation conflicted with basic Trobriand attitudes and practices of rightful soliciting by those in need. Thus, the collapse of the movement's village stores followed the 1972 drought when needy supporters were given food on credit or just 'borrowed' it (Leach 1982:266). What I want to emphasize, however, is that the development initiatives of the movement increasingly involved it in demands, risks and liabilities pertaining to the wider economic system at the national level. The ramifying economic conditions, in terms of capital, information and expertise, escaped local control.

The Kabisawali movement was an attempt by a part of the Trobriand population to take a 'great leap forward' and embrace modern development, and in the same process achieve a self-development that would heighten their esteem, in their own eyes and in those of other Trobrianders and the wider world. In the end all these ventures collapsed. The imagination of Kasaipwalova and at least some of his followers went far beyond economic and administrative realism.

The Kabisawali movement evolved in a complex social and political field that included the traditional order of rank and chieftainship, a modern sphere of educational, bureaucratic and managerial merit and the introduced political institution of the LGC. Further, the movement became unavoidably entangled in relationships with the national political and economic system. Although its aim was to 'do things the Trobriand way', it involved itself in tourism, the import and export of commodities and business ventures as far away as the capital. The schemes and strategies which encountered one another in the movement's planning and performance were influenced by factors ranging from university radicalism to competitive harvest campaigns. The whole political process evinced an interference pattern of external and internal forces producing a series of events which, for some time, transformed the expectations and experience of Trobriand life, although in the end they left little practical result.

CONCLUSION

I have attempted to use this Trobriand case material to show how cultural creativity may be involved in strategies to negotiate discrepancies in a complex field where resources, power and cultural schemes are unevenly distributed. In the case of the kula, innovations were made on the basis of accumulated experience and competence. The central institution of the kula, the circulation of indigenous objects of wealth, has been maintained under adequate local control. Exogenous resources and relationships have been auxiliary to the main project. The transformation of kula practice has therefore been a viable process.

The Kabisawali movement may also be seen as a localizing strategy, an attempt to 'indigenize modernity'. It failed for several reasons. Firstly, its scope was much more ambitious. It attempted to appropriate a comprehensive package of development goals in a short period of time. Secondly, it was a charismatic movement focused on one central leader who was a romantic visionary, not an economic entrepreneur.[5] The expansion of Kabisawali as a business corporation occurred too fast for any consolidated management to be established. One could say that the movement suffered from a surfeit of creativity. Finally, the central modern objectives of the movement made it directly dependent on economic relationships beyond local control.

In the introduction to this chapter I considered the problem of the confrontation of the global and the local. I argued that instead of viewing the two as separate levels or domains, we should attempt a conceptualization that brings out the patterns and processes of a multi-centered field of interference. We should go further than to view their interaction as taking place in a border zone of hybridity. I have attempted to show that the modern or global is not something advancing at the boundary of the local but present and active in the midst of it. And, as we have seen with the Kabisawali, the determining context of ambitious attempts to appropriate modern institutions extends far beyond a local space. Regarding creativity, we have thus seen that its viability is not only dependent on the resonance of a local social environment, but subject to the stark realities of a much wider context.

NOTES

1. This contribution depends on the research of others. My own fieldwork was done mainly on Rossel Island in the same province and I made only a brief visit to the Trobriands.
2. This paragraph is based on a number of references that would encumber it beyond readability. On the consequences of pacification (Macintyre 1983a, Keesing 1990); on iron in the early kula (Austen 1945–6); on Woodlark stone quarries (Damon 1983); on the disappearance of pig tusks from the kula (Malinowski 1922:357); on the bartering of armshells to Europeans (Leach 1983; Macintyre 1983b:77–84); on the import of shell necklaces into the kula by Europeans (Malinowski 1922:357, 468, 507; Liep 1981, 1983).
3. In a recent paper, Martha Macintyre reports that the change of appearance of kula valuables was to a large extent due to the selling off of parts of the traditional ornaments and their decorations to Allied soldiers during the Second World War (Macintyre n.d.).
4. Television films about the Kabisawali were made by the Australian Broadcasting Commission and the BBC (Leach 1982:276,n.1). The movement itself also sponsored the well-known film *Trobriand Cricket* that features Kasaipwalova and other of the leaders (Leach and Kildea 1975).
5. For example, the anti-bureaucratic Kasaipwalova refused to do the paperwork in connection with the tourist business (Leach 1982:277).

REFERENCES

Austen, L. (1945–46) 'Cultural changes in Kiriwina', *Oceania* 16:15–61.
Campbell, S.F. (1983) 'Attaining rank: a classification of shell valuables', in J.W. Leach and E. Leach (eds) *The Kula: New Perspectives on Massim Exchange*. Cambridge: Cambridge University Press.
Damon, F.H. (1983) 'On the transformation of Muyuw into Woodlark', *The Journal of Pacific History* 18:35–56.
Fortune, R. (1932) *Sorcerers of Dobu*. London: Routledge and Kegan Paul.
Friedman, J. (1988) 'No history is an island', *Critique of Anthropology* 8:7–39.
—— (1997) 'Simplifying complexity: assimilating the global in a small paradise', in K.F. Olwig and K. Hastrup (eds) *Siting Culture: the Shifting Anthropological Object*. London: Routledge.
Gregory, C.A. (1982) *Gifts and Commodities*. London: Academic Press.
Keesing, R.M. (1990) 'New lessons from old shells: changing perspectives on the kula', in J. Siikala (ed.) *Culture and History in the Pacific*. Helsinki: Transactions of the Finnish Anthropological Society No. 27.
Leach, J.W. (1982) 'Socio-historical conflict and the Kabisawali movement in the Trobriand Islands', in R.J. May (ed.) *Micronationalist Movements in Papua New Guinea*. Political and Social Change Monograph No. 1. Canberra: Australian National University Press.
—— (1983) 'Introduction', in J.W. Leach and E. Leach (eds) *The Kula: New Perspectives on Massim Exchange*. Cambridge: Cambridge University Press.
Leach, J.W. and Kildea, G. (1975) *Trobriand Cricket: an Ingenious Response to Colonialism*. [Film].
Leach, J.W. and Leach, E. (1983) *The Kula: New Perspectives on Massim Exchange*. Cambridge: Cambridge University Press.
Liep, J. (1981) 'The workshop of the kula: production and trade of shell necklaces in the Louisiade Archipelago, Papua New Guinea', *Folk* 23:297–309.
—— (1983) '"This civilising influence": the colonial transformation of Rossel Island society', *The Journal of Pacific History* 18:113–31.
—— (1990) 'Gift exchange and the construction of identity', in J. Siikala (ed.) *Culture and History in the Pacific*. Helsinki: Transactions of the Finnish Anthropological Society No. 27.
Macintyre, M. (1983a) 'Changing paths: an historical ethnography of the traders of Tubetube'. Unpublished Ph.D. thesis, Australian National University.
—— (1983b) *The Kula: a Bibliography*. Cambridge: Cambridge University Press.
—— (n.d.) 'Substitutions and transformations in exchange systems in the context of economic change: gifts and money on Tubetube and Lihir', paper presented at the session on 'Historical and Contemporary Transformations of Pacific Island Exchange', ASAO Annual Meeting 2000, Vancouver.
Malinowski, B. (1922) *Argonauts of the Western Pacific*. London: Routledge and Kegan Paul.
May, R.J. (1982) 'The Trobriand experience: the TK reaction', in R.J. May (ed.) *Micronationalist Movements in Papua New Guinea*. Political and Social Change Monograph No. 1. Canberra: Australian National University Press.
Munn, N. (1977) 'The spatiotemporal transformations of Gawa canoes', *Journal de la Société des Océanistes* 33:39–52.
Powell, H.A. (1960) 'Competitive leadership in Trobriand political organization', *Journal of the Royal Anthropological Institute* 90:118–45.
Sahlins, M. (1985) *Islands of History*. Chicago: The University of Chicago Press.
—— (1993) 'Goodbye to Tristes Tropes: ethnography in the context of modern world history', *The Journal of Modern History* 65:1–25.
Seligman, C.G. (1910) *The Melanesians of British New Guinea*. Cambridge: Cambridge University Press.

Thomas, N. (1991) *Entangled Objects: Exchange, Material Culture and Colonialism in the Pacific*. Cambridge, Massachusetts: Harvard University Press.

—— (1993) 'Beggars can be choosers', *American Ethnologist* 20:868–76.

Weiner, A.B. (1982) 'Ten years in the life of an island: the anthropology of development policies in the Trobriands', *Bikmaus* 3:64–75.

—— (1988) *The Trobrianders of Papua New Guinea*. Case Studies in Cultural Anthropology. New York: Holt, Rhinehart and Winston.

CONTRIBUTORS

Eduardo P. Archetti is Professor of Anthropology at the University of Oslo.

Robert Borofsky is Professor of Anthropology at Hawaii Pacific University.

James W. Fernandez is Professor of Anthropology at the University of Chicago.

Jonathan Friedman is Professor of Anthropology at the University of Lund and Directeur d'études at the École des Hautes Études en Sciencies Sociales (EHESS), Paris.

Kirsten Hastrup is Professor of Anthropology at the University of Copenhagen and Director of Research at The Danish Centre for Human Rights.

Signe Howell is Professor of Anthropology at the University of Oslo.

John Liep is Senior Lecturer in Anthropology at the University of Copenhagen.

Rolf Lindner is Professor of Ethnology at Humboldt University, Berlin.

Orvar Löfgren is Professor of Ethnology at the University of Lund.

David Parkin is Professor of Anthropology at the University of Oxford.

Marc Schade-Poulsen is Executive Director at the Euro-Mediterranean Human Rights Network.

Susan Reynolds Whyte is Professor of Anthropology at the University of Copenhagen.

INDEX

defined, 2, 27, 32, 46, 48, 62,
68, 106, 145
and development, 131, 168
discontinuous, 46
and discovery, 31
and domestic life, 75–6
dynamic of the categorical, 21–4
ethnographic creativity, 25–6
etymology of, 25
everyday creativity, 2, 6, 72,
146
and experience, 9, 50–2
and exploration, 6
and fashion, 5, 27
forms of, 3
and gender, 75–6
and history of science, 2
and homemaking, 75
and human agency, 26, 31,
42–3
and imagination, 145, 146–7
and improvisation, 2, 160
and innovation, 2, 8, 106
and invention, 7, 11, 31–2,
125–7, 134
iron cage of, 49–50
levels of, 12, 155
linguistic, 136
locative and interlocative, 26–8
and management, 2
as metaphor, 17–18
methods of creativity, 6–7
and modernity, 1, 3–5, 77
modes of creativity, 6
and motivation, 10
and newness, 31, 35, 37
and novelty, 7, 24, 31
and the performative, 134
and pharmaceuticals, 119–31
and poetry, 38
and political ethnicity, 134
as political, negotiated quality,
68
as positive, 5
and postmodernity, 12

and processes, 31
and psychology, 2
as resistance, 5, 73, 77, 156
resources for, 9
rule-governed, 137
and social experience, 48
as a social process, 167
social structural, 120
and sociology, 2
and strategies, 168–9
structural condition, 7
in the structural sense, 59–60
structural variation, 59–60
structure and form, 48–9
and structures of authorization
and justification, 9–10
and subjectivity, 9
and survival, 77 *see also* Whyte,
S.R.
and transcendence, 24–5
and transformation, 6, 24–5,
35–6, 46, 137
'true' creativity, 12, 23, 40, 106
in Uganda, 130–1
in urban slum 49
as weapon of the weak, 5, 73,
77, 156 weapons of the
strong, 156
and the world system, 3–5
creole, 93–7
creoleness, 93
creolization, 9, 34, 36, 63, 93, 94,
97–102, 120, 125, 130, 144,
160, 161
and entanglement, 160
and historical processes, 159
and hybridization, 160, 169
and recontextualization, 144,
156
and the role of institutions, 130
and world systems theory, 159
cultural authenticity, 134, 143
cultural complexity, 93, 98, 159,
160, 166
cultural gap, 6, 8, 127

www.ingramcontent.com/pod-product-compliance
Lightning Source LLC
Chambersburg PA
CBHW032138020426
42334CB00016B/1207